Labour Law in Austria

Labour Law in Austria

Fifth Edition

Nora Melzer

This book was originally published as a monograph in the International Encyclopaedia of Laws/Labour Law and Industrial Relations.

Founding Editor: Roger Blanpain
General Editor: Frank Hendrickx
Volume Editor: Frank Hendrickx

Wolters Kluwer

Published by:
Kluwer Law International B.V.
PO Box 316
2400 AH Alphen aan den Rijn
The Netherlands
E-mail: lrs-sales@wolterskluwer.com
Website: www.wolterskluwer.com/en/solutions/kluwerlawinternational

Sold and distributed by:
Wolters Kluwer Legal & Regulatory U.S.
920 Links Avenue
Landisville, PA 17538
United States of America
E-mail: customer.service@wolterskluwer.com

ISBN 978-94-035-2326-2

e-Book: ISBN 978-94-035-2596-9
web-PDF: ISBN 978-94-035-2606-5

This title is available on www.kluwerlawonline.com

The Author

Dr Nora Melzer is Associate Professor at the Department of Labour Law and Law of Social Security at the University of Graz, Austria, and lecturer at the University of Klagenfurt, Austria, where she teaches Austrian and European Labour Law and the Law of Social Security and Anti-discrimination Law.

She has published a book on remote work and home office, a monograph on minimum wage tariffs and commentaries on continued wage payment, works organization and selected collective agreements, and more than fifty articles, primarily in the fields of Austrian, European and international labour law and the law of social security. Finally, she is the Austrian contributor to the *International Labour Law Reports*.

The Author

Table of Contents

List of Abbreviations

ABGB	*Allgemeines Bürgerliches Gesetzbuch* (General Civil Code)
AG	*Aktiengesellschaft* (Joint-Stock Company)
BABE	Association of Employees in the Field of Private Education Institutions
BGBl	*Bundesgesetzblatt* (Federal Law Gazette)
B-VG	*Bundes-Verfassungsgesetz* (Federal Constitutional Law)
CAP	Common Agricultural Policy
CFREU	Charter of Fundamental Rights of the European Union
EC	European Community
ECHR	European Court of Human Rights
ECJ	European Court of Justice
ECSR	European Committee of Social Rights
EEA	European Economic Area
EMU	Economic and Monetary Union of the European Union
ESC	European Social Charter
EU	European Union
GDP	Gross Domestic Product
GmbH	*Gesellschaft mit beschränkter Haftung* (Limited Liability Company)
GÖD	*Gewerkschaft Öffentlicher Dienst* (Union of Public Services)
idF	*in der Fassung* (current version)
ILO	International Labour Organization
ÖGB	*Österreichischer Gewerkschaftsbund* (Austrian Trade Union Federation)
pm	*post meridiem*
RGBl	*Reichsgesetzblatt*

List of Abbreviations

SMS	Short Message Service
StGBl	*Staatsgesetzblatt*
UWG	*Gesetz über den unlauteren Wettbewerb* (Unfair Trading Practices Act)

General Introduction

Chapter 1. General Background

§1. Geography

1. Austria lies in southern central Europe, mostly within the eastern Alps and the Danube region. The Danube flows through Austria for 350 km of its course. The total area of the country is 32,383 sq. miles (83,871 sq. km). Austria shares common borders with the Czech Republic and Slovakia to the north, Hungary to the east, Slovenia and Italy to the south and Switzerland, Liechtenstein and Germany to the west.

§2. Population

2. According to Statistics Austria, in 2022, Austria has 8,978,929 inhabitants (4,553,444 women and 4,425,485 men). The majority of the population, approximately 51%, are women. The average birth rate is 1.48 children per woman.

3. From the point of view of ethnic grouping, language and religion, the population of Austria used to be very homogeneous compared to that of other European countries, though the latest rise in immigration is changing this; 95.5% of Austrian citizens speak German, which is the official language; however, there are also several recognized indigenous ethnic groups (Croatian, Slovenian, Hungarian, Czech, Slovakian as well as Roma and Sinti) living mainly in the east and south of the country.

4. A large majority of the population (the official figure in 2021 was 55.2%) is still Roman Catholic, though that percentage is declining. It is estimated that approximately 436,700 Orthodox adherents, 745,600 Muslims, 340,300 Protestants and 5,400 Jews live in Austria.

§3. Political and Constitutional System

5. The Austrian Constitution lays down the basic organizational principles of the state. It is primarily regulated by the Federal Constitution 1920 (*Bundes-Verfassungsgesetz* (B-VG)), which mainly sets out organizational provisions such as those for legislative procedures and the form of government.

6. Civil rights are mainly set out within two other constitutional sources: the State Fundamental Law on General Rights of Citizens of 1867 and the European Convention on Human Rights, which has constitutional status under Austrian law. Important rights are those to life, freedom, property, privacy and the right to earn one's living, but in the field of labour law also the right of assembly and of coalition play a major role. The Constitution also contains a provision forbidding arbitrary differentiation between citizens by the legislature and executive (principle of equality). Observance of the Constitution is monitored by the Constitutional Court (*Verfassungsgerichtshof*), which can nullify unconstitutional legislation and executive acts ('negative legislation').

7. The Austrian Constitution itself is not rigid and may be amended quite easily, which is done frequently. Any act of legislation, independent of its content, may be raised to constitutional status by designating it a constitutional provision and by consent of a two-thirds majority in the Parliament (National Council). Acts which otherwise would be considered 'unconstitutional' because of a breach of constitutional principles can be passed in this way and therefore be immune to nullification by the Constitutional Court. For example, this has occurred with regard to the different ages of entitlement to the old-age pension for men and women, which will not be equalized until 2034 (which, by the way, is not a breach of European law, as Austria made a reservation in this respect when joining the European Union (EU) in 1995).

8. According to the Constitution, Austria is a federation of states. This means that the nine provincial governments as well as the central federal government are responsible for certain areas of legislation and administration. However, the most important issues, including labour law, are within the federal government's sphere of competence. In addition, the close connection between executive and legislative action is a particular characteristic of Austrian constitutional law: without legislative backing, the executive may not perform either individual or generalized administrative acts, regardless of whether these grant rights or impose prohibitions or duties.

9. According to the Constitution, Parliament is responsible for legislation. This consists of two chambers, the National Council (*Nationalrat*) and the Federal Council (*Bundesrat*). Members of the National Council are elected in direct, equal and secret ballot elections. 'Simple' (i.e., not constitutional) legislation is passed by the National Council by simple majority (50% of the votes + 1), while constitutional legislation can only be passed by a two-thirds majority, with a quorum of one-half of the elected members. The second chamber, the Federal Council, consists of members elected by the parliaments of the federal states; its task is to represent the interests of the federal states in the process of legislation. In practice the influence of the Federal Council is modest as its decisions may be overruled by the National Council.

10. The members of the federal government (federal chancellor, federal ministers) are responsible for enforcement of legislation and are the highest executive authorities. They are appointed by the federal president, who is similarly elected by the Austrian people in direct, equal and secret ballot elections.

11. The government's subordination to the National Council is most clearly shown in the fact that the latter can initiate the dismissal of the entire government, or individual members thereof, from office by simple majority of votes. Furthermore, government members are obliged to answer Council members' requests for information about their area of responsibility.

12. As already mentioned, the National Council (Parliament), which has 183 members, is the competent federal legislator. The Austrian *Volkspartei* (People's Party) and the *Sozialdemokratische Partei* (Socialist Democratic Party, until 1991 the Socialist Party) formed a coalition (meaning a strong form of cooperation) in the National Council lasting from 1948 to 1966, in which the People's Party had more members than the Socialist Party. Among other things, the coalition had the effect that all legislation was based on a compromise between these two parties. A further consequence was that both federal administration and state-controlled industries either came under the influence of one of them or had their important posts occupied on an 'equal representation' basis (in the same way as on the boards of state companies). In 1966, this coalition (the so-called grand coalition) was replaced by a People's Party government. From 1970 to 1983, the Socialist Party governed on its own, and after that for three years with the participation of the, then, liberal *Freiheitliche Partei* (Freedom Party). In 1985, the Freedom Party began to change into a new type of political party: a populist movement on the right of the political spectrum. This led to new elections and consecutive large coalitions until 1999. The elections of 1999 reflected popular insecurity triggered by profound ongoing economic and social transformation, arising especially from European integration (Austria had joined the EU in 1995) and globalization. The opposing parties made great gains. This resulted in two centre-right coalitions (People's Party and Freedom Party) up to 2006, when a large coalition of the two strongest parties (the Social Democratic Party and People's Party) was formed again. The elections of 2008 resulted in severe losses for the two parties making up the government, whereas the two right wing parties made great gains. In 2013, two new parties stood for election: the *Neos* and the *Team Stronach*. This election again brought heavy losses for the two strongest parties. The Social Democratic Party received 26.8% of the votes and the People's Party 24%. The Freedom Party received 20.5%, while the other right-wing party won only 3.5%. The Green Party received 12.4% of the votes, Team Stronach 5.7% and the Neos 5%. In 2017, the grand coalition between the People's Party and the Social Democratic Party was broken, and in October 2017, one year earlier than the legally specified term, parliamentary elections were held again in Austria. The *Liste Sebastian Kurz* – the new Austrian People's Party (formerly People's Party) emerged as the largest party in the National Council; it received 31.5% of the votes (winning 62 of the 183 seats). The Social Democratic Party finished second with 26.9% (52 seats), slightly ahead of the Freedom Party, which won 26% (51 seats). The Neos won 5.3% (10 seats), and the *Liste Peter Pilz* (which had split from the Green Party at the start of the campaign) came into parliament for the first time with 4.4% (8 seats). The Green Party failed to pass the 4% threshold and therefore lost all their seats, thirty years after their first entrance into parliament. Again, as in 1999, this has resulted in a coalition of the (*Liste Sebastian Kurz* – the new Austrian) People's Party and the Freedom Party). This coalition broke up as a result of the so-called Ibiza affair in May 2019; therefore, parliamentary elections were to be held in September 2019, which was – again – earlier than legally required. In the interim period, a government of experts was formed that depended on the support of all parties in parliament. In the election of September 2019, the *Liste Sebastian Kurz* has received 37.5% of the votes and is the largest party in the National Council again (71 seats). The election has resulted in severe losses for the Social Democratic Party, which received only 21.2% of the votes (40 seats), and especially for the Freedom Party, which received 16.2% of the votes (31 seats). The Green Party, alternately, made great gains and re-entered parliament with 13.9% of the votes (26 seats). The *Neos* has received 8.1% of the votes (15 seats), while the *Liste Jetzt*, earlier the *Liste Peter Pilz*, has failed the 4% threshold and has not entered the parliament. This election result has led to the first coalition of the *Liste Sebastian Kurz* and the Green Party in Austria, who have been working together since the beginning of January 2020. After corruption allegations in autumn 2021, the coalition threatened to break up but remained intact after party leader *Sebastian Kurz* withdrew from national political life.

13. Austria is composed of nine federal states or provinces (*Länder*): Vienna (which also serves as its national capital), Lower Austria, Upper Austria, Tyrol, Carinthia, Vorarlberg, Burgenland, Styria and Salzburg. As mentioned above each province has its own competence as regards legislation and administration. It is headed by a provincial governor as head of administration, and a provincial parliament in charge of legislation and with control over the governor. Only the members of the provincial parliament are elected by direct, equal and secret elections.

14. The third territorial entity below the level of the federation and the state is the municipality (*Gemeinde*). Its organs, the mayor and the municipal council, are democratically elected.

15. As for civil and criminal law (including also most parts of labour law), the highest court in Austria is the Supreme Court (*Oberster Gerichtshof*), which is the last resort of appeal against court decisions. It has no power to rule on the constitutionality of Acts on its own but may initiate a procedure before the Constitutional Court if the Supreme Court would otherwise have to apply law which it assumed to be unconstitutional. There are 4 higher regional courts of appeal (*Oberlandesgerichte*); 20 regional courts (*Landesgerichte*) of which 16 are – besides civil law matters in general – also the first recourse for labour and social security matters (*see also* paragraphs 91 et seq.); and 115 district courts (*Bezirksgerichte*). The Administrative Court (*Verwaltungsgerichtshof*) is the supreme administrative court, competent to rule on the legality of the actions of the government and the administration. In 2014, lower administrative courts were introduced to guarantee a 'fair trial' in administrative procedures as well: the Federal Administrative Court (*Bundesverwaltungsgericht*) and the Provincial Administrative Courts (*Landesverwaltungsgerichte*). Now parties adversely affected by administrative decisions or acts must file their complaints with these courts before going to the Administrative Court.

16. As indicated earlier the Constitutional Court rules on whether the national and state legislators are within their material and/or territorial competences, when enacting laws or decrees, and also on whether laws interfere with individual constitutional rights (e.g., equal treatment or property rights). The court has the power to annul laws, as well as administrative acts, which are deemed unconstitutional ('negative legislation').

17. The highest organs of Austrian executive action (administration) are the federal president, the federal government and the federal ministers, of which those chiefly competent in labour and social matters are the Federal Minister of Labour and the Minister of Social Affairs. Inferior administrative organs (or authorities), that is to say, those subordinated to the Federal Minister of Labour are the Federal Conciliation Board (*Bundeseinigungsamt*), a tripartite administrative body consisting of impartial members designated by the state and representatives of (almost) all professional groups (such as employees, employers, liberal professions such as physicians, architects or attorneys), and the works inspectors (competent for supervising and controlling establishments with regard to workers' health protection).

§4. Employment Statistics

I. General Information on Austria's Economy

18. The Austrian economy is a market economy; private ownership of the means of production is constitutionally guaranteed. Many of the country's largest enterprises in the iron and metal manufacturing industries, most electricity companies and large banks, the post office and telephone services, broadcasting, the railways, and most other transport undertakings were often state-owned, as a result of their nationalization in the early post-war period. For many decades, the government and its state-owned industry conglomerate played a very important role in the Austrian economy. However, starting in the early 1990s, state-owned companies began operating largely as private businesses, and a great number of them were at least partially privatized.

19. This is not least attributable to Austria becoming a member of the EU in 1995. Membership brought economic benefits and challenges and has drawn an influx of foreign investors attracted by Austria's access to the single European market. Austria has also made progress in generally increasing its international competitiveness. As a member of the Economic and Monetary Union of the European Union (EMU), Austria's economy is closely integrated with that of other EU member countries, especially Germany. On 1 January 1999, Austria introduced the new euro currency for accounting purposes. In January 2002, euro notes and coins were introduced and replaced the Austrian schilling.

20. Austrian farms, like those of other west European mountainous countries, are small and fragmented, and production is relatively expensive. Since Austria became a member of the EU in 1995, the Austrian agricultural sector has been undergoing substantial reform under the EU Common Agricultural Policy (CAP). Although Austrian farmers provide about 80% of domestic food requirements, the agricultural contribution to gross domestic product (GDP) has declined since 1950 to about 1.2% in 2021.

21. Although some industries are global competitors, such as several iron and steelworks, chemical plants and oil corporations that are large industrial enterprises employing thousands of people, most industrial and commercial enterprises in Austria are relatively small-scale from an international perspective. In 2021, the industrial sector, with the building industry, contributed approximately 28.5% to Austria's GDP.

22. The service sector is the most important for Austria, generating the vast majority of its GDP (in 2021, about 70.3% in total). Vienna has grown into a finance and consulting metropolis and in recent decades has established itself as the gateway to the east. Viennese law firms and banks are among the leading corporations in doing business with the new EU Member States. Tourism, especially winter tourism, is very important for Austria's economy; it accounted for 7.6% of Austria's GDP in 2019 (46,195,388 arrivals and 152,709,084 overnight stays in 2019). Due to the COVID-19 pandemic, it accounted only for 4.5% of the GDP in 2020 (25,030,207 arrivals and 97,875,868 overnight stays in 2020).

23. Austria's economy therefore features a large service sector, a sound industrial sector, and a small, but highly developed agricultural sector. Following several years of solid foreign demand for Austrian exports and record employment growth, the global economic downturn in 2008 led to a recession that persisted through the following years. The government's stabilization measures increased the budget deficit to 5.4% of GDP in 2009 and to 4.5% in 2010, from about 1.5% in 2008. In the following years, the budget deficit settled down to a stable level and amounted to 1% of GDP in 2015. In 2018, a zero deficit has been reached for the first time in forty-four years, and in 2019, a small budget surplus of 0.6% has been achieved. With regard to the COVID-19 pandemic, there was a budget deficit of 8% in 2020 and one of 5.9% in 2021.

24. As already mentioned the Austrian economy has benefited greatly in the past from strong commercial relations with central, eastern and south-eastern Europe, especially in the banking and insurance sectors, but these sectors have been vulnerable to recent international financial instability, and some of Austria's largest banks have required government support.

II. General Information on Austria's Labour Force

25. According to Statistics Austria, in 2021, Austria's average labour force was 4,306,000. For more detailed information *see* Tables 1–8.

Table 1 Employed Population by Professional Status, 2020–2022 (000)

Quarter	*Total*	*Employees*							*Self-Employed and Family Workers*		
Total	*Apprentices*	*White-collar workers*	*Blue-collar workers*	*Public servants*	*Employee-like persons*	*Total*	*Self-employed with workers*	*Self-employed without workers*	*Family workers*		
Total											
1st quarter 2020	4,288.0	3,756.4	108.6	2,255.1	978.3	390.3	24.0	531.6	266.1	215.4	50.1
1st quarter 2021	4,189.9.8	3,694.0	105.7	2,270.2	906.5	375.9	35.8	495.9	263.1	181.4	51.3
2nd quarter 2021	4,247.1	3,746.6	100.1	2,262.5	974.7	379.8	29.4	500.5	262.0	176.6	61.9
3rd quarter 2021	4,399.8	3,871.2	109.7	2,317.4	1,032.6	372.9	38.5	528.7	272.7	185.8	70.1

Quarter	*Total*	*Employees*							*Self-Employed and Family Workers*		
Total	*Apprentices*	*White-collar workers*	*Blue-collar workers*	*Public servants*	*Employee-like persons*	*Total*	*Self-employed with workers*	*Self-employed without workers*	*Family workers*		
Total											
4th quarter 2021	4,386.8	3,860.3	111.0	2,316.4	1,030.5	369.6	32.7	526.5	274.2	190.9	61.5
1st quarter 2022	4,374.1	3,831.0	106.2	2,326.7	994.0	376.8	27.3	543.1	288.9	191.4	62.8

Source: https://statistik.at/fileadmin/publications/SB_5-9-Arbeitsmarkt-2022Q1.pdf.

Table 2 Employees in Different Areas of the Economy

	2004	2013	2018	*2020*	*2021*
Agriculture, forestry and fishing	26,600	21,018	24,606	24,800	25,753
Total primary sector	**26,600**	**21,018**	**24,606**	**24,800**	**25,753**
Mining	13,022	5,615	5,965	5,935	5,695
Production of real assets	585,127	583,305	619,152	619,525	623,401
Supply of energy;	26,456	26,908	25,594	25,947	26,063
Supply of water and waste management	7,364	15,340	16,832	17,857	17,862
Construction	235,523	247,126	261,418	271,072	285,003

	2004	2013	2018	*2020*	*2021*
Total secondary sector	**867,492**	**878,294**	**928,961**	**940,336**	**958,024**
Commerce; maintenance and repair of motor vehicles	498,629	528,008	548,413	548,827	562,146
Hospitality	159,019	195,896	216,402	178,025	186,716
Transportation and communication	214,350	262,135	296,293	301,486	305,138
Banking and insurance	109,882	117,711	113,462	112,798	111,370
Real estate, scientific, technical and economic services	294,359	383,367	446,592	441,894	465,984
Public administration, military, social insurance	449,866	544,400	578,255	583,165	588,000
Education	144,213	98,564	107,273	110,262	110,113
Health, veterinary and social industry	171,972	234,279	269,893	276,856	295,266
Other public and personal services, arts, entertainment and recreation	142,555	123,694	126,418	120,789	121,074
Private households	3,375	3,077	2,769	2,744	2,759
Exterritorial organizations	2,741	660	764	807	850
Total tertiary sector	**2,190,961**	**2,491,791**	**2,706,534**	**2,677,653**	**2,749,416**
Military duty	11,169	6,689	4,823	4,885	4,791
Persons paid sickness benefits	110,786	84,609	75,534	68,353	65,788
Unknown areas		1,053	1,037	1,149	1,180
Total	**3,207,008**	**3,483,454**	**3,741,495**	**3,717,176**	**3,804,952**

Sources: http://wko.at/statistik/jahrbuch/JAHRBUCH_2022.pdf.

https://www.sozialversicherung.at/cdscontent/load?contentid=10008.763576&version=1642424141.

Table 3 Employed Population by Age, 2010–2020 (000)

Years	*Total*	*15–24*			*25–34*	*35–44*	*45–54*	*55–64*			*15–64*	*65+*
	Total	*15–19*	*20–24*				*Total*	*55–59*	*60–64*			
Total												
2010	4,016.8	519.3	181.9	337.3	866.7	1,103.7	1,065.1	389.1	292.5	96.6	3,944.0	72.8
2011	4,052.6	528.0	180.1	347.9	883.0	1,082.5	1,097.5	391.5	298.5	93.0	3,982.5	70.1
2012	4,084.6	527.0	178.4	348.6	902.0	1,050.6	1,119.2	414.6	320.2	94.4	4,013.5	71.1
2013	4,104.8	521.0	165.6	355.4	902.3	1,019.6	1,145.1	442.2	338.1	104.1	4,030.1	74.7
2014	4,112.8	508.2	158.7	349.5	917.6	990.3	1,153.6	464.7	355.7	108.9	4,034.3	78.4
2015	4,148.4	500.0	149.6	350.4	940.1	977.7	1,159.5	490.4	379.7	110.7	4,067.7	80.7
2016	4,220.3	501.2	145.1	356.1	970.8	969.0	1,163.7	538.1	406.5	131.5	4,142.8	77.6
2017	4,260.5	483.7	137.1	346.6	970.5	977.0	1,172.3	581.9	443.5	138.4	4,185.4	75.1
2018	4,319.1	480.7	139.0	341.7	972.9	991.2	1,161.6	634.8	472.5	162.2	4,241.2	77.9
2019	4,355.0	472.6	132.0	340.6	986.2	1,001.4	1,156.9	663.1	493.8	169.2	4,280.3	74.7
2020	4,296.9	454.3	133.9	320.4	968.0	992.4	1,121.6	687.8	514.3	173.5	4,224.1	72.9

Source: https://statistik.at/fileadmin/pages/360/Tab1_erwerbstaetige_nach_alter_und_geschlecht_seit_1994.ods.

Table 4 Employed Population by Professional Status, 2010–2021 (000)

Years	*Employed Population*	*Employees Thereof*			
		Total	*Apprentices*	*Blue-Collar Workers*	*White-Collar Workers, Public Servants*
	Total				
2010	4,016.8	3,462.0	131.3	1,018.5	2,312.1
2011	4,052.6	3,514.5	138.4	1,029.8	2,346.3
2012	4,084.6	3,550.6	130.0	1,040.1	2,380.5
2013	4,104.8	3,563.0	126.2	1,053.6	2,383.1
2014	4,112.8	3,566.3	119.1	1,025.1	2,422.0
2015	4,148.4	3,609.2	118.0	1,025.4	2,465.8
2016	4,220.3	3,683.5	111.9	1,050.8	2,520.8
2017	4,260.5	3,733.2	106.2	1,053.6	2,573.4
2018	4,319.1	3,800.6	108.3	1,075.8	2,616.5
2019	4,355.0	3,825.4	104.6	1,074.1	2,646.7
2020	4,296.9	3,772.1	113.1	984.3	2,674.7
2021	4,306.0	3,793.1	106.6	986.1	2,700.4

Source: https://statistik.at/fileadmin/pages/257/3_Erwerbstaetigkeit_Zeitreihen_bis2021.ods.

Table 5 Self-Employed by Professional Status, 2010–2021 (000)

Years	*Total*	*Self-Employed and Family Workers*			
		Total	*Self-Employed*	*In Agriculture and Forestry*	*Family Workers*
	Total				
2010	4,016.8	554.8	468.2	108.6	86.7
2011	4,052.6	538.0	456.2	109.8	81.8
2012	4,084.6	534.0	455.3	104.3	78.7
2013	4,104.8	541.9	466.2	102.3	75.6
2014	4,112.8	546.5	463.6	104.4	82.9
2015	4,148.4	539.2	472.4	102.7	66.8
2016	4,220.3	536.9	473.2	100.6	63.7
2017	4,260.5	527.3	465.0	88.5	62.3
2018	4,319.1	518.5	465.1	87.2	53.4
2019	4,355.0	529.6	482.7	88.2	46.9
2020	4,296.9	524.8	471.7	90.4	53.2
2021	4,306.0	512.9	451.7	77.3	61.2

Source: https://statistik.at/fileadmin/pages/257/3_Erwerbstaetigkeit_Zeitreihen_bis2021.ods.

Table 6 Registered Unemployed and Unemployment Rates According to National Definition, 1994–2021

Years	*Registered Unemployed*			*Unemployment Rates According to National Definition*			
	Total	*Males*	*Females*	*Total*	*Males*	*Females*	*Non-nationals*
	Thousand			%			
1994	214.9	120.6	94.4	6.5	6.4	6.7	8.0
1995	215.7	120.0	95.7	6.6	6.4	6.8	7.7
1996	230.5	128.0	102.5	7.0	6.9	7.3	8.4
1997	233.3	128.6	104.8	7.1	6.9	7.4	8.4
1998	237.8	129.4	108.4	7.2	6.9	7.5	8.7
1999	221.7	121.5	100.2	6.7	6.5	6.9	8.2
2000	194.3	107.5	86.8	5.8	5.8	5.9	7.5
2001	203.9	115.3	88.6	6.1	6.2	5.9	8.4
2002	232.4	134.4	98.0	6.9	7.2	6.4	9.8
2003	240.1	139.7	100.4	7.0	7.5	6.5	9.9
2004	243.9	140.3	103.6	7.1	7.5	6.6	10.0
2005	252.7	144.2	108.4	7.3	7.7	6.8	10.6
2006	239.2	135.8	103.4	6.8	7.1	6.4	9.8
2007	222.2	124.3	97.9	6.2	6.5	6.0	8.8
2008	212.3	118.8	93.4	5.9	6.1	5.6	8.0
2009	260.3	153.6	106.7	7.2	8.0	6.4	10.2
2010	250.8	145.1	105.7	6.9	7.5	6.3	9.6
2011	246.7	139.1	107.6	6.7	7.1	6.3	9.4
2012	260.6	148.4	112.3	7.0	7.4	6.5	9.7

Years	Registered Unemployed			Unemployment Rates According to National Definition			
	Total	Males	Females	Total	Males	Females	Non-nationals
	Thousand			%			
2013	287.2	165.2	122.0	7.6	8.2	7.0	10.7
2014	319.4	183.5	135.8	8.4	9.0	7.6	12.1
2015	354.3	205.1	149.3	9.1	9.8	8.3	13.5
2016	357.3	204.5	152.9	9.1	9.7	8.3	13.5
2017	340.0	192.8	147.2	8.5	9.0	7.9	12.5
2018	312.1	174.8	137.3	7.7	8.0	7.3	11.3
2019	301.3	166.6	134.7	7.4	7.6	7.1	10.8
2020	409.6	224.0	185.7	9.9	10.1	9.7	15.3
2021	331.7	180.8	150.9	8.0	8.1	7.9	11.9

Source: https://www.ams.at/content/dam/download/arbeitsmarktdaten/%C3%B6sterreich/berichte-auswertungen/001_ub-al-alq_geschl_77-21.xls. https://www.ams.at/content/dam/download/arbeitsmarktdaten/%C3%B6sterreich/berichte-auswertungen/001_aml77-21.xls.

Table 7 Unemployed and Unemployment Rates According to ILO Definition, 1995–2021

	Unemployed					Unemployment Rate				
Years	Total	15–24	25–44	45–54	55–64	Total	15–24	25–44	45–54	55–64
	Thousand					%				
1995	139.3	30.6	69.3	30.0	9.4	3.7	5.2	3.2	3.8	3.8
1996	155.4	36.0	76.7	31.3	11.3	4.1	6.3	3.6	4.1	4.5
1997	158.9	34.8	82.1	31.3	10.6	4.2	6.3	3.8	4.1	4.2

	Unemployed					*Unemployment Rate*				
Years	*Total*	*15–24*	*25–44*	*45–54*	*55–64*	*Total*	*15–24*	*25–44*	*45–54*	*55–64*
	Thousand					*%*				
1998	159.6	30.6	82.6	34.0	12.3	4.2	5.8	3.8	4.4	4.7
1999	141.6	26.7	69.8	31.7	13.5	3.7	5.1	3.2	4.0	4.9
2000	133.8	26.3	64.8	28.8	13.9	3.5	5.1	2.9	3.6	5.2
2001	137.1	28.6	67.8	27.5	13.1	3.6	5.6	3.1	3.3	4.9
2002	156.2	31.8	75.3	33.5	15.6	4.0	6.2	3.4	3.8	5.4
2003	169.6	36.5	81.6	35.2	16.4	4.3	7.0	3.7	3.9	5.3
2004	213.5	57.3	107.6	36.7	11.7	5.5	10.5	5.0	4.2	4.3
2005	223.5	62.6	110.3	38.6	11.7	5.6	11.0	5.1	4.2	4.0
2006	211.7	55.7	103.9	39.0	12.8	5.3	9.8	4.8	4.1	4.0
2007	200.3	55.2	94.8	38.3	11.8	4.9	9.4	4.4	3.9	3.4
2008	172.0	50.1	79.7	33.8	8.2	4.1	8.5	3.8	3.3	2.2
2009	222.9	62.7	105.2	44.5	10.2	5.3	10.7	5.0	4.2	2.7
2010	203.4	54.3	97.4	41.6	9.9	4.8	9.5	4.7	3.8	2.5
2011	193.8	51.9	89.4	37.6	14.6	4.6	8.9	4.3	3.3	3.6
2012	208.9	54.7	96.2	43.0	14.8	4.9	9.4	4.7	3.7	3.4
2013	231.3	55.8	110.0	48.0	17.3	5.4	9.7	5.4	4.0	3.8
2014	244.9	58.2	116.7	50.9	18.4	5.6	10.3	5.8	4.2	3.8
2015	251.8	59.2	115.0	53.0	24.3	5.7	10.6	5.7	4.4	4.7
2016	270.0	63.5	124.2	53.8	28.1	6.0	11.2	6.0	4.4	5.0
2017	247.9	52.6	115.2	53.8	25.8	5.5	9.8	5.6	4.4	4.2

	Unemployed					*Unemployment Rate*				
Years	*Total*	*15–24*	*25–44*	*45–54*	*55–64*	*Total*	*15–24*	*25–44*	*45–54*	*55–64*
	Thousand					%				
2018	220.1	49.8	99.2	45.0	25.4	4.9	9.4	4.8	3.7	3.9
2019	204.6	44.1	100.4	36.4	23.2	4.5	8.5	4.8	3.0	3.4
2020	243.5	53.2	117.2	43.8	28.9	5.4	10.5	5.6	3.8	4.0
2021	283.7	55.3	133.5	55.4	38.9	6.2	11.0	6.3	4.8	5.2

Source: https://statistik.at/fileadmin/pages/261/Arbeitslose_2021.ods.

Table 8 Unemployed and Unemployment Rates by Age and Sex According to ILO Definition, 2010–2021

Males

	Total	*15–24*	*25–44*	*45–54*	*55–64*	*Total*	*15–24*	*25–44*	*45–54*	*55–64*
		Thousand						%		
2010	112.7	29.3	53.0	23.5	6.7	5.0	9.6	4.9	4.0	2.9
2011	103.0	27.3	44.9	20.2	10.5	4.6	8.8	4.2	3.4	4.4
2012	112.7	29.5	47.8	25.3	9.9	5.0	9.6	4.5	4.1	3.9
2013	123.7	28.6	55.6	28.2	11.3	5.4	9.4	5.3	4.5	4.2
2014	134.7	31.4	59.5	30.5	12.8	5.9	10.6	5.6	4.9	4.5
2015	142.2	32.9	62.2	30.3	16.9	6.1	11.1	5.8	4.8	5.7
2016	153.5	36.6	67.9	29.7	19.2	6.5	12.1	6.3	4.7	5.9
2017	141.6	30.3	64.5	29.9	16.2	5.9	10.8	6.0	4.7	4.6
2018	121.4	26.4	53.2	26.4	14.9	5.0	9.4	4.9	4.3	3.9

	Total	*15–24*	*25–44*	*45–54*	*55–64*	*Total*	*15–24*	*25–44*	*45–54*	*55–64*
		Thousand						%		
2019	111.7	25.4	51.6	19.6	14.8	4.6	9.2	4.7	3.2	3.8
2020	132.1	30.5	60.3	23.3	17.7	5.5	11.3	5.5	3.9	4.4
2021	152.3	29.4	69.7	29.3	23.6	6.3	10.7	6.3	5.0	5.6

Females

	Total	*15–24*	*25–44*	*45–54*	*55–64*	*Total*	*15–24*	*25–44*	*45–54 years*	*55–64 years*
		Thousand						%		
2010	90.7	25.0	44.4	18.1	(3.1)	4.6	9.4	4.5	3.5	(1.9)
2011	90.8	24.6	44.4	17.4	(4.1)	4.6	9.1	4.5	3.2	(2.5)
2012	96.2	25.2	48.4	17.7	(4.8)	4.8	9.2	4.9	3.2	(2.7)
2013	107.6	27.2	54.4	19.8	6.1	5.3	10.0	5.6	3.5	3.2
2014	110.2	26.8	57.2	20.4	(5.6)	5.4	9.9	5.9	3.5	(2.8)
2015	109.6	26.3	53.0	22.7	7.4	5.3	10.0	5.5	3.9	3.4
2016	116.6	26.9	56.3	24.1	9.0	5.6	10.2	5.7	4.1	3.8
2017	106.3	22.2	50.7	23.9	9.5	5.0	8.7	5.2	4.0	3.7
2018	98.7	23.5	46.0	18.6	10.5	4.7	9.4	4.7	3.2	3.8
2019	92.8	18.7	48.8	16.8	8.5	4.4	7.8	4.9	2.9	2.9
2020	111.4	22.7	56.9	20.5	11.2	5.2	9.5	5.8	3.6	3.6
2021	131.4	25.9	63.7	26.1	15.2	6.1	11.3	6.4	4.6	4.6

Source: https://statistik.at/fileadmin/pages/261/Arbeitslose_2021.ods.

§5. Social and Cultural Values

26. The social and cultural values which co-determine the nature of labour law and industrial relations in Austria largely coincide with the legal foundations of economic power in a free enterprise and an open market economy. There are various legal bases for civil or human rights in the Austrian Constitution, and the different pillars of the economic system originate from different periods of time.

27. The right to property enables proprietors to dispose of, exploit and benefit from their property, and to make a profit from it. This basic right was established in one of the first constitutional documents, the Fundamental Law on General Rights of Citizens 1867 (*Staatsgrundgesetz* 1867), which is still in force. It is also part of the First Protocol of the European Convention for the Protection of Human Rights and Fundamental Freedoms, which is directly applicable in Austria.

28. The freedom of occupational choice was also introduced in the above-mentioned law from 1867. According to this fundamental law, all persons may freely decide which economic activity to carry out to gain their living: every citizen can freely engage in commerce, industry or any other activity of his/her choice.

29. Of major importance, too, is the notion of 'private autonomy' (legal self-determination), which is not directly guaranteed under the Constitution but nonetheless represents a major principle of civil law. However, interpreting the constitutional 'right to property' in a modern way, it can be understood as the right to conclude contracts (freedom of contract; *see* paragraph 39) and the main legal basis for the principle of private autonomy. Everybody has the right to determine their own legal relationships according to their own will. Everybody can decide whether and with whom they want to make a contract and what the content of this contract should be. The partner in any contractual relationship also has private autonomy; thus, the making of a contract requires both parties' consent. The legal system assumes that a contract which was the subject of a free bargaining process takes into account the interests of both parties and therefore constitutes a fair balance. However, this only works in situations where both parties have the same bargaining power. If this is not the case, the law restricts private autonomy in favour of the weaker party.

30. Labour law also follows these fundamental principles but has to take into account that in practice most employment contracts are not negotiated but are predetermined by the employer. Especially in times of higher unemployment, the employee has no choice but to sign the contract as proposed by the prospective employer, or not to enter into an employment relationship with this employer. Apart from the amount of remuneration, there is usually no real opportunity to negotiate the terms of an employment contract.

31. Austrian lawmakers have chosen two alternative concepts to protect the employee in the position of the economically weaker partner in the contractual relationship:

(1) the lack of bargaining power of the individual employee is balanced at a higher level, that is to say at the collective level, where negotiations take place between employees' and employers' organizations. Collective bargaining is seen as an appropriate means to equalize the imbalance at the individual level, without interfering too much with the private autonomy of the parties in the individual employment contract;
(2) laws provide a set of statutory rules that may only be changed in favour of the employee. This measure is usually only taken to provide for a minimum standard in favour of the employee, any further being achieved through collective bargaining (*Günstigkeitsprinzip*).

32. The Austrian economy is very open to the rest of the world, and two-thirds of all exports are destined for the EU Member States. The societal choice of a free market has been exemplified and strengthened by Austria's membership of the EU since 1995.

33. Austria is a pluralistic society in which individuals are allowed the freedom to promote their own interests. Consequently, social conflict is inevitable. Austrians usually opt for a resolution model that is very much based on maintaining – externally – an image of harmony and common understanding. This is evidently a reality in the Austrian industrial relations system: although employers and employees are not prevented by any legal regulations from taking collective action (strikes and lockouts), these means of applying pressure are hardly ever used in practice. In recent decades (with only a few exceptions such as a general transport strike against pension reform), Austria has had a strike incidence of less than one minute's strike per employee per year. Collective conflicts of interest between employers and employees in Austria are resolved in the rather unique setting of 'social partnership', a system based on close, voluntary, high-level cooperation between representatives of employers, employees and the state (*see* paragraph 639). These principles and notions of cooperation have also been applying during the COVID-19 pandemic where the employers' side and the employees' side found solutions to support all economic players, that is enterprises, employees, consumers, social insurance bodies and so on.

Chapter 2. Definitions and Notions

34. Social law or social legislation in Austria comprises labour law on the one hand and social security law on the other.

§1. Social Security Law

35. Austrian legislation provides for a compulsory social security system, which covers:

- insurance against illness and pregnancy/childbirth, inability to work caused by illness and pregnancy/childbirth (health insurance);
- insurance against work-related accidents and occupational diseases (accident insurance);
- insurance to cover retirement, disability and survivors' pensions (pension insurance);
- unemployment insurance;
- insurance against the employer's insolvency;
- allowances in the case of need for long-term care;
- family allowances.

36. The first three branches of the social security system (so-termed social insurance, based on the German system developed by *Bismarck* at the beginning of the twentieth century) are administered by public law bodies called social security agencies, which are 'self-governed'. This means that representatives of the employees and employers concerned, who administer these agencies, are delegated by the respective statutory interest groups, the chambers of labour and the economic chambers. The Minister of Labour has no direct power to issue directives but controls the legality and the expediency of the actions of these social security agencies. Unemployment insurance, alternately, is the direct responsibility of the competent minister. However, here, too, both sides of the 'social partners' are represented in advisory boards.

37. Employers are obliged to pay the required contributions both on their own behalf and on behalf of their employees (which the employer may deduct from wages). Table 9 illustrates the financial obligations incurred for social security contributions (as a percentage of gross wages).

Table 9 Social Security Contributions (%)

	Total	*Employer*	*Employee*
Health insurance			
Employees	7.65	3.78	3.87
Free employees	7.65	3.78	3.87
Self-employed persons	7.65		
Farmers	6.80		
Pensioners	5.10		
Apprentices	3.35	1.68	1.67
Accident insurance			
Employees	1.20	1.20	
Free employees	1.20	1.20	
Self-employed persons	EUR 10.64 per month		
Farmers	1.90		
Pension insurance			
Employees	22.80	12.55	10.25
Free employees	22.80	12.55	10.25
Self-employed persons	18.50		
Farmers	17.00		
Apprentices	22.80	12.55	10.25
Unemployment insurance			
Employees	6.00	3.00	3.00
Free employees	6.00	3.00	3.00
Self-employed persons (optionally included)	6.00		
Apprentices	2.40	1.20	1.20

§2. Labour Law

I. Definition

38. Labour law is the sum of all the rules regulating the legal relationships of ‘dependent employed persons’. Essentially, anybody who is obliged to work for someone else as a result of an employment contract is dependent, or not self-employed. However, labour law regulates not only the relationship of (a) individual employees and individual employers, but also comprises regulations on (b) the state as the public authority and employer, whereby the individual employee is the object of protection, (c) the individual employee and the personnel of the establishment where they work, and between (all the) employees and the establishment owner, (d) individual employees and their supra-establishment trade association, and between the associations, as well as (e) procedures for dealing with employment disputes and (f) the employment market (*see also* paragraph 25).

II. Features of Labour Law

39. From a legal point of view, an employment contract is based on freedom of contract under civil law. According to this principle, it is up to the parties whether and with whom they conclude a contract and what this agreement entails. In the final analysis, the economic power of the parties also determines the contents of the contract. In the past, in Austria, as in other countries, the validity of the freedom of contract principle, when extended to employment contracts, has had negative consequences for the economically weaker party, the employee. The need to avoid such consequences has led to the development of labour law. The function of labour law is to compensate for the differences in bargaining power between employer and employee which arise from economic conditions and to protect the employee. Austrian labour law seeks to achieve this aim in a variety of ways and on various levels. In essence, it is a matter for the state to create obligatory rules specifying the content of individual employment contracts. Moreover, the associations of employees (and employers) must be given the opportunity to influence the contents of employment relationships (e.g., by means of collective agreements). Last, the personnel in an establishment must be able to legally organize themselves and enjoy specific powers restricting the employer's freedom of decision (e.g., by means of co-determination by the works council).

40. The purpose of labour law is to protect employees from the consequences of their economic dependence. However, the application of labour law does not depend on the existence of economic dependence *per se*, as labour law covers all employees. The status of an employee is connected to the so-termed personal dependence: that is, working under the leadership and control of another person (paragraph 52) Insofar, the Austrian definition of employee is not only in accordance with the European understanding (*see* only '*Lawrie Blum*'); furthermore, it takes into account that also modern forms of work, such as (digital) work at the home office, and even sometimes crowd work, might fulfil the criteria of personal dependence, and, therefore, constitute work protected by labour law regulations.

III. Demarcation of Labour Law and Social Security Law

41. Despite their close historical and sociological connections labour law and social security law are independent areas of law. Social security law primarily regulates the application of rights and duties between individuals and state or self-governed institutions such as the social insurance bodies. It is concerned with offsetting social risks, which exist for a variety of reasons, in the personal affairs or the financial situation of people who are economically weak and in need of protection. The disadvantages and potential threats which social security law is primarily intended to address are illness, unemployment, old age, disability, work accidents, occupational diseases, motherhood, care dependency and family burdens. Protection is mainly facilitated via (compulsory) insurance and welfare services provided by the state, or at least promoted and supervised by it.

42. From a historical or a sociological point of view, employment law and social security law have pursued the same aims: the safeguarding and protection of persons who are at a disadvantage in the economic struggle. Yet social security law is not restricted to protecting (economically) dependent employed persons; it also embraces self-employment. Since 1957, the self-employed have been brought into the pension insurance system, and since 1966 into the health insurance system. Farmers have been compulsorily insured for health services since 1965 and for pensions since 1969. Further steps to widen the range of the social security system were undertaken in 1998, when all forms of self-employed business activities were included in the compulsory system of social insurance ('inclusion of all kinds of income' in the health, accident and pension system). In 2008, 'free' or 'independent workers' (*see* paragraph 54) were also included in the unemployment insurance system and new system of severance pay. To sum up: from this point onwards, everybody who is gainfully employed and earning more than the minimum income limit concerning social insurance contributions (in 2022: EUR 485.85 per month) is covered by the social security system.

IV. Individual and Collective Labour Law

43. Traditionally, Austrian labour law is divided into two major parts, which are further subdivided. The main division is between individual labour law and collective labour law.

44. Individual labour law primarily comprises employment contract law: the rules regulating the relationship between individual employers and individual employees. It also includes provisions relating to safety at work, which are directed primarily at the employer. Their purpose is to protect employees from employment-related hazards to their life, health and morality (i.e., rules limiting the hours of work, the employment of children and young persons, and rules concerning protection against technical dangers). Observance of these rules is supervised by state authorities, and their breach is punished by administrative sanctions such as fines. But it is recognized that these rules can also be a part of individual employment contracts and thus form the basis of employees' contractual rights (paragraph 275).

45. Collective labour law is divided into the law of trades representation (law of 'associations' or 'affiliations') and the law of works representation. The former consists of standards regulating the relationship between employees or employers and their representative associations at the branch or national level (trade unions, chambers of labour, chambers of commerce). Trades representation law also includes rules relating to the so-termed collective creation of law, in particular collective agreements. It also encompasses the law of industrial disputes. Finally, it embraces rules providing state assistance in the settlement of industrial disputes (conciliation law).

46. Trades representation law concerns supra-enterprise relationships, that is to say, whole economic branches. By contrast, the second part of the statute on collective labour law relating to works representation concerns relationships in individual establishments or undertakings. Works representation law creates organizational possibilities for the personnel in an establishment, giving the right to participate in its management, and thereby restricting the owner's freedom of decision.

V. Legal Nature

47. Austrian labour law mainly comprises general rules binding only in one direction – the parties may deviate from the law either by individual or collective agreement only in favour of the employee. Therefore, the law regularly sets minimum standards which can only be improved upon. Legal acts that impair or reduce the rights of the employee are invalid. However, this usually means 'relative nullity' – it can only be invoked by the protected party (the employee). A period within which legal steps have to be taken is not laid down in the law, but jurisprudence imposes an obligation to act within due time.

48. Misbehaviour or deviance of the employer is not often sanctioned by penalty. Administrative penalties (mostly fines) apply to deviance which is counter to a strong public interest, such as that concerning the employment of foreign workers without administrative permission or the protection of employees as regards their life and health, such as deviances relating to working time, rest periods and especially workplace safety. In 2011, the lawmaker stipulated, for the first time, that non-compliance with rules on minimum wages should not only lead to consequences according to civil law, but also allow for an administrative penalty (for details, *see* paragraphs 412 et seq.).

49. The fines are mainly imposed by administrative bodies rather than by labour courts. The core body of labour law contains no criminal sanctions, however, as it concerns the individual or collective employment relationship.

50. Modern labour legislation (especially concerning working time restrictions) aims for increased flexibility, leaving it to the social partners to deviate from legal standards by way of a collective or a works agreement, in order to adapt certain regulations to the needs of a branch or even an enterprise.

§3. PERSONS

I. The Term 'Employee'

51. The Austrian Civil Code defines an employee only as a person who undertakes to perform work for an amount of time (which may or may not be specified) for another, without referring explicitly to the criterion of personal dependence/subordination which plays a major role in practice (*see* §1151 General Civil Code). This criterion is not legally defined, however. For decades, both literature and jurisprudence have interpreted this definition as follows: an employee is a person obliged to do work for another in a state of 'personal dependence' as a consequence of a contract under Austrian civil law. Performing work in a state of personal dependence means that work is carried out in a position of subordination, in other words, under the command, authority and control of another and using the resources belonging to another, namely, the employer. Employees cannot freely decide when, where or which work they are to perform, as this depends on the employer's orders. If work is performed in such a manner, the employee enjoys the full protection of labour law (including collective agreements) and social security.

52. Fundamentally, personal dependence means that employees cannot do what they prefer during working hours. Therefore, a contract which does not oblige an individual to render services in person, or which provides that a substitute may be deployed, cannot be qualified as an employment contract. In other words, a characteristic feature of an employment contract is the employee's integration into an employer's organization. The person providing the work performance is subject to the employer's managerial authority as regards working hours, the place of performing work and personal conduct while working. An employee is subject to the employer's supervision and disciplinary authority. Since the concept of personal dependence is seen as indicative, not all the above-mentioned criteria have to exist at the same time in a particular case. An overall assessment determines whether a contractual relationship can be considered an employment contract or not. If the features which are characteristic of an employment contract outweigh the others, the contract is considered to be an employment contract.

53. The obligation to perform dependent work must be based on a contract under civil law. If the activity is not based on an employment contract, labour law is not applicable. For instance, the work relationship of civil servants (federal officials, *Beamte*) is based on an act of state under public law. Therefore, they are not employees in the sense of labour law. In principle, the same applies to work by members of the family, because such work is frequently based on family law duties. However, (additional) employment contracts between family members are possible.

54. Persons who work for others based on a contract under civil law but not in a position of (complete) personal dependence, that is to say, who are not subject to (comprehensive) command or control, are not employees but are so-termed free employees or quasi-employees. Examples for this group are manual home workers, free-lancing journalists, members of the board of a joint-stock company or independent commercial representatives. Yet, in part, such free employees or independent workers can be covered by labour law protection. These may happen in three ways:

(1) Labour law statutes can explicitly refer to 'free employees' or 'quasi-employees' and cover them, such as in §1164a General Civil Code, according to which the employer also has to provide a written record outlining the essential rights and obligations arising from the employment to free employees. Furthermore, the Equal Treatment Act or the Maternity Protection Act applies likewise to free employees.
(2) Several general rules apply to free employment contracts *per analogiam*, such as the rules and principles on termination of contracts without substantive reason. In such cases, an immediate termination is not allowed; rather, an adequate period of notice must be observed (§1159 *Allgemeines Bürgerliches Gesetzbuch* (ABGB) analogously). Due to legal changes in the course of the convergence of blue-collar and white-collar workers (*see* below, paragraph 58), even longer periods of notice of at least six weeks and termination dates are to be observed.
(3) Several statutes do not refer to 'free employees' (quasi-employees) as such but explicitly cover 'employee-like' persons (*see* below, paragraph 55). If free employees (additionally) fulfil the conditions of employee-similarity, they are covered forthwith by those labour law regulations. The main examples of the inclusion of employee-like persons are the Employees' Liability Act or the Act on Labour and Social Courts. As a result, such employee-like persons are not subject to general civil procedure law (only). Therefore, for example, compensation for damages to employers caused by quasi-employees during work may be reduced, and, furthermore, they can file suits before the Labour Courts (*see* paragraphs 247 et seq.).

55. The applicability of the term 'employee' – and therefore of labour law – is closely tied to the employee's personal dependence. For the main part, economic dependence in the sense that the employee depends on a salary to earn a living is legally insignificant. However, economic dependence in another sense is a crucial feature in the case of 'employee-like' persons to whom some acts of labour law apply. These are persons who have no employment contract but work for others in a reduced kind of personal independence. Employee-like workers do not perform their duties in a relationship of comprehensive subordination – mostly they can organize for themselves when to work. They have only one, or a few, contractees/principals, and they do not have at their disposal their own establishment, essential work equipment or even their own employees/subcontractors. This includes home workers, some forms of franchisees and so-termed commercial representatives. Furthermore, new forms of work such as crowd working, UBER-drivers, etc. might be covered by regulations for employee-like persons.

II. Categories of Employee

56. Austrian employees are divided into two main categories, blue-collar and white-collar workers (for further categories and details *see* paragraphs 154 et seq.). The distinction between them has legal consequences on several levels. From a formal point of view, there still exist nomenclatures and separate Acts for each group, especially the White-collar Workers Act 1921 and the Industrial Code 1859. Moreover, there are material differences between the various categories as regards some claims against the employer.

57. The criteria used in drawing the line between these two categories of workers are based on the essential characteristics of the work performed: predominantly manual work is blue collar, and predominantly intellectual effort represents white-collar activities. The White-collar Workers Act (*Angestelltengesetz*) refers to the work performed – if this concerns primarily commercial or higher non-commercial functions or office work, the employee is a white-collar worker. If not, the employee is deemed a blue-collar worker.

58. This distinction still exists nowadays, but at least its implications have been levelled by legislation bit by bit. The working programmes of many previous governments have for a long time included the project of a unified labour code or at least the equalization of the blue- and the white-collar workers' legal situation. For example, in 2000, a first step was taken towards convergence concerning the continuation of payment in the event of illness. Furthermore, several collective agreements were concluded that are applicable to both groups of workers. The main reason for the failure to adopt a unified labour code for all employees, or at least a material convergence of the differently named groups, has been the increased costs for the employers (such as in the case of longer termination periods for blue-collar workers), which is claimed to weaken the competitiveness of Austrian companies in a globalized economy. But there have also been reservations on the other side, because the (complete) abolition of all distinctions between various types of employees would have consequences in the area of works council organization and within trade unions. Irrespective of such long-held positions, in autumn 2017, only a few days before the national election, the Social Democratic members of Parliament filed a bill that was supported by two parties of the opposition (i.e., the Freedom Party and the Green Party) and, therefore, passed. Mainly, the new rules result in a convergence of blue- and white-collar workers in the fields of continued wage payment due to sickness (effective from 1 July 2018, by which the different periods of payment in the event of illness and accident were abolished) and termination by notice (originally, they should have been effective from 1 January 2021, in fact, they only became effective from 1 October 2021). The rights and duties of the various categories of employees are, however, still laid down in separate acts, of which there exist a great number, and in which, from a material point of view, some rules also still differ.

59. In summary, the remaining differences are as follows:

- different nomenclature (white-collar workers, blue-collar workers) and different acts for each group;
- different catalogues of grounds for summary dismissals;
- different structures of the trade unions, and therefore differently applicable collective agreements within the same economic branch;
- different bodies of representation at the enterprise level if both groups do not vote for a joint works council;
- differences in the social security system as to access to pensions due to incapacity for work.

III. Senior Personnel and Supervisors

60. Senior personnel and supervisors, even top managers like the general managers of a limited liability company (if they do not own a majority of the shares), are classified as white-collar workers under Austrian law. Only members of the executive board of a joint-stock company are generally excluded from the range of labour legislation. This means that principally senior personnel and supervisors benefit from the full range of protective labour legislation. However, due to the function of these employees, there are exceptions. Also, some statutes with different aims specify different criteria for senior personnel and supervisors.

61. The most important examples of exclusion from the scope of application of labour law provisions can be found in the Labour Organization Act, concerning the works organization in the establishment, and in the Working Time Act. The first exclusion concerns senior personnel that have 'significant influence' on the management of the enterprise or establishment. According to case law, employees who are in charge of running the daily business of this entity are excluded from the scope of application of its works organization. The function of such an employee is similar to that of an employer. Consequently, these employees are neither eligible to serve as nor have the right to vote for, works council representatives and are not represented on the works council. The so-termed general protection against dismissals is construed as a co-determination right of the works council. As a result, senior personnel are not covered by works agreements and have no possibility of contesting their dismissal in court for reasons of social injustice (*see* paragraph 478). Hence, the employment contracts of such employees may be terminated freely by serving notice and without due cause.

62. The Working Time Act also excludes senior personnel, but its definition differs from that of the Work Organization Act. Senior personnel or other employees who have been granted considerable autonomous decision-making powers are excluded from the scope of the Working Time Act if they have sufficient working time autonomy. As a result of the exemptions from the Working Time Act, for example, such managers are not bound by the rules on limited overtime, as white- and blue-collar workers in general are, but they are also not entitled to statutory overtime premiums.

63. Collective (bargaining) agreements may define their own applicability as long as they concern employees in the legal sense. In practice, these agreements usually cover also the above-mentioned groups, explicitly excluding only general managers of limited liability companies.

Chapter 3. Sources of Labour Law

64. Austrian Labour law is both international and national in origin.

§1. International and European Sources

I. International Organizations

65. As a member of various international and supranational organizations, such as the United Nations, the International Labour Organization, the Organisation for Economic Cooperation and Development, the Council of Europe, and particularly the EU since 1995, Austria has undertaken increasing international obligations in the field of labour law. For example, it has ratified a great many of the 190 International Labour Organization (ILO) conventions.

II. European Organizations

A. The Council of Europe

66. The European Social Charter (ESC) sets out diverse social rights and freedoms and establishes two monitoring mechanisms, guaranteeing their implementation in the contracting states. States party to the charter must regularly submit reports on the implementation of the charter in law and in practice (reporting system). National reports are examined by the European Committee of Social Rights (ECSR), which decides whether the national situations they describe comply with the charter. Moreover, this body monitors compliance through collective complaints lodged by the social partners and other non-governmental organizations (collective complaints procedure),

67. The original 1961 ESC has been undergoing a gradual change: it was revised in 1996 and came into force in 1999, replacing the initial Treaty. The Revised Charter was signed by Austria in 1999 and ratified in 2011.

B. The European Union

68. Since Austria's accession to the EU the impact of EU legislation on Austrian labour law has been of major significance and has often been an important impetus to developing national regulation. Besides the free movement of workers, which is established at Treaty level, the EU mostly regulates issues relating to the employment relationship by way of directives which have to be implemented by separate national legislative acts. Until recently, the EU has, for example, acted in the following areas:

- non-discrimination (free movement of labour, equal pay, and equality of treatment);
- health and safety (including working time and teleworking);
- workers' participation in transnational companies or groups of companies;
- protection of workers in the event of the transfer of businesses as well as mergers and demergers;
- mass redundancies;
- the employer's obligation to inform workers of the conditions applicable to the employment relationship;
- protection of workers in the event of employers' insolvency;
- precarious employment relationships (contracts for limited time, part-time work and temporary employment);
- protection of new forms of work such as platform work and telework;
- transparent working conditions;
- data protection;
- transnational posting of workers.

69. In these fields, the European Court of Justice (ECJ) has the monopoly on interpreting European law, whereby its task is to secure uniform application of this law in all Member States. Since, broadly speaking, this law must be implemented in domestic legislation and applied in domestic courts, the ECJ jurisprudence has a strong impact on national legal practice. Only recently, for example, the ECJ stated that the Austrian Good Friday Regulation contradicted EU law because this had been a day off only for specific religious groups; as a result of this, the discriminating regulation in the Hours of Rest Act was amended and changed to provide a 'personal holiday' for every employee (*see* paragraphs 338, 346).

70. The importance of provisions concerning employment and industrial relations has increased over time. Originally, there was hardly any regulation of these fields in the Treaties of Rome. Therefore, the large majority of EU law on employment and industrial relations can be found in other EU legal measures, particularly in directives. Following the amendments to the Treaties of Rome by the Single European Act, the Treaty of Maastricht (Treaty on European Union), the Treaty of Amsterdam and the Treaty of Nice as well as the Treaty of Lisbon, the Treaty provisions in the area of employment and industrial relations now have a more constitutional function. They determine the competences of the EU in these areas and govern the exercise of these competences: for example, through legislation, through the European social dialogue or the Open Method of Coordination. It is also important to mention that the EU has no express competence in matters concerning pay, the right of association, the right to strike or the right to impose lockouts (Article 153 section 5 Treaty on the Functioning of the EU).

71. The Charter of Fundamental Rights of the European Union (CFREU), proclaimed at the European Council at Nice on 7 December 2000, includes provisions that are also of importance to employment and industrial relations: they concern the protection of personal data (Article 8), freedom of association (Article 12), freedom to choose an occupation and the right to engage in work (Article 15), non-discrimination (Article 21), equality between women and men (Article 23), workers' rights to information and consultation within the undertaking (Article 27), the right of collective bargaining and collective action (Article 28), protection in the event of unjustified dismissal (Article 30), fair and just working conditions (Article 31) and the prohibition of child labour and protection of young people at work (Article 32) as well as the reconciliation of family and professional life (Article 33). After the entry into force of the Lisbon Treaty in 2009, the charter acquired a legally binding status, placing it on equal footing with the treaties. Pursuant to Article 51 section 1 of the charter and the case law of the ECJ, it became binding not only upon EU institutions but also upon the Member States, insofar as their domestic measures fall under the scope of EU law. Furthermore, in 2017, the twenty-eight Member States of the EU committed themselves to the European Pillar of Social Rights, delivering new and more effective rights for citizens. The declaration is built upon twenty key principles, divided into three main categories: equal opportunities and access to the labour market, fair working conditions, and social protection and inclusion. How the individual principles will actually be implemented remains to be seen. However, it has to be mentioned that already two directives, the Directive (EU) 2019/1158 on work-life balance for parents and carers and the Directive (EU) 2019/1152 on transparent and predictable working conditions, have been adopted within the framework of the European Pillar of Social Rights.

§2. National Sources

I. Statutes

72. The most important areas of Austrian labour law are regulated in detail by statute. However, there is no unified code regulating this branch of law in its entirety. A multitude of different statutes exists, particularly in individual labour law. In part, they only apply to particular groups of employees (e.g., white-collar workers or construction workers); however, in part they apply to all employees but concern only certain aspects of employment conditions (e.g., continuation of payment in the event of sickness and accident, and vacations).

73. Those statutory provisions which regulate rights and duties arising from employment relationships are mostly binding to the employee's advantage ('relatively' or 'one-sided' binding rules/effect). Hence, neither collective agreements nor works agreements, nor individual contracts may contain terms diverging from these statutes insofar as they are less advantageous to the employee. As a rule, this effect is laid down in the statute itself. Only a few statutes allow the arrangement of conditions which are less favourable to employees by collective agreement ('optional' or 'dispositive' rules/effect; for example, §1155 General Civil Code). A few other statutes do not allow any changes by inferior provisions in any direction, that is to say neither in favour nor to the disadvantage of the employee or employer ('absolutely' or 'two-sided' binding rules/effect; *see* the following paragraphs). Both statutory regulations which do not imperatively protect employees, and those which also prevent agreements that are more beneficial to employees (binding in all directions), are rare exceptions.

74. In the field of collective labour law, the multitude of statutes and diversity were considerably reduced when the Labour Organization Act (*Arbeitsverfassungsgesetz*) came into force in 1975. This legislation has – despite its name (*Verfassung*) – nothing to do with the Constitution or even constitutional rights; rather, the term '*Verfassung*' means 'organization' (e.g., of the labour force, the establishment, or the social partners) in this context. The Labour Organization Act regulates the collective creation of law (collective agreements and works agreements), works representation and conciliation law. In most cases, statutory regulations in collective labour law are absolutely binding for both parties. For instance, no form of employees participation can be agreed upon validly between employers and employees if it is not (explicitly) allowed under the Labour Organization Act.

II. Collective (Bargaining) Agreements

75. Collective agreements are of great importance; they cover about 95% of employees (*see also* paragraphs 392, 655). In the field of (minimum) wages, about 450 collective agreements are bargained and changed annually. Collective agreements are essentially concluded by supra-establishment associations. As a rule, they apply to employers and employees in a particular branch of the economy all over Austria, or at least in one or several federal provinces.

76. A collective agreement has the same effect as a statute. Its provisions are directly and legally binding, independent of the employer's or employee's will. Principally, they can be neither overruled nor changed for the worse (for the employee) by individual or works agreements. Unless employees benefit from the deviating provisions, individual or works agreements can only derogate from collective agreements if the law (or the collective agreement or both) explicitly provides for deviations by such lower-ranked provisions. The main significance of collective agreements lies in the settlement of (minimum) wages which are regularly bargained and changed (mostly annually or every two years). However, they usually also cover other subjects, such as working hours, vacation rights, periods of notice, expense allowances, grounds for continued payment, and so on.

77. Collective agreements are concluded by bodies which have been given this right either by statute or by decision of the competent authorities (paragraphs 677 et seq.). In practice, most collective agreements are concluded between the mandatory organization on the employers' side (chambers of economy) and the trade union, that is to say an association on the employees' side. Austrian collective agreements cover the majority of employees and employers. This prevalence of collective agreements is rooted in the fact that they are usually concluded by employers' organizations with mandatory membership. Moreover, §12 of the Labour Organization Act specifies that such collective agreements also apply to employees who do not belong to the concluding body on the employees' side of it (outsiders or free-riders).

78. In the rare case in which employers do not belong to a collective bargaining body, an executive authority (the Federal Conciliation Board) can extend the scope of a collective agreement (*Satzung*) under certain circumstances. This 'charter' then also applies to employment relationships originally not covered by the agreement's scope, for example, to outsiders on the employers' side (*see* paragraphs 651, 691, 710).

79. Minimum wages can be laid down by an executive body (the Federal Conciliation Board), for employees in whose favour no collective agreement can be concluded because there is no organization on the employers' side with any entitlement to conclude such collective agreements. These 'minimum wage tariffs' (minimum wage rates) have the same effect as a statute or a collective agreement. They are of practical significance primarily for carers, *au pairs*, domestic servants and janitors, as they work for employers who are generally not organized within the statutory chambers of economy or any associations (for more details, *see* paragraphs 746 et seq.).

III. Works Agreements

80. Collective agreements are essentially concluded by supra-establishment associations. As a rule, they apply to employers and employees in a particular branch of the economy, all over Austria or at least in one or several federal provinces. By contrast, works agreements are written agreements between the owner of a particular establishment and a works council. Their application is restricted to this establishment. Moreover, works agreements can only regulate matters as allowed for in either a statute or collective agreement. Like a statute or collective agreement, a works agreement is directly binding. In areas which are covered by a works agreement, an individual contract can only lay down conditions which are more favourable to the employee than those in the works agreement. Other changes by individual contract are not permitted.

IV. Individual Contracts of Employment

81. An individual employment contract is a contract under civil law creating and (insofar as it is permissible) regulating the individual employment relationship. Since the most important conditions of employment are regulated by statutes and collective agreements the role of an individual contract might be restricted to specifying the type of work and the point in time at which employment commences. It is of course possible, and common in practice, that other matters might also be regulated in the employment contract (such as wages, workplace and work hours). For the most part, the employment conditions determined by statute, collective agreement or works agreement lay down minimum standards and therefore cannot be worsened (from the employees' point of view) by the employment contract.

82. The so-termed establishment or employment practice (*Betriebsübung*), that is to say the procedures in certain matters common to the whole establishment (such as the time of starting work and the rendering of certain services to employees not specified in the collective or works agreement), are not an autonomous source of law in Austria. Establishment practices are only binding for employer and employees if these practices can be qualified as an implicit individual agreement according to civil law principles.

83. In any case, numerous decisions of the Austrian Supreme Court have held that employees may have implicit contractual entitlements in the light of long-standing employment practices. Thus, employers who repeatedly grant benefits to employees without a contractual or statutory basis become obliged to continue this practice, on the basis of an implicit contractual agreement ('conclusive' agreement; as to 'free works agreements' as basis of establishment practice, *see* paragraph 649). To prevent such an implicit agreement, the employer must explicitly state the discretionary character of the benefit granted each time, or reserve the right to cease granting such benefits.

V. Employer's Orders

84. Insofar as the employee's duties are not regulated by statute or collective, works or individual agreements, an employer can specify these duties by giving orders to individual employees or to the labour force in general (such as to serve a specific client at a specific time).

§3. The Hierarchy of the Sources of Labour Law

85. The order of precedence of the various national sources of law is, for the most part, already discernible in the outline presented above. Regulations which may not be deviated from by a collective, works or individual agreement have the highest precedence. They are followed by statutes binding in favour of the employee; in other words, these statutes take precedence over all less favourable agreements, including collective ones. Below binding statutes are collective agreements, which can only be derogated from by works agreements or individual employment contracts in favour of the employee. Below the collective agreements, there are works agreements, which can, for the most part, only lay down conditions more favourable to the employee than those laid down by statutes binding to the employee's advantage or by collective agreements. The rights and duties of the individual employment contract only apply if there is no regulation in binding statutes or collective agreements, or if the individual agreement deviates from them in favour of the employee. The penultimate position in this hierarchy is held by the few optional statutory provisions in labour law that can be deviated from, either in favour or to the disadvantage of the employee. Only if there are no other types of regulation can the employer's right to give orders be exercised. These principles are to be considered in all cases. Furthermore, if and insofar as a statute (or, as it is generally termed, a regulation of higher priority) does not regulate a particular question, the collective, works or individual agreement (regulations of inferior priority) can regulate it in any way.

86. The principle that sources of law of inferior priority can only improve and not worsen the employee's position applies not only to the relationship between individual employment contracts and binding statutes, collective agreements and works agreements but also to the relationship between all of these general legal instruments.

87. Deciding whether or not an arrangement is more advantageous to the employee can be difficult – the problem is solved by applying the 'principle of comparative advantage': if the advantage is in doubt, the socio-political purpose of the legal provision, rather than the subjective interest of the individual employee, are decisive. For instance, an agreement entailing more working hours than permitted by the Hours of Work Act is invalid, even if the increased hours of work would be in the interests of the individual employee concerned (hence, even if this would increase the pay). If no clear decision can be made on the basis of the purpose of the regulation, the question has to be asked: in whose interests is the changing of the higher-ranking provision, those of the employer or those of the employee? If this cannot be answered, it is crucial to establish who made the suggestion of a different employment arrangement.

88. Furthermore, it is important to note that it is not permissible to compare the agreed conditions as a whole with the prescribed conditions as a whole. On the contrary, it is also prohibited to see the divergent arrangements in complete isolation from other provisions. Only a comparison of those employment conditions that concern the same topics leads to a valid result. For instance, an agreement under which an employee agrees to waive the right to severance pay in order to receive higher earnings or more vacation time is disadvantageous and therefore invalid.

89. In general, directly applicable EU labour law (as laid down in the EU Treaty or in regulations) takes precedence over domestic labour law – but this does not happen very often, since the usual source of EU law concerning employment and industrial relations are directives that have to be implemented by the national legislator. Where rights conferred by a directive are violated by the state or emanations of the state (especially in cases of lacking or incorrect national implementation), a citizen may claim the 'vertical direct effect' of this directive and the resultant rights against the state (or against an emanation of the state). Horizontal direct effect does not apply to EU directives, as these are generally only enforceable against the state, and the ECJ has refused to extend the direct effect of directives to claims by individuals against other private individuals, including private employers.

Chapter 4. Procedures in the Event of Individual and Collective Labour Disputes

§1. Individual Labour Law

I. General

90. Legal disputes concerning individual employment relationships in Austria are predominantly settled by state authorities, in particular by special labour courts. Private arbitration tribunals are of minimal significance, primarily because the proceedings of state authorities do not last excessively long, and the potential costs for an employee are usually low (cost-free legal representation is available, provided by the trade union as well as by the statutory chamber of labour for its members). Furthermore, the validity of arbitration clauses is restricted by statute where matters of labour law are concerned (*see* §9 Act on Labour and Social Courts). Any agreement to submit a dispute between an employer and a staff representation body (especially works council) to private arbitration is void. Any clause agreed by the employer and employee to submit a future dispute between them is equally void, insofar as the dispute concerns the labour relationship. Hence, with the exception of arbitration clauses of board members of corporations and theatre employees, disputes related to the individual labour contract may only be submitted to arbitration by the parties after the dispute has occurred.

II. Labour and Social Courts

91. Essentially, labour and social courts decide – in addition to their competence in matters concerning social security benefits – legal disputes between employers and employees arising from employment or training relationships, and disputes between employees arising from their work together. These courts are also competent in disputes concerning employment-like contractual relationships (involving employee-like persons). The labour court system and the rules of procedure were fundamentally reorganized in 1986 by the Act on Labour and Social Courts (*Arbeits- und Sozialgerichtsgesetz*). Since then, the labour and social courts have also been able to hear actions against unfair dismissal, and decide disputes between employer and staff representation bodies (e.g., a dispute over a participation right).

92. The competent Courts of First Instance are sixteen of the twenty regional courts (*Landesgerichte*), which act as labour and social courts along with their other areas of jurisdiction (with the exception of Vienna, which has a special labour and social court; *see also* paragraph 15).

93. Labour courts hear cases and reach a decision in panels, with a professional judge as chairperson, and two associate judges, each representing the employer or the employee side. The vote of each of these lay judges has the same weight as that of the professional judge. They are designated in advance by the professional judges from lists made by the appropriate statutory representative bodies (e.g., the chambers of commerce, labour or physicians). The lay judges do not receive remuneration for their activities, only the payment of expenses.

94. Appeals against the first instance Labour Court are heard by a special section of one of the four higher regional courts of appeal (*Oberlandesgerichte*). Appeals against their decisions are heard by two special sections of the Supreme Court (*Oberster Gerichtshof*). In both instances, the appeal court consists of boards with professional judges and lay judges (as for their designation see above). Appeals usually only concern the legal aspects of the case and do not take the form of a complete rehearing of the case.

95. Besides the usual option of an action in court being filed by the person (e.g., an employee) who is actually affected by the dispute and who is the bearer of the claimed right, it is also possible for a works council or a representative organization (here, by virtue of its right to conclude collective agreements) to initiate one of the two types of 'model litigation':

(1) a staff representation body (e.g., a works council) may litigate with the employer over a matter of individual labour law before the Labour Court. The dispute has to concern more than two employees (although there is no necessity to give their names). In the same way, the employer may litigate against the staff body. In such cases, the court is only empowered to decide (or, actually, to state) whether or not one of the parties to the individual labour contract has a right against the other party to this contract. Therefore, the court has no power to order anyone to do something or to refrain from doing it. Furthermore, the court's decision in such cases is not legally binding for subsequent court proceedings between employer and employee. The procedure therefore only allows the legal situation to be clarified;
(2) the second type of model litigation is similar to the first one above, but it works at a higher level. An employees' or employers' organization, which is capable of concluding collective agreements (*see* paragraphs 677 et seq.), may bring an action against the social opponent. The aim of this action is also the court's decision, whether or not an individual employee has a right against their employer or vice versa. The claimant (association) has to submit a sample of facts which is not (necessarily) related to individual employees, but which could possibly affect more than two employees. The court's decision is therefore merely an answer to a quite abstract question of law. Motions of this kind are heard by the Supreme Court.

§2. Collective Labour Law

I. General

96. In the area of collective disputes, according to the literature, there is a distinction between 'disputes of rights' and 'disputes of interest'. Disputes of interest are defined as disputes about whether a future collective or works agreement should be concluded and/or which rights and duties should be laid down in it. Hence, after resolving such a dispute, law might actually be created by the deciding institution, because the result of the dispute or arbitration might be, for example, a collective or a works agreement. In contrast, disputes of rights are always about dissenting interpretations of (already existing) rules. Different authorities are responsible for the two types of disputes. The procedures for settling them are also different.

II. Disputes of Interest

A. *Works Agreements*

97. State intervention or decision is only allowed for a small fraction of disputes of interest within the framework of works democracy. Essentially, these disputes are called 'enforceable co-determination' and are listed exhaustively in the Labour Organization Act (*see* paragraphs 809 et seq.). If the conclusion of a works agreement between an establishment's owner and its works council cannot be achieved, in terms of the conclusion, amendment or cancellation of a works agreement, the so-termed conciliation board (*Schlichtungsstelle*) conciliates between the parties, at the request of one of them; it makes suggestions, strives for agreement, and where necessary, also makes a ruling. The ruling serves as a works agreement.

98. This conciliation board is not a permanent institution. It is established after one of the parties files a motion with the head of the competent labour and social court. Each board consists of a chairperson and four other members. The chairperson of a conciliation board is appointed by the head of the labour and social court, either as a result of an agreement to this effect between the disputing parties or, if no agreement can be achieved, the chairperson is chosen from among the professional judges. The other members are appointed by the parties to the dispute.

99. Two further institutions are provided for in works representation law and may be brought into action in specific disputes of interest. A conciliation committee (*Schlichtungskommission*) can be created to conciliate in the event of disputes between an establishment owner and a works council about certain economic measures. In a few specific cases, a works council can also file a protest with the (central) State Economic Commission (*Staatliche Wirtschaftskommission*), which then also conciliates and, where necessary, renders an opinion on the legitimacy of the protest (for the details *see* §§111, 112 Labour Organization Act). However, at present, these institutions have not yet acquired practical significance.

B. *Collective Agreements*

100. Disputes on conclusion and amendment of collective agreements are dealt with by the Federal Conciliation Board, on the request of either party to the intended collective agreement. The decision of this Board may be treated as a collective agreement, if both parties agree in advance, in writing, to abide by the Board's decision. In practice, the parties to collective agreements hardly ever use the services of the Federal Conciliation Board to aid in the conclusion or the amendment of collective agreements. What the Board does more often is to provide an expert opinion on the interpretation of collective agreements, upon requests by courts or administrative bodies.

III. Disputes of Rights

A. Works Representation Law

101. The labour and social courts (*see* paragraph 91) are – among other issues – responsible for deciding legal disputes arising from works representation law. These include disputes concerning a works council's right of co-determination; disputes about the election of staff bodies; disputes relating to the management of staff bodies and the ending of their activities; and the interpretation of rights or duties laid down in works agreements.

B. Trades Representation Law

102. There is no special state authority responsible for legal disputes in trade representation law. If disputes arise, they are decided by general procedures, partly by labour courts and partly by administrative courts. For example, if the employer does not pay the minimum wage laid down in the collective agreement, the employee files an action in court. If an association is denied a decree on the acknowledgement of the right to conclude collective agreements, the association may contest the decision before the Federal Administrative Court.

Chapter 5. The History of Labour Law

§1. At the Time of the Austrian Empire

103. As in other European countries (and in particular, Great Britain and what was then called Prussia), the development of labour law was a consequence of the industrialization process which had begun in the 1800s. A considerable movement of agricultural workers and manual workers to the factories led to a superfluity of labour. This, along with the fact that contemporary law adhered to the principle of unrestricted freedom of contract, resulted in a massive pauperization of a large part of the population, and in particular of factory workers. In Austria, the first state reaction to this situation came in 1842. The employment of children under the age of nine in factories was prohibited. The next attempt to improve the situation only came in 1859, by way of the Industrial Code (*Gewerbeordnung*), which essentially regulated entitlement to run an undertaking and also laid down several necessary rules concerning employment. The main reason for such a late state intervention was lagging industrialization in Austria – it started later than in Great Britain. However, another important reason was that employees were only allowed to create affiliations to promote their interests in 1867 (with the Fundamental Law on General Rights of Citizens, a constitutional act concerning, *inter alia*, the freedom to form associations), and the main penalties in criminal law against industrial action were first removed in 1870.

104. The legal situation of employees improved strongly between 1884 and 1888. Special authorities were created to supervise compliance with the employment regulations, which limited the daily hours of work to a maximum of eleven hours, forbade the employment of children under 14 in factories, and specified that young people under 16 could only be given light work. The beginnings of social welfare law also date back to this period. In 1887 and 1888 respectively, statutory accident and health insurance were introduced. In 1895, a statute followed which specified rest on Sundays and on public holidays.

105. In 1901, the nine-hour shift was introduced into coal mining. In 1910, an Act was passed that extensively regulated white-collar employment relationships in the private sector (paragraphs 164 et seq.). This gave white-collar workers advantages compared to other workers, whose rights still do not entirely match those of the white-collar workers. During the First World War in 1914–1918, an amendment of the Austrian General Civil Code was introduced, defining the employment contract in §1151 *leg cit* in contrast to the works contract and bringing certain improvements for manual workers (such as the continuation of wage payment in the event of illness).

§2. 1918–1938

106. The most significant advances in labour law were introduced after the end of the First World War, which at the same time saw the end of the Austro-Hungarian Empire. In 1918, the eight-hour day for factories was established, as well as statutes concerning blue-collar workers' vacation rights, and special statutes for home workers, white-collar workers, artistic theatrical employees, journalists and so on. In collective labour law, works representation was first statutorily regulated in 1919, and works councils were given certain rights of participation. Moreover, at the end of 1919, the collective agreement and its specific effects were embodied in law for the first time. The creation of statutory representation for employees (chambers of labour) also dates from this time. In 1921, the White-collar Workers Act was introduced, which can be seen as the first labour law code that regulates rights and duties of employees and employers in a comprehensive way; such as termination, holidays, severance pay and so on. However, it only applied to white-collar workers who were a minority of workers at that time.

107. The period after the dissolution of Parliament in 1933 and the introduction of an authoritarian Constitution resulted in the deterioration of industrial relations. The free collective agreement system was abolished. A single trade union was created which enjoyed a legal monopoly to conclude collective agreements. A drastic remodelling of labour law then followed during the annexation of Austria into Germany in 1938. Numerous Austrian statutes were repealed in 1938 and replaced by German ones. A fundamental change took place, particularly in collective labour law: trade unions were deactivated and instead of collective agreements, state ordinances laid down by special authorities specified the conditions of employment.

§3. Since 1945

108. After 1945, the previous legal situation was re-established with various improvements. Statutory works representation was introduced, and the previous collective agreement situation as well as statutory employee representation (chambers of labour) were re-established. Subsequently, there was continuous introduction of further improvements for employees or new statutes pulling together diverse regulations for the sake of a better general regulation were continuously introduced. The efforts to codify labour law particularly deserve mention. In 1974, their first success was achieved. The Labour Organization Act is a codification of collective labour law and regulates works representation law as well as the law of collective bargaining for almost all types of employees. The influence of works councils in both personnel and social matters was strengthened.

109. Nevertheless, despite intensive efforts, attempts to codify individual labour law have not yet succeeded in all fields. All the same, appropriate minimum standards and above all socio-political improvement in favour of all groups of employees have been achieved in the recent past. In 1974, the continuation of full pay during illness was statutorily guaranteed for blue-collar workers. Two years later, a unified statute was passed regulating vacation rights, which applies equally to white- and blue-collar workers. In 1977, an Act was passed protecting employees' interests in the case of employer insolvency, and in 1979, an Act was adopted specifying the equal treatment of the sexes in settlement of remuneration.

110. The Labour and Social Courts Act of 1986 has reorganized these courts and their procedure. In 1987, the Parliament enacted the much-disputed Temporary Work Act (*Arbeitskräfteüberlassungsgesetz*), which dealt for the first time with the 'lending' of the employee's services to another business. In 1990, Parliament adopted the first regulation of retirement benefits paid by the employer ('private' occupational pension scheme), which are not mandatory and are only additional to state pensions in Austria. This Company Pension Act (*Betriebspensionsgesetz*) secures the employee's claims to a private pension, insofar as it has been promised, in the event of premature termination of the contract. Furthermore, the Act restricts employers' opportunities to interfere with pension agreements. In the same year, Parliament improved the legal position of employed parents of a child: the right to 'maternity leave' (period of unpaid vacation connected with the right to return to work) was extended to two years after the child's birth. In addition, the right of a child's father to claim this leave was laid down at that time ('parental leave'). In 1990, moreover, the first attempt was made to introduce a right to parental part-time work in lieu of parental leave, in other words, to reduce the working time to allow for the care of a child. After the (originally rather rigid) model acquired some flexibility in 1999, the 2004 legislation introduced a right to working-time reduction until the seventh year of age of the child or the child's enrolment in school.

111. One of the most important events, with regard to labour law as well, was Austria's accession to the European Economic Area (EEA) in 1994 and to the European Community (now the EU) one year later. As a consequence, Austria had to adapt its national employment law to European standards: this was particularly applicable to the laws on the employment of EU citizens, the legal impact of transfers of businesses on the employment relationship, and the law concerning equal opportunities, as well as health and safety rules. In the aftermath of the accession, the impact of EU law remained an important impetus for further development of labour regulation. New laws concerning the following subjects mostly represent implementation of European directives: contracts for limited time and part-time workers, the European works council, workers' participation in the *Societas Europaea* and the European cooperative society, as well as in the event of transnational mergers, and – perhaps most importantly – laws combating discrimination based on ethnicity, age, sexual orientation, disability and religion.

112. Among the predominant national trends in Austria, there have to be mentioned the unification and simplification of the existing legal situation of employees, for instance by means of step-by-step harmonization of the continuation of payment of wages in the event of illness of blue-and white-collar workers, which regulations were adopted in 2000 and 2017, and the equalization of the periods for giving notice. However, the nomenclature still differs (white-collar workers, blue-collar workers) and differently termed statutes apply. The second important trend has represented a reaction to the need for employment relationships to adapt quickly to changing conditions: there have been attempts to add more flexibility to the employment relationship (especially at the beginning of the 1990s, concerning working time) while also trying to add more security in the event of termination, or payments to compensate for this flexibility (like premiums for extra work carried out by part-time workers, introduced in 2007). Another main feature of Austrian labour law is the integration of several forms of free employees or quasi-employees into some areas of labour law and the most fields of social insurance law.

Chapter 6. Equal Treatment and Anti-discrimination

§1. Introduction

113. Equal treatment of men and women is a subject of ongoing concern at international and European as well as at Austrian level. It has been extended to include other prohibited grounds of discrimination and these now constitute a general framework of anti-discrimination regulation. Furthermore, due to their neutral wording, most equal treatment rules concerning gender also include the protection of intersex employees.

114. Austrian law contains different sets of rules at different levels of legislation that provide general protection against discrimination by an employer. The constitutional principle of equal treatment outlaws different treatment without good cause (Article 7 Federal Constitution Act). The Austrian Constitutional Court holds that different treatment is only justified if it is based on objective characteristics. The constitutional principle of equal treatment binds only the legislative and executive powers. Moreover, it provides only Austrian citizens and Austrian legal entities with a subjective right. As to labour law, Austrian courts have established that the constitutional equality principle is also applicable to collective agreements and works agreements. However, the parties to an employment contract are not bound by this constitutional principle.

115. European legislation also prohibits discrimination. Article 157 of the Treaty on the Functioning of the European Union provides that all parties to the treaty are bound to apply the principle that men and women should receive equal pay for equal work. Additionally, the Charter of Fundamental Rights contains various principles of equal treatment in its third chapter and thus is considered to be an important legal basis for discrimination law. At the level of secondary law, several European Directives forbid discrimination based on gender, family status, religion and belief, sexual orientation, race and ethnic origin.

116. At the national level, equal treatment of men and women used to be the sole subject of the Equal Treatment Act 1979 (*Gleichbehandlungsgesetz*), which was restructured and extensively amended in 2004. This law now deals not only with discrimination based on gender but also with that based on religion and belief, sexual orientation, age and ethnic origin. This Act implements the above-mentioned secondary law, EU Directive 2000/78 (Framework Directive) as well as EU Directive 2000/43 (the Anti-Racism Directive). Only the equal treatment of employees with disabilities is dealt with in a special act, the Employees with Disabilities Act (paragraphs 287, 509 et seq., 552 et seq.).

117. Further legal provisions concerning equal opportunities are found in certain other Acts. They cover, for example, members of the works council, foreign employees, part-time workers, issues in connection with company pensions, and employees performing tasks in connection with work security. Protection against discrimination due to a reason not mentioned in either of these provisions is laid down in §879 of the General Civil Code, according to which discriminatory acts are *contra bonos mores* and, therefore, void. Moreover, the implied contractual 'duty to treat employees equally' has to be mentioned which is derived from the employer's 'duty of care' and goes beyond the prohibited grounds outlined above. It forbids an employer to treat particular employees less favourably than others without material reasons (paragraphs 284 et seq.).

§2. Scope of Application and Content of the Equal Treatment Act

118. The Equal Treatment Act covers most persons in the private sectors (including, since 2021, also directly the agricultural sector); similar regulations exist for the public sector. With regard to employment issues, the Equal Treatment Act covers employers, the parties to collective agreements (e.g., unions and chambers of commerce) and works agreements (e.g., the works council). It also extends the scope beyond the traditional employment relationship to include 'employee-like' persons who are not personally dependent (paragraph 54) but who are economically dependent on their contractual partner.

119. The Act covers most persons in the private sector in relation to:

- employment issues;
- access to all forms of occupational counselling and training;
- membership or involvement in an employers' or employees' organization, or any organization of which the members practise a certain profession, including the benefits these organizations offer;
- access to all activities of self-employed workers.

120. The parts concerning anti-racism extend the scope of application to:

- the supply of goods and services which are available to the public (including living space or accommodation);
- social protection including social security and healthcare;
- social benefits;
- education.

121. As for employment matters, the Act applies to, among other things and not limited to:

- the conclusion of the contract of employment;
- determination of remuneration;
- granting of fringe benefits, which do not constitute remuneration;
- training measures;
- promotion;
- all other working conditions; and
- the termination of the employment relationship (*see* paragraph 476).

122. Women and men must be treated equally. Discrimination on the basis of gender is forbidden, and discrimination based on civil status is, by legal definition, a form of gender discrimination. Though not explicitly forbidden, it is a long-standing practice of Austrian courts as well as the ECJ that discrimination on the basis of pregnancy, birth, maternity or change of gender is also a form of gender discrimination. Additionally, it has to be pointed out that the Austrian Constitutional Court recognizes the third sex as a gender; therefore, discrimination of intersex employees can also be a form of gender discrimination.

123. As mentioned above, amendments to the original Equal Treatment Act from 1979 extended its scope: since 2004, discrimination on the ground of age, sexual orientation, religion or belief as well as ethnic origin has been forbidden.

124. Both direct and indirect discrimination are prohibited. Direct discrimination occurs when the different treatment is based directly on the prohibited grounds outlined above, and when this treatment cannot be justified by reference to legitimate and proportionate grounds. Indirect discrimination occurs when an apparently neutral provision, criterion or practice puts persons of one sex, of particular age or sexual discrimination, or persons having a particular religion or belief at a disadvantage compared to other persons, unless this different treatment can be justified, as it pursues a legitimate aim, by means that are appropriate and necessary to achieve this aim.

125. Equally forbidden are:

- an instruction to discriminate;
- harassment: unwanted conduct related to any of the above-mentioned forbidden grounds with the purpose or effect of violating the dignity of a person that creates either an intimidating, hostile, degrading, humiliating or offensive environment, or that subsequently results in disadvantages at work due to the victim's reaction (rejection or toleration);
- sexual harassment: any form of sexually related unwanted conduct with the purpose or effect of violating the dignity of a person, that creates either an intimidating, hostile, degrading, humiliating or offensive environment, or that subsequently results in disadvantages in the job because of the victim's reaction (rejection or toleration);
- the failure to take reasonable means to prevent discrimination or (sexual) harassment by a third party (e.g., a colleague or customer);
- discriminatory job advertisements.

§3. Affirmative Action and Income Reports

126. With a view to ensuring full equality in practice, the principle of equal treatment does not prevent any employer or collective or works agreement from maintaining or adopting specific measures to prevent or compensate for possible disadvantages linked to any of the mentioned grounds, for example, the introduction of a quota system stipulating mandatory recruitment of equally qualified women up to a quota of 40% in a certain professional sector. These measures are referred to as 'affirmative action' or 'positive discrimination'.

127. Since 2011, employers with more than 150 workers have to prepare an 'income report' every two years (§11a Equal Treatment Act). This report must contain information on the number of women and men in each remuneration group, as well as the average pay of men and women in each of these groups. The report is anonymous and must not allow any attribution to individual employees. The report has to be sent to the (central) works council; in the event of its lacking, the report must be published on the blackboard (bulletin board) in order to inform the employees of the establishment. In any case, the employees are obliged to maintain secrecy about the contents of the report. However, they are allowed to use the data, if needed, for example, in the event of legal consultation by the chambers or attorneys.

§4. Enforcement and Remedies

128. For the most part, infringements of the Equal Treatment Act neither constitute criminal offences in themselves nor are they subject to imprisonment and/or penalty payments. The Act provides for civil liability of the discriminating person. Contractual provisions which are contrary to the principle of equal treatment are null and void. Yet, according to §218 section 2 of the Criminal Code, anyone who 'intensely' touches sexually related parts of another person's body against their will also faces imprisonment of up to six months.

129. If discrimination is (directly or indirectly) based on sex or other prohibited grounds, the Equal Treatment Act provides diverse remedies depending on the different forms of discrimination:

- if the employment relationship was not finalized due to a discriminatory reason, the employee may claim damages of a minimum of two months' pay, if they would have been employed in the event of a non-discriminatory hiring procedure. If the employee would not have been hired anyway, they may claim up to EUR 500 compensation for immaterial damages;
- if the employee did not receive the same wage or fringe benefits as other employees due to sex or other forbidden grounds, the employee has the right to be paid the difference and compensation for immaterial damages;
- if an employee does not get promotion due to a breach of the Equal Treatment Act, this employee is entitled to damages of a minimum of three months' worth of the difference between the remuneration the employee would have earned after the promotion and their actual remuneration. If the employee would not have been promoted anyway, he or she may claim up to EUR 500 compensation for immaterial damages;

- an employee who has been (sexually) harassed may file a suit against the harasser and the employer, if the employer has negligently failed to put an end to the harassment (e.g., in knowing of the harassment and not taking disciplinary measures against the harassing employee). If the damage is not merely a financial loss, the employee is also entitled to compensation for the injury to dignity (minimum EUR 1,000);
- if the employment of an employee is terminated, or not prolonged, for discriminatory reasons, the termination can be challenged in court within fourteen days. An employee who accepts the unlawful termination can claim compensation for financial loss and for immaterial damages.

130. An employee claiming direct or indirect discrimination due to reasons laid down in the Equal Treatment Act has to substantiate that the given reason has been 'more probable' for the discrimination than the reasons given by the defendant ('reduced standard of proof'). Hence, the complaint will be dismissed if there is 'much stronger' evidence that the less favourable treatment results from lawful factors.

131. Job advertisements by employers, private employment agencies, and even public law bodies which arrange placement services on behalf of others, must not be discriminatory or fail to use gender-neutral language (§9 Equal Treatment Act). For example, unless one gender is an absolutely necessary prerequisite for the job, the advertisement must not refer to one gender only or explicitly exclude a gender. Furthermore, since 2011, vacancy advertisements have to contain information about the minimum wages applicable to the job publicized. In both cases, 'job advertisement' includes all forms of internal or external announcements of vacancies, such as on the blackboard (bulletin board), both on the intra- and on the internet, in newspapers and so on.

132. The information on the minimum wage has to comprise the (initial) basic amount in numbers, and also information about the working time or job-related premiums. It also has to be given for jobs with employers who are not subject to a collective norm on minimum wages, such as collective agreements or minimum wage tariffs. Furthermore, if this exists, the advertisement has to contain information on the employer's willingness to pay an amount exceeding the (collective) minimum level.

133. Job applicants have no individual rights in the event of non-compliance of the advertisement with these rules. However, each applicant, as well as the Ombudsperson's Office for Equal Treatment, may initiate administrative penal procedures. In this procedure, the Ombudsperson for Equal Treatment enjoys the status of a party. The administrative fine for vacancy announcements not meeting these requirements entails fines amounting up to EUR 360.

Chapter 7. Employment of Foreign Workers

134. The restrictions on the employment of foreign workers in Austria aim primarily to safeguard the employment opportunities of Austrian national employees against uncontrolled immigration of labour. The law gives the competent minister the ability to adapt labour immigration to the needs of the labour market by means of ordinances. The possibility of a foreigner obtaining employment in Austria depends, to a great extent, on nationality.

§1. Freedom of Movement for EU–EEA Nationals

135. Within the framework of the EU and EEA, nationals of Member States enjoy complete freedom of movement. This means that without the need for a permit, they can leave their own country and look for work in the labour market of another Member State. If they accept a job, they have equal legal standing with the workers who are nationals of that country.

§2. The Regulation of Other Foreign Workers, Non-nationals of a Member State of the EU–EEA

136. The admissibility of employing persons who are not Austrian nationals or citizens of an EU or EEA Member State is regulated by the Foreign Nationals Employment Act (*Ausländerbeschäftigungsgesetz*). According to this Act, any work by an alien employed in Austria is forbidden, unless the alien has specific permission (work permit), issued by the Public Employment Service; however, there are deviations for the employment of Turkish citizens and close relatives of Austrian or EU citizens.

137. Employment of an alien without valid permission is a statutory offence (but normally not a criminal one, according to criminal law), and the employer can be fined. In order to prevent wage or social dumping, permissions to employ foreign workers usually have the condition attached that the same wage and working conditions must apply as for Austrian employees. Among others, the following types of permission are noteworthy.

138. For a third-country worker who has not previously been employed in Austria, permission has to be sought by the prospective employer. The permission (*Beschäftigungsbewilligung*) has to be granted, if the present and presumed future situation of the (appropriate) labour market allows for the employment of this third-country worker, and if this employment does not conflict with public interests. This type of permission is limited in time (not more than one year) and covers only one particular place of employment. The employer may apply for an extension. The permit can be cancelled for substantive reasons.

139. The Red-White-Red Card (*Rot-Weiß-Rot-Karte*) aims to facilitate the immigration of qualified third-country workers and their families with a view to permanent settlement in Austria, based on personal and labour market related criteria. Very highly qualified workers, skilled workers in shortage occupations, and graduates of Austrian universities and colleges of higher education are deemed eligible for a Red-White-Red Card (§20d Foreign Nationals Employment Act). However, one of the additional requirements that must be fulfilled for any residence title to be granted is adequate means of subsistence. This means that applicants must have fixed and regular income of their own, enabling them to cover their living costs without resorting to welfare aid from local authorities. At the time of application, the regular monthly income must be equal to the amount of the standard rates of the General Social Insurance Act. Holders of a Red-White-Red Card may subsequently also apply for the Red-White-Red Card plus (*Rot-Weiß-Rot-Karte plus*) which entitles third-country nationals to fixed-term settlement and unlimited labour market access (self-employment and gainful employment not limited to a specific employer).

140. Third-country nationals may be granted an EU Blue Card (*Blaue Karte EU*), if they:

- have completed studies at a university or another tertiary educational institution with a minimum duration of three years;
- have received a binding job offer for at least one year in Austria and the employment corresponds to the applicant's education;
- will earn a gross annual income of at least one-and-a-half times the average gross annual income of full-time employees (in 2022: at least EUR 66,593 per year, which is about EUR 4,756 gross monthly income plus special payments);
- and an examination of the labour market shows that there is no equally qualified worker registered as a jobseeker with the Public Employment Service (*Arbeitsmarktservice*) available for the job.

Chapter 8. International Private Labour Law; the Application of Austrian Law to Foreign Nationals

§1. The Competent Judge

141. As a rule, the Austrian labour and social courts are competent, if the dispute involves an employee working (or having worked) in Austria. However, in cases with European reference, the Regulation (EU) no. 1215/2012 of the European Parliament and of the Council of 12 December 2012 on jurisdiction and the recognition and enforcement of judgments in civil and commercial matters determines, if Austrian courts are competent. The Regulation includes a number of detailed provisions concerning individual employment contracts (Articles 20–23) and differentiates between claims against employers and employees. For the most part, the latter may only be sued by their employer in the country in which they are domiciled. Additionally, the regulation contains rules on employers not domiciled in a Member State but who have a branch, agency or other establishments in one of the Member States.

§2. The Proper Law of Contract

I. Conflict of Laws Rules

142. Depending on their date of conclusion, for employment contracts concluded before 18 December 2009, the Austrian International Private Law Act (*Internationales Privatrechtsgesetz*) and the European Convention of the Law Applicable to Contractual Obligations are applicable. The Convention contains special rules regarding conflict of laws for 'employment contracts' in Article 6. For employment contracts concluded after 17 December 2009, the Regulation (EC) no. 593/2008 on the law applicable to contractual obligations (Rome I) applies, which also includes provisions for 'individual employment contracts' (Article 8). As the underlying principles of both the Convention and the Regulation are similar, they will be explained together, with the differences between them identified.

143. Which rules for the application of public labour law are valid in these circumstances is not expressly stated or explained. The application of public law does not depend on which legal system is decisive in questions of private law, but solely on the intended validity that can be derived from the Austrian provisions themselves. Austrian employee protection law, such as work bans for certain persons (children, expectant mothers), during certain times (night work), health and safety regulations and rules about Sunday and public holiday work are, as a rule, only applicable to Austrian places of work, as infringements of these can only be sanctioned by the Austrian authorities if they have taken place in Austria.

144. The European Convention and the Rome I Regulation both establish freedom of choice of the applicable law as the general rule: a contract is governed by the law chosen by the parties. The choice may be made expressly or clearly demonstrated by the terms of the contract or the circumstances of the case. The parties can choose to select the law applicable to the whole or to part of the contract. The parties may agree to change the applicable law at any time.

145. Because labour law is mostly legislation protecting the employee, the effects of the choice of law are limited in this field: the choice of law may not have the result of depriving the employee of the protection afforded to them by provisions, if these cannot be derogated from by agreement under the law that would have been applicable in the absence of choice.

146. If the law applicable to the individual employment contract has not been chosen by the parties, the contract shall be governed by the law of the country in which – or, failing that, from which – the employee habitually carries out work in performance of the contract (this passage is only included in the directive). The country where the work is habitually carried out shall not be deemed to have changed, if the employee is temporarily employed in another country. If the employee does not habitually carry out work in any one country, the contract shall be governed by the law of the country where the place of business is situated, through which the employee was engaged. If, however, it appears from the circumstances as a whole that the contract is more closely connected with another country, the contract shall be governed by the law of that country.

II. The Posting of Workers

147. The Directive 96/71/EC of 16 December 1996 concerning the posting of workers in the framework of the provision of services, amended by Directive (EU) 2018/957, aims to prevent 'social dumping' by means of hiring workers in one Member State and sending them temporarily to another to carry out their work there. If only the rules relating to conflict of laws were applied, this would result in the workers taking with them all the labour standards of the posting country, even if those were lower than the standards in the country where they are working now. The EU therefore sets up certain minimum standards, irrespective of the applicable law. Member States must ensure that, whatever the law applicable to the employment relationship, employers guarantee workers posted to their territory its terms and conditions of employment concerning:

- maximum work periods and minimum rest periods;
- minimum paid annual holidays;
- the minimum rates of pay, including overtime rates (excluding supplementary occupational retirement pension schemes);
- the conditions of hiring-out of workers, in particular the supply of workers by means of temporary employment undertakings;
- health, safety and hygiene at work;

- protective measures with regard to the terms and conditions of employment of pregnant women or women who have recently given birth, of children and of young people;
- the conditions of workers' accommodations where provided by the employer;
- allowances or reimbursement of expenditure to cover travel, board and lodging expenses;
- equality of treatment between men and women, and other provisions to prevent discrimination.

148. Originally, Austria had implemented the directive in the Employment Contract Law Adaptation Act. In 2016, a specific statute, the Law against Wage and Social Dumping, was implemented (for details, *see* paragraphs 412 et seq.).

§3. Collective Labour Law

I. Collective Creation of Rules

149. Essentially, Article 6 of the Convention/Article 8 of the Regulation also applies to collective agreements. Therefore, Austrian collective agreements always apply where Austrian labour law is decisive according to the conflict of laws rules. In the case of work abroad, it must be taken into consideration whether Austrian collective agreements can or are intended to cover work abroad.

150. The application of a collective agreement to an individual employment relationship always presupposes as a minimum requirement that the employer is a member of the employer association concluding the collective agreement (paragraphs 705 et seq.). But even if the employer is not a member, because it does not have a base in Austria, by law, a minimum wage has to be paid, based on the collective agreement that covers comparable employees (*see* §3 Law Against Wage and Social Dumping; §7 Employment Contract Law Adaptation Act).

II. Works Representation Law

151. There exists no express conflict of laws rule for statutory works representation law, as neither the Convention nor the Rome I Regulation is applicable. Austrian works representation law applies to every establishment in Austria, irrespective of whether the owner is Austrian, and whether or not the employment relationships of the employees working in the establishment are subject to Austrian law according to conflict of laws rules. Austrian works representation law is only applied to workplaces abroad in the case of dependent elements of an Austrian establishment. For an independent establishment abroad, Austrian works representation law does not even apply if the employment relationships of the employees working there are overwhelmingly subject to Austrian labour law according to the conflict of laws rules.

152. Nevertheless, individual employees who are only (temporarily) posted abroad always continue to be fully subject to Austrian works representation law. Foreign works representation law is taken into account in all cases if it covers the place of work (in the particular country). This applies regardless of the legal system applicable according to the Convention or the Rome I Regulation.

Part I. Individual Labour Law

Chapter 1. Definitions and Concepts

§1. Different Categories of Employees

I. Occupational Classification

153. In Austria, there is no unified labour code for all employees, and individual employment relationships are not uniformly regulated by statute. There are some general rules laid down in the General Civil Code, but they are subordinate or subsidiary, which means that they are applicable only when no special statutes apply. The special statutes vary, in that some of them contain comprehensive regulations for a specific group of workers or the type of work carried out, and others regulate only certain matters (such as vacation or sickness leave). In the first case, the statutes make distinctions between whether an employee performs mainly manual work or not (white- or blue-collar worker; *Angestellter* or *Arbeiterin).* Due to further legal steps towards a convergence of white- and blue-collar workers in 2017, differences in the area of individual labour law have mostly been abolished, but the rights and duties are still regulated in separate acts, and the nomenclature of the categories of employees differs (for details, *see* paragraphs 56 et seq.).

A. *Blue-Collar Workers* (Arbeiter, Arbeiterinnen)

1. Industrial Workers (*Gewerbearbeiter, Gewerbearbeiterinnen*)

154. The most important, and by far the largest, group of blue-collar workers are those who work in industrial or commercial enterprises covered by the Industrial Code 1859 (*Gewerbeordnung*), as qualified craftsmen, assistants, factory workers, apprentices and unskilled workers – that is, primarily doing manual work. Employees who perform higher duties, office or commercial and trading work, are excluded from the Industrial Code.

155. Such employment relationships are still governed by some sections of the 'old' Industrial Code dating back to 1858 (put into effect in 1859). Among other things, these old statutes specify weekly wage payments and the right to cash payment, and set down valid reasons for dismissal and resignation. The fourteen-day period of notice in §77 of the Industrial Code became ineffective on 1 October 2021 and was replaced by §1159 General Civil Code that provides a period for giving notice of a least six weeks.

156. Construction workers from a special group within that of industrial workers, because their holiday rights and their severance pay are regulated in a special act (Construction Workers' Holiday and Severance Pay Act – *Bauarbeiter-Urlaubs- und Abfertigungsgesetz*), and there are several statutory regulations governing wage payments in the event of a lack of work because of bad weather (Construction Workers' Bad Weather Compensation Act – *Bauarbeiter-Schlechtwetterentschädigungsgesetz*).

2. Other Provisions for Special Groups of Blue-Collar Workers

157. As regards health and safety of mine workers' employment relationships, the *Mineralrohstoffgesetz* refers to the general provisions of the Health and Safety Act (*ArbeitnehmerInnenschutzgesetz*).

158. There are some special provisions for workers in bakeries, especially for workers in night bakeries. They lay down the hours of night work, breaks, overtime work and Sunday work.

159. Until the end of 2019, agricultural and forestry workers were a special group within blue-collar workers: according to the Austrian Constitution (Article 12 section 1 no. 4 of the Federal Constitution, former version), the competences for legislation regulating the employment relationships of this group were divided between the state and the provinces. According to this abolished regulation, the federal Parliament was responsible for fundamental legislation (framework legislation), and the provincial parliaments for regulatory statutes. The fundamental federal statute, the Agricultural Employment Act 1984 (*Landarbeitsgesetz*), was nevertheless so extensive and detailed that there was hardly any room left for individual deviation by the provinces. As of 2020, the statutes of the provinces became federal law which applied only to the respective province. In 2021, a new act, the Agricultural Employment Act 2021, a federal statute, was established which lays down the same rights and duties for all agricultural and forestry workers in Austria.

160. The Agricultural Employment Act 2021 covers employees of establishments in forestry and agricultural production. This includes, for example, hunting estates and fisheries, as well as agricultural and forestry trading cooperatives. As already mentioned, the Agricultural Employment Act contains an extensive and detailed set of standards governing employment relationships. For instance, it regulates the probation period, the due date of payments, payments in kind, service accommodation, the continuation of payment to workers unfit to work because of illness or accident and the termination of employment relationships. Furthermore, the Agricultural Employment Act regulates agricultural collective labour law in detail. This statute is therefore virtually a labour code for agricultural and forestry workers; like the White-collar Workers Act it almost completely governs the employment relationship.

161. Domestic servants (*Hausgehilfen*), that is to say workers who carry out routine manual work in their employer's household, such as carers or cleaning staff, are covered by the Domestic Employees Act (*Hausgehilfen- und Hausangestelltengesetz*). The same Act applies to employees who perform higher duties in households as well, such as teaching (for details on these, *see* paragraph 176). It does not matter whether or not the employees are actually a part of their employer's household (e.g., sleeping or eating there). Furthermore, the term 'household' does not only include households of private persons or families, but also retirement homes, private kindergartens, student dormitories and so forth, that is to say (non-commercial) establishments which provide meals, accommodation, care and so on. The Act regulates these employment relationships in considerable detail: for example, among other things, the issue of a duty card on the settlement of a contract, the due date of payments and the continuation of payment in the event of illness or accident, as well as containing special regulations about working hours and overtime and the termination of the employment relationship. Concerning the care of older people in households new rules have been established in 2007 (the so-termed House Care Act – *Hausbetreuungsgesetz*), intending to make the organization of such employment between private persons and mostly foreign workers simpler (especially '24-hour care'). Its rules mostly apply in addition to the Domestic Employees Act.

162. Janitors (*HausbesorgerInnen*), that is to say employees who carry out the cleaning, servicing and supervision of a house, used to be covered by the Janitors Act (*Hausbesorgergesetz*). This regulates the duties of janitors in relative detail, places them under a special duty of discretion, and provides for the determination of their remuneration by the Federal Conciliation Board. It also makes stipulations about the janitor's duty accommodation and termination, in which the (valid) termination of the employment relationship by the house-owner's giving notice must be based on substantive grounds, if the janitor has the use of duty accommodation. However, contracts with janitors concluded after 30 July 2000 are not covered by the Act anymore, and fall under the scope of the (less favourable) general provisions for blue-collar workers (such as the General Civil Code or the Industrial Code).

3. Blue-Collar Workers Not Covered by Any Special Provisions

163. The employment relationships of those employees who are neither white-collar workers nor covered by any special provisions for blue-collar workers are regulated by the general provisions in the Austrian Civil Code mentioned above (paragraph 153).

B. White-Collar Workers (Angestellte)

1. General Provisions on White-Collar Workers

164. Besides industrial workers, this group is Austria's most important category of employees. The employment relationships of white-collar workers are regulated by the White-collar Workers Act (*Angestelltengesetz*).

165. White-collar workers as defined in the Act are employees in the service of trading and commercial establishments ('merchants') or other enterprises explicitly listed as employers in the Act. For example, according to the Act, attorneys, physicians, dentists, architects, funds, foundations and so forth can be employers of white-collar workers. Moreover, the work of the covered employees is also defined: white-collar workers are employees 'who primarily perform commercial or higher non-commercial functions or office work' for one of the types of employers mentioned above. Therefore, the status of a white-collar worker depends primarily on the sort of service to be rendered, but also on the type of employer.

166. The Act does not further define the various sorts of activities, and they are only described in general. For this reason, the (extensive) past court decisions (still) have particular weight. According to decisions of the Supreme Court, 'commercial duties' are activities which require some skill in trade, or training and practice in the nature of goods turnover. Basically, the buying and selling of goods, warehousing and the supervision of stocks count as commercial duties, as do carrying out correspondence, bookkeeping, cash accounting, advising customers, marketing and so on.

167. According to current views, office work includes all clerical work other than simple copying. However, completely ancillary work, such as simply handling files and office materials, is not included.

168. In legal practice, the 'higher non-commercial activities' are the most difficult to tie down. In general, these include work which requires special prior knowledge and skill and which cannot be carried out by just 'any' substitute.

169. For example, higher, and thus white-collar, work is done by (designing) technicians, teachers, classical musicians in an orchestra, or managing and senior staff, including some forepersons, workshop superintendents, driving instructors in a driving school or nurses, so long as they do not perform only manual duties. On the contrary, this does not apply to drivers, railway signalpersons, football players or any other workers who perform mainly manual functions.

170. The White-collar Workers Act almost completely governs the employment relationship. It regulates the general content of employment contracts and non-competition clauses, specifies claims in the event of inability to work because of illness, accident and other impediments and regulates commission payments, profit-sharing and termination (notice periods, grounds). In the last context, it grants the employee the right to severance pay in certain cases, if the contract was concluded before the end of 2002 (paragraphs 376 et seq.).

171. In comparing the legal positions of white- and blue-collar workers, it is noteworthy that essential changes occurred in 2017, which resulted in the abolition of the main differences in individual labour law between the two groups. This happened partly by granting blue-collar workers the advantages of white-collar workers, such as longer periods of notice (for the employer) in the case of termination (effective from 1 October 2021). Partly, the white-collar workers' claims have been aligned to the blue-collar workers' situation, such as in the event of an occupational accident or disease, which grants them extra continued payment in these cases. Alternately, the longer period of white-collar workers' continuation of payment in the case of normal sickness has been considerably reduced (effective from 1 July 2018). The distinction between the two groups of employees, so far, has not been abolished in collective labour law, as regards employees' representation and co-determination (*see* paragraph 775). Therefore, in most branches there still exist different collective agreements for blue- and white-collar workers; the same applies to works agreements at the business level.

2. Other Provisions for Special Groups of White-Collar Workers

172. White-collar workers in agriculture and forestry (so-termed estate employees (*Gutsangestellte*)), are covered by the Estate Employees Act (*Gutsangestelltengesetz*) which, with regard to content, only slightly differs from the White-collar Workers Act.

173. Artistic theatrical employees are persons contracted to a theatre undertaking to perform artistic functions in connection with the production of stage performances. This includes, for instance, actors, actresses, (opera) singers and musicians, but also directors, costume designers, producers and musical directors. Their employment relationships are regulated by the Theatrical Work Act (*Theaterarbeitsgesetz*). For example, there are specific regulations on trial periods (which are forbidden altogether), the continuation of payment in the event of illness or accident (including explicit rules on menstruation and pregnancy), provision of work equipment (such as costume and 'jewellery'), payment of travelling expenses, as well as specifying the theatrical undertaking's obligation to give the artist work ('right to actual work'), regulating disciplinary and contractual penalties and governing the fate of the employment relationship in the event of permanent or indefinite shutdown of the theatrical undertaking due to 'fire or other fundamental events'. Furthermore, unlike in most other fields of labour law, it is also allowed to conclude arbitration clauses (*see* paragraph 90).

174. Journalists, for the purposes of labour law, are those employees in a newspaper undertaking entrusted with the writing of texts and drawing of pictures who are employed at a fixed salary and do not merely carry out the work as a sideline. Employees in news agencies, broadcasting stations or film businesses also count as journalists if they are entrusted with the preparation of pictures or the creation of texts covering current events. This also applies if the newspaper is published (only) online. The Journalists Act (*Journalistengesetz*) lays down special regulations about their employment relationships, in particular in the event of the sale of the newspaper or a change of its political slant. In other respects, however, the White-collar Workers Act regulates their employment relationships.

175. Because their payment system is especially regulated, pharmaceutical employees make up a distinct group of employees. According to the Salary Fund Act (*Gehaltskassengesetz*) all employers (owners of a pharmacy) are obliged to pay salary contributions into a central fund out of which pharmaceutical workers are then paid. As to other rights and duties, pharmacists are subject to the provisions of the White-collar Workers Act.

176. The employment relationships of white-collar workers in households (*Hausangestellte*), that is to say employees who perform higher functions in the employer's household (such as teachers or secretaries), are also governed by the Domestic Employees Act (*Hausgehilfen- und Hausangestelltengesetz*; *see* paragraph 161). Yet, the regulations differ from those for domestic servants mainly performing manual work, as it stands, for example, in terms of longer periods of notice.

177. Contractual public servants (*Vertragsbedienstete*) are employees who have concluded an employment contract with a public law body, such as the Federal Government. They are governed by the Contractual Public Servants Act (*Vertragsbedienstetengesetz*), which contains detailed regulation of their employment relationships. In particular, the employer can only give notice in writing and referring to a legally laid down reason. Similar legal regulations exist for the contractual public servants of provincial governments and local councils, for whom the individual provinces are responsible, as to legislation.

II. Classification According to the Particular Purpose of the Employment Relationship

A. Apprenticeship

178. Apprenticeship (*Lehre*) is an employment relationship which serves the purpose of educating apprentices in a particular profession. Apprenticeship is regulated in detail by the Vocational Training Act (*Berufsausbildungsgesetz*). According to §1 of this Act, apprentices are employees being trained according to a training contract by an employer entitled to train apprentices in one of the occupations named in the official list of apprenticing professions, and who actually learn to perform their specific profession within the context of this training. The apprenticing professions are laid down by ordinance of the competent Federal Minister in the Apprentice Professions List. In Austria, the apprenticeship is organized in a Dual System; the apprentice trains and practices in the company and in vocational school

(*Berufsschule*) as well. In the company, the apprentice acquires the knowledge and skills of the profession; in the vocational school he or she acquires also theoretical skills and general education.

179. Among other matters, the Vocational Training Act specifies conditions which the employer must fulfil before being permitted to train apprentices. The Act also specifies the duration of an apprenticeship (averaging three or four years). Furthermore, the Vocational Training Act provides for the creation of ordinances, setting out in detail in which specific activities the apprentice in a particular profession is to be instructed. The Act does not govern other forms of trainee or intern relationships.

180. An apprenticeship is entered into for a specified time. Premature termination of the training relationship, by either apprentice or employer, is only possible for particular reasons named in the Act. The employer may also terminate the employment contract at the end of any year of training, as long as an attempt at mediation has been made (for more details *see* §§14–15a Vocational Training Act).

181. Duties of both accredited apprentice trainer (employer) and apprentice are standardized in the Vocational Training Act. For instance, an apprenticeship contract must be drawn up in writing, and it requires, in the case of minor apprentices, the consent of the legal guardian (§12 *leg cit*). The employer is not permitted to use an apprentice for activities which are not a part of the training. The trainer is also obliged to urge the apprentice to attend school as prescribed, as well as to give the necessary time off to do so. The employer must also pay the apprentice the 'apprenticeship remuneration', the amount of which is, for the most part, determined by collective agreements (but *see also* paragraph 751). At the end of the apprenticeship, the employer must issue a training certificate which should contain details of the profession in which the apprentice has been trained and the length of the apprenticeship. After it, the employer is obliged to employ the apprentice in the business for three months in order to gain work experience (§18 Vocational Training Act).

B. Other Training Relationships

182. Apart from legal apprenticeships, there are other forms of training relationships which are not specifically regulated by law, for example, the '(unpaid) trainee' (*Volontär*). Unpaid trainees are people being trained in an enterprise, but neither in an apprenticeship profession nor for later employment in the establishment – they simply wish to acquire skills and knowledge for other purposes. The trainee is not obliged to work, and the quasi-employer is only obliged to pay the minimum rate, if anything. Thus, trainees have no employment contracts.

183. Much the same applies to interns (*Praktikanten*). These are people acquiring practical experience, supplementary to their school or university education. Their training relationship is only subject to labour law if they are obliged to work during their internship, for example, at specific times or premises.

184. Finally, many collective agreements have defined a special group of 'on-the-job trainees'. These are employees who are trained for a certain length of time in specific activities, so that afterwards they fulfil the conditions for better payment on the grounds of better qualifications. Their contractual relationship is a regular employment relationship in the sense of §1151 of the General Civil Code.

C. Probationary Employment Relationship

185. Trial employment relationships are normal employment relationships, although they possess the special characteristic that they can be terminated at any time in the first month by either of the contractual partners. The trial period can last one month at most and must be especially agreed upon (or provided for in the applicable collective agreement; for more details, *see* paragraphs 201 et seq.).

§2. The Individual Employment Contract

I. The Capacity to Be a Party to an Employment Contract

A. Age

186. Only at the age of 18 do people have the full capacity to conclude a contract. However, there are anomalies related to the conclusion of employment contracts: persons above 14 can already contract themselves for services, but minors, that is to say teenagers from 14 to 18, may, without their parents' involvement, only spend their income, insofar as the satisfaction of their basic needs is not at risk.

187. Other requirements apply to the conclusion of apprenticeship and other training contracts. In such cases, the agreement of the legal guardian is necessary for the conclusion of these contracts. Furthermore, there are some restrictions concerning the concluding of non-compete clauses which would bind the minor employee in an improper way (e.g., young athletes playing for a sports club on the bases of an employment contract).

B. Foreign Nationals

188. The admissibility of employing persons who are not of Austrian nationality is regulated by the Foreign Nationals Employment Act (*Ausländerbeschäftigungsgesetz*, paragraphs 136 et seq.).

II. Form and Content

A. Form

189. As in civil law, 'freedom of form' is basic to employment contract law. Therefore no special form is required for employment contracts. They can be concluded (explicitly) verbally or in writing, or by implied consent. But the contracting parties can also agree on the use of a particular form, in which case, in the event of dispute, it will be presumed that the agreed form is a condition of validity (§884 General Civil Code). However, the contracting parties can also deviate from the agreed form by arrangement, which is usually done implicitly by offering a change of contract without observing the form agreed upon.

190. The law requests a written form only for certain sorts of agreements; for example, an apprenticeship contract must be drawn up in writing and requires, in the case of minor apprentices, the consent of the legal guardian (§12 Vocational Training Act). Some specific provisions in contracts of employment must also be in writing, for example an agreement to make a deposit as security for future claims by the employer for damages (§1 Provision of Caution Money Security Act), as well as provisions obliging the employee to refund costs for advanced professional training, in the event of the termination of the employment contract (§2d Employment Contract Law Adaptation Act). Also, an agreement by which employee inventions are to belong to the employer is only valid in written form (§7 section 1 Patents Act). As of 2021, it has also been explicitly laid down that agreements on working in the home office have to be in writing (§2 Employment Contract Law Adaption Act).

191. Numerous decisions of the Austrian Supreme Court have held that employees may have implicit contractual entitlements in the light of long-standing employment practice (*Betriebsübung*). Thus, employers who repeatedly grant benefits to employees without a contractual or statutory basis become obliged to continue this practice. To prevent such an implicit agreement, the employer must explicitly state the discretionary character of the benefit granted, or reserve the right to cease granting such benefits (*see also* paragraphs 83, 649).

B. Content

192. An employment contract comes into existence as a result of concordant declarations of legal intent. The substance of the agreement of intent need be no more than that one of the parties to the contract committing him- or herself to work for the other. It is enough that the type of work can be established by interpreting the purpose of the contract or looking at common practice. In particular, it is not necessary for specific remuneration to be agreed; §1152 of the Civil Code specifies that fair payment should be made if the agreed work is not expressly without remuneration.

193. In areas where nothing has been agreed, employment conditions are derived from legislation, collective agreements and works agreements; or from supplementary interpretation based on equitable common practice. However, as already stated, wherever these legal standards are binding in favour of the employee, any agreement which deviates from them to the employee's disadvantage is null and void (paragraphs 47, 73). In addition to the unfavourable arrangements as such, the provisions in an employment contract which are connected to them, whether objectively or subjectively (i.e., according to the intentions of the contractual parties), are also null and void. Other provisions remain effective just as the employment relationship itself does (principle of partial nullity).

194. As a matter of fundamental principle applying to all contracts, any contract or contractual provision which is *contra bonos mores* or contradicts criminal law is null and void. The concept of *bonos mores* (§879 Civil Code) is a part of the general fundamental principles of law. It is, therefore, the essence of all legal standards which are not expressly stated in a statute.

III. The Duration of an Employment Contract

A. Employment Contracts for an Indefinite Period

195. In Austria, most employment relationships are still entered into for an indefinite period. They last until they are terminated by a unilateral statement of intent (notice, premature termination on substantial grounds) or by agreed termination (contract of termination). An employment relationship for an indefinite period always exists, if the parties have not agreed upon a specific period of validity (*see also* paragraph 441).

B. Fixed-Term Employment Contracts

196. The agreement of a definite period of employment is valid in principle. Its end can be determined by objective conditions such as the reaching of a specific date, the completing of a specific task or the occurrence of a specific event (*see also* paragraph 442); for example, an employment contract can be concluded between employer and a replacement worker for the duration of a (permanent) employee's illness.

197. Fixed-term employees are often treated less favourably than comparable permanent workers. Many employees' rights only exist after a certain duration of employment, or otherwise depend quantitatively on the duration of employment (periods of notice, vacation rights). Above all, there is no actual job security for fixed-time workers, as only a termination by giving notice or by summary dismissal may be contested in court if it is 'socially unjust' (paragraph 479). So far, there is no legislative Act explicitly limiting the possibility of concluding successive fixed-term contracts, but the courts have been maintaining for decades that the employer has to prove legitimate material reasons for such a 'chain of contracts'. Otherwise, successive fixed-term contracts are considered to be a contract of indefinite duration. Additionally, current amendments lay down that the employer shall inform fixed-term employees about vacancies which become available in the undertaking (§2b Employment Contract Law Adaptation Act).

198. Consequently, if the contracts are regarded as being a contract of indefinite duration the employer has to give the period of notice as stated in the law, collective agreement or employment contract. Otherwise, the employer has to pay indemnification ('compensation for notice', which is equal to the remuneration for the period of notice; *see also* paragraphs 529, 535).

199. It is also possible to combine the two sorts of contract – the parties may explicitly agree on a fixed-term contract, which additionally contains a clause that it may be terminated by observing the applicable notice periods. To prevent abuse, the courts have held that for such a combination to be not undue, there has to be an appropriate correlation between the duration of the contract and the termination options.

C. Lifetime Employment Relationships

200. Lifetime employment relationships cannot be terminated by the employer's giving notice, whereas the employee can resign by giving a six months' notice, any time after the contract has been in operation for five years. However, both parties can terminate for substantive reasons.

D. Probationary Employment Relationships

201. A trial employment relationship must be agreed, that is to say, not all employment is initially agreed on trial (*see* paragraph 185).

202. Due to the 'easy' termination of the trial employment relationships, there exist several restrictions: the main feature of the probationary employment relationship (trial period) is that the contract can be terminated by either party without notice, and also without a reason being given. In general, a trial period can only be agreed upon for one month after the commencement of the employment relationship (§1158 section 2 General Civil Code; §19 section 2 White-collar Workers Act). Furthermore, there are restrictions in relation to the termination of probation contracts with pregnant women.

E. Permanent Employment Relationships

203. In principle, it is permissible to include in an employment contract that the employer or employee waives the right to give notice. Yet, the law provides that the employee can resign in any case, by giving six months' notice after the employment contract has been in operation for at least five years (*see also* the lifetime employment relationships in paragraph 200).

Chapter 2. Rights and Duties of the Parties in the Course of the Employment Relationship

§1. Duties of the Employee

I. Duty to Work

A. General

204. An employee is obliged to carry out the agreed duties meticulously and according to the employer's instructions. This means that the employee is not committed to achieving a specific success or result, but merely committed to careful and conscientious work (for the liability of the employee in the case of neglect of duties as an employee, *see* paragraphs 262 et seq.).

B. The Duty to Carry Out Work in Person

205. The employee must perform the duties him- or herself, insofar as the employment contract does not specify otherwise (§1153 General Civil Code). This means that in the event of incapacity to work, the employee is neither permitted nor obliged to provide a replacement.

206. Without a specific agreement, the employer's right to the employee's work is not transferable. Therefore, the employee cannot be made to work against their will for anybody other than the contractual partner. However, there are two major exceptions: the transfer of a business and temporary agency work.

1. Transfer of Business

207. The Austrian legal provisions in §§3–6 of the Employment Contract Law Adaptation Act regulating the effects of a transfer of a business originate from EU law, in particular, Directive 2001/23/EC. A transfer of a business takes place if an economic entity – that is to say, an organized group of persons and assets facilitating the exercise of an economic activity which pursues an objective specific to it – is transferred to another employer and retains its identity, following the transaction in question. In this event, the employer's (the transferor's) rights and obligations, arising from a contract of employment existing on the date of the transfer, shall be transferred automatically to the new employer (transferee). Furthermore, the employees must not lose any of their rights due to the transfer; the new owner of the business enters into all the rights and duties of their predecessor (automatic or *ex lege* entry).

208. In order to determine whether or not the conditions for the transfer of a business are met, it is necessary to consider all of the facts characterizing the transaction in question, including, in particular:

- the type of undertaking or business;
- whether or not its tangible assets, such as buildings and moveable property, are transferred;
- whether or not its intangible assets are transferred, and their value at the time of the transfer;
- whether or not the majority of its employees are taken over by the new employer;
- whether or not its customers are transferred;
- the degree of similarity between the activities pursued before and after the transfer; and
- the period, if any, for which those activities were suspended.

209. It has to be mentioned that these are individual factors in the overall assessment, and should not, therefore, be considered outside of the overall context. Furthermore, in certain labour-intensive sectors (such as cleaning or janitor work), even a group of workers engaged in activities which they carry out together on a permanent basis may constitute an economic entity. Such an entity is capable of maintaining its identity after it has been transferred, where the new employer does not merely pursue the activity in question but also takes over a significant proportion of the employees, in terms of their numbers and skills, of those specifically assigned by the former employer to that task. In such circumstances, the new employer takes over a body of assets enabling them to carry on the activities or certain activities of the transferor's undertaking on a regular basis.

210. Both the former and the new owner of the business might try to avoid the costs arising from the full entry into all rights and duties by terminating the employment relationships with the employees concerned; therefore, such dismissals with a connection to the termination would be *contra bonos mores* and considered undue. Alternately, employees have the right to object to the transfer of their employment relationship or even the right to terminate an employment contract (e.g., in the case of certain impairments by an unfavourable collective agreement which would be applicable after the sale of the undertaking).

211. The effects of transfers of businesses on the applicable collective agreement are determined in accordance with the general regulations on collective agreement membership (*see* paragraph 705). In particular, the following cases can be identified:

- The applicable collective agreement remains the same after the transfer of business, namely if the new employer is a member of the same employer organization.
- If a collective agreement applies to the old employer but not to the new one (e.g., because the new employer is not a member of the employer organization), the new employer remains bound to the collective agreement which applied to the old

employer. However, the content of the collective agreement is maintained the same after the transfer of business (freezing effect); that means that if the collective agreement was changed by the contracting parties (e.g., an increase in remuneration is agreed upon), these changes would not affect the new employer.
- If the new employer is a member of a different employer organization, the collective agreement corresponding to the membership of the new employer shall apply after the transfer of business. It does not matter whether these regulations are more favourable or not. However, the employees are legally protected in such a way that their regular remuneration may not be reduced.

2. Temporary Agency Work

212. The Temporary Agency Work Act (*Arbeitskräfteüberlassungsgesetz*) applies when the employer assigns the employee to 'user' undertakings, to work there temporarily. According to such an agreement in the labour contract, the employee is obliged to work for somebody other than the contractual partner. An employer who assigns employees professionally as a for-profit business (temporary work agency) needs a public licence to do so. The temporary worker has a legal right to fair pay, which might be determined, *inter alia*, by the minimum wage set forth in the collective agreement applicable to the user undertaking. If, however, the provisions of the collective agreement of the temporary work agency (Arbeitskräfteüberlasser-Kollektivvertrag) are more favourable than those in the user enterprise, they shall apply. For example, this might be the case regarding the calculation of vacation benefit and Christmas pay, for which the collective agreement of the temporary work agency makes special provisions. The user of the temporary agency worker is liable as a guarantor for the employee's remuneration. Additionally, various statutes invalidate unfair stipulations on temporary agency workers and provide them with the same rights and duties as regular employees.

C. The Type of Work to Be Done

213. The type of work that is to be done by the employee derives from the employment contract. However, in practice, the employment contract usually lays down or determines the type of work only in a quite general way (clerical, unskilled, and so on).

214. The employee is not obliged to do other work than that agreed upon contractually. Only one exception exists: in the case of an emergency or urgent need, the employee can be obliged to carry out different work on grounds of duty of loyalty (*see* paragraphs 223 et seq.).

D. The Workplace

215. The employment contract also determines where work is to be done. The workplace can usually be determined by considering the circumstances in which the contract is concluded and also its purpose. The premises of the establishment into which the employee is integrated will usually be the workplace agreed upon. As a rule, therefore, the employee is neither allowed nor obliged to perform duties at another place. This principle still applies though – due to the COVID-19-pandemic-measures – working in the home office has increased. The dwelling of an employee as a workplace has to be agreed upon in writing by employer and employee. Furthermore, in the event of a relocation of the business premises, the Supreme Court has decided that the employee is obliged to work on the new site ('duty to follow').

216. If agreed upon, the employee must work at different or varying sites (e.g., construction workers and commercial travellers). In these cases, the employer can determine the actual workplace by order. The contractual agreement may be derogated in cases of urgent necessity (*see* paragraph 245).

E. The Amount of Work: Working Time

217. Daily, weekly or monthly (normal) working time, in other words, the time spent at work, is also principally regulated by contract. The same applies to the question of whether or not the employee is obliged to work overtime. If the parties did not agree on a certain amount of working time, and the contract does not indicate otherwise, a full-time employment contract is deemed to be concluded.

218. Freedom of contract is considerably restricted, particularly as regards stipulation of the number of working hours. These restrictions arise for the most part from the Working Time Act (*Arbeitszeitgesetz*) and collective agreements. Again, there are exceptions in cases of urgent need (on the grounds of the employee's duty of loyalty) and where special statutory regulations exist (*see also* paragraphs 223 et seq., 245).

219. The beginning and end of work time on individual days of the week as well as the time for breaks have to be agreed upon, if no provisions exist in collective agreements or works agreements. The employer may only change these provisions unilaterally if such a right has been granted, a notice period of at least two weeks has been observed and if no substantial interests of the employee are opposed (§19c Working Time Act). Therefore, contracts stipulating 'employment on call' or 'on demand' are illegal in Austria.

II. The Duty of Obedience

220. As mentioned above, the employee's duties are only laid down by an employment contract in general terms. The exact particulars of the employee's activities, the way of working and the actual workplace arise from the employer's orders. The employer's right to give instructions corresponds to the employee's duty of obedience.

221. The extent of the duty of obedience and the right to give orders depend on the type of employment arranged, as well as on the kind of relationship with the employer. For example, traditionally, white-collar workers are considered to be closer to the management than blue-collar workers, in terms of responsibility, trustworthiness and the establishment's image (*see* the specific ground for dismissal of 'untrustworthiness' for white-collar workers).

222. Basically, an employee only has to obey orders related to the job. The right to give instructions concerns the performance of work, the use of machinery or cooperation with fellow workers. Alternately, the right to give orders does not cover the employee's private affairs or free time. Furthermore, the right to give orders and the duty of obedience are even more restricted. For instance, an instruction may not contravene statutory or legal collective standards (collective or works agreements). Besides this, the right to give orders is also limited by the specific individual employment contract, that is to say, an employee does not have to obey orders which contravene contractual terms agreed with the employer.

III. The Duty of Loyalty

A. General

223. Various additional employees' duties make up the duty of loyalty. All these duties have in common a goal that an employee is obliged to protect the employer's business interests. The duty of loyalty does not oblige the employee to show personal loyalty to the employer as a private person.

224. There are no express statutory regulations which would generally impose a duty of loyalty as such on all employees, but the duty of loyalty can be deduced from various legal provisions (e.g., §27 no. 1 White-collar Workers Act: 'disloyalty' as a ground for dismissal, which also constitutes a reason for premature dismissal of even specially protected groups of employees).

225. The duties covered by the term 'duty of loyalty' are primarily the duties of abstention: the duty of secrecy and respect for professional secrets, the ban on accepting presents from clients and so forth, restraint on competition, the ban on a disreputable private life, and the ban on inciting other employees to breach of duty. By comparison, duties of a positive nature are the exception as regards the duty of loyalty: the duty to notify the employer of imminent danger, the duty of aid and assistance in cases of urgent necessity.

B. The Duty to Respect Professional Secrets

226. An employee is obliged to keep the employer's professional secrets, in other words, facts and knowledge in the secrecy of which the employer has an objective and subjective interest. Professional secrets include, for example, technical processes, sources of supply, calculations, customer lists and so on. However, it is not only a matter of the employer's wishes whether certain facts are to be treated as secret or not. It must also be possible for employees to know that their employer has a justified interest in keeping them secret. Also, revealing criminal practices in an establishment and informing competent superiors or authorities (such as several forms of 'whistleblowing') are not breaches of the duty of secrecy.

227. The duty of secrecy does not only apply for the duration of employment but, according to certain statutory provisions, also after its end. Additionally, most employment contracts explicitly include duties of secrecy in relation to the time after the end of the employment relationship.

228. If the employee's breach of secrecy occurs for the purposes of commercial gain, the employee is liable to a fine, as laid down in the Unfair Trading Practices Act (*Gesetz über den unlauteren Wettbewerb* (UWG)). A specific duty of secrecy applies to works council members (*see* paragraph 789), the breach of which is similarly punishable with an administrative fine. Otherwise, a breach of the duty of secrecy is only liable to sanctions according to civil law, or may constitute a substantive ground for termination.

C. The Ban on Accepting Presents in the Course of One's Duties

229. All employees are forbidden to accept illicit benefits without the knowledge and consent of their employer. The acceptance of a benefit is illicit when it would tend to compromise the employee's independence. On the contrary, acceptance of a gift is not forbidden, where the gift is generally customary (e.g., tips or Christmas presents which do not exceed the bounds of normality).

230. §13 of the White-collar Workers Act contains a special prohibition which applies to employees charged with the conclusion or arrangement of business deals. Without their employer's consent, such employees are not permitted to accept any commission or reward from third parties, with whom they are concluding or arranging business deals on behalf of their employer. If such employees do accept such payment, the employer can demand the handing over of the reward.

231. §10 of the Unfair Trading Practices Act contains a general ban on the acceptance of presents: anyone who demands, accepts the offer of, or accepts gifts or other benefits in the course of business, and consequently gives another person preferment in the procurement of goods or services by way of unfair business behaviour, faces criminal sanctions such as imprisonment. The same applies to the person who gives or offers the employee the gift.

D. Restraint on Competition

1. During the Employment Relationship

232. Employees of a merchant, or other forms of trade enterprises, may not conduct any sort of independent commercial undertaking. In addition, they are also forbidden to do business for their own or another's benefit in the employer's line of business (§7 section 1 White-collar Workers Act). Actual or potential damage to the employer does not need to have occurred.

233. If such employees act in a way contrary to this prohibition, they are liable to the employer for damages. The employer may also demand the handing over of payments received, instead of compensation for damages. Furthermore, the employee can be summarily dismissed.

234. For other groups of employees, in particular blue-collar workers, there is no explicit statutory restraint on competition. Nevertheless, a general restraint on competition condition has been recognized in Supreme Court decisions, based on the duty of loyalty. Therefore, all employees are obliged to refrain from activities in their employer's line of business, if it could prejudice their employer's business interests.

235. The restraints on competition mentioned above can be intensified or reduced by agreement. For example, clauses of liquidated damages (contractual penalties) in an employment contract are an additional safeguard to comply with the contractual obligations. In the event of one party's failure to comply with its obligations under the contract, this party will compensate the other, as agreed.

2. After the End of the Employment Relationship

236. The ban on competition ends with the employment relationship. If the employer also wants to prevent competition by the employee after the end of the employment relationship, the employer must conclude a corresponding agreement (non-competition clause, restrictive covenant) with the employee.

237. However, in order to protect employees, the validity of non-competition clauses is statutorily limited (§§36, 37 White-collar Workers Act, §2c Employment Contract Law Adaptation Act) as follows:

- No valid restrictive covenant agreement can be made with minors at all.
- For all other employees, the restraint cannot last for more than one year after the end of the employment relationship. Only activities in the previous employer's line of business can be forbidden to employees.
- The restrictive covenant is only valid if the employee's wages exceed a certain amount (twenty times the daily maximum basis for social security contributions, that is, in 2022, EUR 3,780 per month).

– Finally, as regards the type of activity, period and place, in relation to the employer's business interests, the agreement must not unreasonably impede an employee's advancement (e.g., general ban on subsequent sales activities all over Austria).

238. Moreover, the employer is restricted from enforcing a non-competition clause, if the circumstances leading to the immediate or ordinary termination of the employment were caused by the employer (such as delay in paying remuneration), or if the employer has terminated employment without just cause. In the latter case, the employer may still invoke the restrictive covenant if willing to continue full payment to the former employee for the period of the restrictive covenant.

239. Frequently, non-competition clauses are secured by penalty clauses. If such a contractual penalty has been agreed, in order to ensure observance of the restraint on competition, the employer may only demand payment of the penalty, because the penalty clause legally restricts the employer from enforcing the non-competition by any further means (such as cease-and-desist orders or additional damages). Hence, there is no complementary right to contractual performance; the main advantage for the employer is that the actual damage does not have to be estimated.

240. According to current legislation, the agreed upon amount of penalty compensation must not exceed six times the employee's net wages. Furthermore, the (agreed) penalty can also be reduced in court, according to the principles of equity.

E. The Ban on a Disreputable Private Life

241. Basically, employees may organize their free time as they wish. One exception derives from the restraint on competition mentioned above. Also, there are further limitations in several cases which are not regulated in detail by statute.

242. Employees may not do anything in their free time to prejudice the reputation of the business establishment or their own reputation in the eyes of colleagues or subordinates.

243. Employees are also forbidden to perform activities in their free time which negatively affect their ability to work. Therefore, somebody who is occupied during the day may not also be professionally active through the night (whether they are employed or self-employed).

F. The Duty to Notify

244. An employee is obliged to report to the employer any damage threatening the 'normal' course of work process. The same applies to pending loss within the business establishment, where the employee him- or herself is not active. It is a matter of debate, in which cases an employee has a duty to report past damage caused by other employees (e.g., theft) to the employer. A particular duty to notify exists if the employee is entrusted with an inspection function, as well as when the employer is threatened by the danger of further damage. Otherwise, there is no general duty to inform on colleagues, but there is certainly a duty to notify in the case of preventable damage (threatened but which has not yet happened), and felonies as well.

G. The Duty to Perform Overtime and Exceptional Functions

245. In cases of urgent necessity, an employee is obliged to work overtime (on grounds of the duty of loyalty), and can also be obliged to perform functions other than those contracted. However, a general statutory basis for these obligations does not exist. Urgent necessity only exists in the case of an unusual situation, where the employer is threatened with severe loss. The emergency may neither be foreseeable, nor may the employer's urgent need be satisfied other than by calling on the employee.

246. Principally, if an employee's important personal interests conflict with the employer's necessity, there is no obligation to work overtime or perform exceptional functions.

IV. Employee Liability

A. General

247. Principally, if an employee fails to work at all or does not work duly, thereby prejudicing the employer, they can be held responsible for the damages. However, this civil law liability is considerably modified by a special statute, the Employees' Liability Act (*Dienstnehmerhaftpflichtgesetz*). Employees, and 'employee-like' persons as well, are to be protected from excessive risk of compensation of damages caused by the performance of their work because, in many cases, they have to deal with work equipment and machinery which is very expensive. The entrepreneurial risk must not be transferred to them.

248. According to the rules of civil law, an employee would be liable to the employer for all culpably and wrongfully inflicted damages. The degree of fault would thereby be of no significance as regards the amount of compensation. The Employees' Liability Act has reduced this liability for (free) employees. It applies to all damage caused during the performance of work. In its details, the Act is complex. One must first of all differentiate between damage to the employer caused directly and damage caused indirectly.

B. Direct Damage to the Employer

249. The employer is directly prejudiced if an employee harms the employer or the employer's property while performing his or her work.

250. If an employee's damaging behaviour is an 'excusable fault' in the legal sense, the employee is not liable to the employer at all (§2 section 3 Employees' Liability Act). This covers cases where the damage happened due to the circumstances of the delivery of the work (e.g., particular stress because of the lack of employees) and could only have been avoided by exceptional attention on the part of the employee.

251. If an employee's behaviour is not 'excusable' but still not grossly negligent, there is a right of judicial mitigation (§2 section 1 Employees' Liability Act): the court can either decide to drop liability for damages completely, reduce it, or leave it unchanged (in relation to civil law). There are several criteria for deciding whether or not, and to what extent, an employee is liable: whether the employee's work can be expected to lead to damage (dangerous or risky work) is of relevance, and furthermore, the employee's level of training and payment have to be taken into account. The question of whether or not an employee's behaviour is grossly negligent cannot be precisely answered, in general. In any event, the employee can only be held liable if there has been a mistake on the employee's part which could also have been made by an otherwise conscientious employee.

252. Even if the employee's behaviour was grossly negligent, the court may reduce (but not completely drop) the employee's liability (§2 section 1 Employees' Liability Act). In case of deliberate damage, the employee always has to pay full compensation to the employer.

253. An employer's right to claim compensation for damage that is not due to gross negligence lapses six months after the time when the claim could first be asserted in court. Furthermore, settlement by an employer of such a claim, namely the employer's 'self-service' by setting-off against the employee's claims, is only permissible if the employee does not make any objection.

C. Indirect Damage to the Employer

254. An employer is indirectly prejudiced if the employee culpably causes harm to a third party in the performance of work, and the employer is liable to the third party under civil law; for instance, when an employee in an automobile workshop damages a vehicle belonging to one of the employer's customers during a test-drive.

255. According to civil law in general, the injured third party can hold the employee liable for damage. However, in specific cases regulated by civil law, the injured party can also claim compensation from the employer (instead of the employee, who is usually poorer). If this happens, the employer – again according to civil law – has the right to reimbursement of the full amount from their employee.

256. However, in combination with the law on the limitation of the employee's liability, the employer must eventually bear the loss, according to the rules outlined under paragraphs 248 et seq.

257. That means, in detail, that if the injured third party holds the employee responsible for damages according to civil law, the employee has a right of recourse against the employer. In the case of excusable fault, the employee can demand from the employer the full amount of the compensation to the third party. If the employee is found negligent, the claim depends on the criteria for equity mentioned above. Only in case of deliberate damage must the employee indemnify the loss; in other words, they have no recourse against the employer.

258. If the prejudiced third party claims compensation for damages from the employer, the employer can only fully recover damages from their employee in cases of deliberate damage. In the event of 'excusable carelessness', the employer has no right of recourse. In cases of negligence, the employer's right of recourse can be lessened in court, according to the criteria of equity mentioned above.

259. However, it is important that in the event of damage to third parties, the employee's liability is only reduced if the employer is liable to the third party under civil law. That is essentially the case, if an employee is active in the fulfilment of a contract concluded between the employer and the injured third party (§1313a General Civil Code), and also when the employee causes damage when driving a vehicle belonging to the employer.

V. Sanctions for Neglect of Duty

A. The Right to Fulfilment

260. According to civil law, an employer has a right to expect an employee to perform his or her duties. This right can basically be enforced by action and subsequent execution: for example, if an employee ignores the duty to abstain from competing with the employer, the employer can bring an action against the employee to enforce abstention. Where necessary, the judgment will be enforced by duress.

261. The duty to work itself is an important exception to this rule. The general view is that the duty to work cannot be enforced by lawsuit and subsequent execution. The enforcement of the duty to work by coercion, such as by fines or imprisonment, would be a severe restriction of the employee's personal freedom. It is ruled out for this reason, although there is no express statutory provision which would exclude such a measure.

B. Compensation for Damage

262. If an employee culpably neglects his or her duties, and the employer's assets are therefore detrimentally affected, the employee must compensate for the loss. The conditions and extent of the claim are governed by civil law.

263. However, if the loss occurs due to careless performance of the duty to work, the employee's liability might be limited according to the Employee's Liability Act (paragraphs 247 et seq.).

264. A right to fulfilment does not exclude a claim for compensation.

C. Summary Dismissal

265. The strongest sanction against an employee's breach of duty is the employer's right of summary dismissal (termination without notice). However, not every breach of duty by an employee gives the employer this right. There are reasons which justify the employee's absence from work and thus the neglect of his or her duties (such as their own sickness, a sick child, or a visit to authorities when summoned). Hence, the right to lawfully dismiss an employee only exists if the breach of duty is a valid reason for summary dismissal (paragraph 522 et seq.).

266. If the breach of duty is a valid reason for summary dismissal in a particular case, the employer can also claim damages, in addition.

D. Disciplinary Action

267. The imposition of disciplinary measures is another possible sanction for breach of duty. 'Disciplinary action' is taken to mean that the employer inflicts a legally permissible disadvantage on the employee. The purpose of the measure must be to retaliate for a breach of duty on the part of the employee and to deter them and other employees from any further breaches of duty. Fines, a promotion ban and warnings are a few practical examples.

268. A disciplinary measure can only be imposed if it is lawfully permissible. It is only lawful if it is allowed in a statute, collective agreement, works agreement or in the individual employment contract.

269. At the moment, there is no statute regulating the lawfulness of disciplinary measures which is applicable to all employees, and there are only a few collective agreements which provide for them. However, works agreements and individual employment contracts have more practical significance. Individual employment contracts are significant, because the legal basis of a disciplinary measure can also be the employer's right to give orders. This means, for instance, that an employee can receive a warning or be banned from promotion at will, because to that extent, the employer has the right to give instructions.

270. Special protection from disciplinary measures is given to individual employees by works representation law: the introduction of an establishment disciplinary code (including several types of 'codes of conducts') requires the approval of the works council. The imposition of disciplinary measures in individual cases also requires the co-determination of the works council. Moreover, a disciplinary measure can only be imposed if it is allowed in a collective or works agreement. All this only applies to business establishments to which works representation law applies (paragraph 768).

§2. The Employer's Duties

I. The Duty to Provide Remuneration

271. The employer's duty to provide remuneration will be dealt with in Chapter 4 (*see* paragraphs 357 et seq.).

II. The Employer's Duty of Care

A. General

272. An employer is not only obliged to provide remuneration, but also to take care of its employees. Various employer's duties are collected under the heading 'duty of care'. They have in common that the employer must provide and arrange working conditions in a way that the employees' health, integrity, morality and lives are protected as far as possible. Furthermore, employers are also obliged to safeguard their employees' other material and non-material interests.

273. The duty of care has various statutory bases. For blue-collar workers, §1157 of the General Civil Code applies. This provision states that employers must regulate working conditions so as to ensure (in connection with the workspace and machinery they provide) at their own expenses that the employees' health, integrity, morality and lives are protected as far as possible. Similar standards are laid down by §18 of the White-collar Workers Act.

274. Both statutory regulations are very general; therefore, they may also be the basis for claims of protection against health and safety risks of the employee in cases that have not been determined by laws explicitly (e.g., specific needs such as eyeglasses for working in front of a monitor). More detailed duties result from the rules for protecting employees' health and safety from technical dangers under public law. The Employee Protection Act (*ArbeitnehmerInnenschutzgesetz*) and numerous ordinances by the federal minister applicable to different types of enterprises and work are decisive in this context. In these regulations, more or less concrete measures for the protection of employees' lives, integrity and health are prescribed for employers. A special authority, the Works Inspection Office (*Arbeitsinspektorat*) is responsible for safeguarding observance of the regulations.

275. Furthermore, it is recognized that the duties of employers laid down in these regulations are obligations not only towards the state but at the same time towards the employee. This means that an employer's infringement of these regulations can also be considered to be a breach of the individual contract of employment (duty of care).

276. Besides numerous regulations on health, integrity, morality and safety, court decisions and legal literature play a major part in defining the duty of care in practice. For instance, the employer's duty not to differentiate arbitrarily between employees in dealings with them (the principle of equal treatment) goes back to court decisions and legal literature. One, or a few, employee(s) must not be treated less favourably in any way than all the others or the majority of the employees (*see also* paragraphs 284 et seq.).

B. The Protection from Dangers to Employees' Life and Health

277. According to the Employee Protection Act *(ArbeitnehmerInnens-chutzgesetz)*, places of work must be so equipped and run as to avoid work-associated accidents and illness. The life, health, integrity and dignity of the employee have to be safeguarded by the employer. The employer is also obliged to identify and evaluate (prospective) risks in the enterprise ('workplace evaluation'). Additionally, the Employee Protection Act contains provisions on the protection of non-smokers at the workplace. According to these regulations, smoking is prohibited in workplaces in buildings if non-smokers are working there as well. The employer may, however, set up individual rooms in which smoking is permitted. Finally, with the general smoking ban in gastronomy, in force since 1 November 2019, the workers employed in gastronomy also receive appropriate protection against harmful passive smoking Moreover, further smoking prohibitions can result from other standards such as the Tobacco and Non-smoker Protection Act (*Tabak- und Nichtraucherinnen- bzw. Nichtraucherschutzgesetz*) or the Maternity Protection Act (*Mutterschutzgesetz*).

278. Accordingly, employees must be informed of risks and dangers connected with their work and workplaces. The employer must provide any necessary protective equipment (such as helmets or safety glasses); furthermore, drinking water, washing facilities and toilets must be provided. The employer is also obliged to provide equipment for the use of employees during breaks (tables, seating and so forth).

279. As a result of the Employee Protection Act, there are numerous further ordinances by the federal minister for particular establishments and jobs. They contain precise rules about measures to protect employees' life and health.

C. The Protection of Morality and Personality

280. All employees must be protected from annoyance, harassment, or damaging influence. Their dignity and private sphere must be protected, for example, the differences between the sexes have to be taken into account in the provision of sanitary facilities and where applicable, living quarters.

281. The duty to respect an employee's person, dignity and personal sphere also forbids, among other things, an employer's permanent monitoring, or data storage of the employees' private telephone calls, their being on the internet or all their whereabouts in the workplace.

D. The Protection of Employees' Property

282. An employer must provide for the protection of property such as is normally brought into the establishment by an employee, for example, the employer must provide facilities for its safekeeping.

283. Jurisprudence has ruled that the employer is held liable, even without fault, for loss and damages suffered by the employee, if employees have used their own resources for business purposes under the following conditions: the employee's property was used in the clear interest of the employer for the fulfilment of the employee's duties and thereby damaged. For example, the employer has to pay damages if the employee uses his or her own car to carry out work, and the car is damaged on this occasion. The amount of compensation to which the employee is entitled is reduced if the employee caused the damage negligently. Additionally, the rules governing the employee's liability are applied here, too.

E. The Duty to Treat Employees Equally

284. Fundamentally, an employer has the opportunity to treat employees differently, in the design of their contract or the giving of orders. The main limits are set by statutory or collective regulations (e.g., collective agreements and works agreements).

285. However, the duty of care also means that an employer has the duty to treat all employees equally: one or a few employees must not be treated less favourably than all the others or the majority of the employees, without a material reason. An unequally treated (in other words, a discriminated against) employee can claim equal treatment.

286. The duty of equal treatment is of most practical importance in the area of employers' 'voluntary' benefits, that is to say, the provision of advantages which the employer is not obliged to provide according to statutory or collective regulations.

These voluntary benefits include additional payments (bonuses) or wage rises. An employer may not exclude individual employees from such benefits without material reasons.

287. The duty of equal treatment is also specifically regulated by statute, yet only for special cases: according to the Equal Treatment Act (*Gleichbehandlungsgesetz*), discrimination based on sex, age, sexual orientation, ethnic origin or religion is prohibited (*see* paragraphs 113 et seq.). The Employees with Disabilities Act forbids discrimination on the grounds of disability.

F. *The Duty Actually to Provide Work*

288. There is no general and express statutory rule obliging an employer actually to occupy an employee in line with the agreement reached. Court decisions have supported the view that employers who do not occupy employees are only in default of acceptance and thus do not breach the contract: they must continue payment, but the employee has no right to fulfilment by actually being given work. Only if the employee has a specific interest in actually performing and delivering the work is the employer's duty actually to provide work assumed. This is, for example, the case with:

- airline pilots, who would otherwise lose their licences if they cannot prove a certain amount of flying time;
- apprentices, because of the aim of their employment relationship (which is professional training);
- surgeons, who would otherwise lose their skills;
- actors and professional athletes (e.g., football players), because their market value depends largely on them actually delivering their services.

G. *The Duty to Provide Holidays*

289. The duty to provide holidays will be dealt with in paragraphs 341 et seq.

H. *The Duty to Provide Information on Essential Aspects of the Employment Contract* (Dienstzettel)

290. According to Directive 91/533/EEC (Employment Information Directive) and Directive (EU) 2019/1152 on transparent and predictable workings conditions, the employer has to inform employees of the conditions applicable to the contract or employment relationship. Austria has implemented these directives mainly via §2 and §2f Employment Contract Law Adaptation Act. After the commencement of employment, the employer has to provide the employee, without undue delay, with a written record outlining the essential rights and obligations arising from the contract of service. In Austria this statement is referred to as *Dienstzettel*. According to current Austrian legislation, the written record must contain the following information:

(1) name and address of employer;
(2) name and address of employee;
(3) date of commencement of the employment relationship;
(4) where the employment is for a fixed period, the end date of the employment;
(5) period of notice and termination date (in other words, the date on which the employment relationship may end);
(6) fixed or main place of work (with an indication of changes in places of work where applicable);
(7) if a general salary scheme (e.g., a collective agreement) exists, the employee's classification in such a salary scheme;
(8) types of services to be performed;
(9) initial basic amount (in numbers), with the other component elements of the compensation, as well as due dates of the salary;
(10) holiday entitlement and amount of paid leave;
(11) agreed daily or weekly normal working hours;
(12) reference to applicable agreements and works agreements and similar legal instruments of collective labour law;
(13) the identity of the fund to which the employer pays contributions according to the new system of severance pay;
(14) it remains to be seen whether the duration and conditions of the probationary period, if any; and the training entitlement, if any, will also become mandatory explicit content of the information about the employment relationship.

291. In addition, if an employee will have to work for more than a month abroad, the written record must contain the following additional information:

(1) the duration of the employment abroad;
(2) if the employee is not paid in euro, the currency to be used for the payment of remuneration;
(3) where appropriate, the conditions for the employee's return to Austria;
(4) where appropriate, the additional remuneration attendant on the employment abroad.

292. If any of the above-mentioned terms and conditions written down in the record change, the employee must be given the information on the changes in writing, or be given an updated written record within one month.

293. The employer does not need to provide such a written record, if the employment is for a fixed period of not more than one month, or if a written employment contract exists that covers all necessary issues.

294. The information described above in paragraph 290 (5), (6), (9)–(11) and in paragraph 291 (1)–(4) may be given in the form of reference to the laws, the collective agreements or works agreements applicable. In such cases, there is also no requirement to update the written record, if such conditions change. However, a mere reference is not allowed concerning the initial basic amount.

295. The employer has to provide the employee with the written record without undue delay after the commencement of the employment relationship. If the employer fails to provide this, the employee may sue the employer before the labour and social court to make them issue the written record. Where the decision of the court states that the employee has the right to a written record, the court itself cannot provide the employee with the written record as such. However, failure to comply with this decision of the labour court will make the employer subject to sanctions for contempt of court. Furthermore, current amendments lay down that an employer who does not give appropriate information on the initial basic amount (in writing) but pays 'all-in' instead may be sued. In this case, the employee would have to be granted the amount that average employees get for this job, including 'usual' extra payment (de facto wages) in this region.

I. The Duty to Provide Pay Slips

296. According to §2f section 1 Employment Contract Law Adaptation Act, the employer is obliged to provide each employee with a written, comprehensible and complete settlement of all remuneration and reimbursement of expenses, when their salary is due. This (usually monthly) bill can also be provided by means of information technology.

J. The Duty to Provide a Copy of the Social Insurance Registration

297. According to §2f section 2 Employment Contract Law Adaptation Act, the employer is obliged to hand over a copy of the social insurance registration immediately after the commencement of the employment relationship.

K. Provision of a Certificate at the End of the Labour Contract

298. The employer is obliged to provide the employee with a certificate at the end of the employment relationship. This certificate must contain a description of the job which the employee performed, as well as details about the beginning and end of the employment relationship. The employer is not obliged by law to assess the employee's performance on the job. However, if the employer comments on the performance, the certificate may only contain favourable comments. The employer has to refrain from any comment that may make it more difficult for the employee to find a new job. In practice, a certain language used in these certificates has been developed, in order to give hints at the performance of the employee by omission of commonly used phrases or by stressing platitudes such as the worker's punctuality.

III. Rights and Duties in the Event of Employees' Inventions

299. The legal situation as to employees' (technical) inventions is regulated in detail by the Patents Act (*Patentgesetz*). Generally, employees have a right to be granted a 'patent' for their inventions during an employment relationship ('professional invention'). However, the Act permits other agreements. A collective agreement or written individual agreement can lay down that the employees' professional inventions belong to the employer, or that the employer has the right to make use of them. Inventions which are not made in the course of employment always belong to the employee (inventions without any connection to work).

300. According to the definition in the Patent Act, employee inventions are inventions by an employee which are by their nature of value in the undertaking's field of activities if:

- the activity which led to the invention is part of the employee's official duties;
- the employee's invention is inspired by their activities in the undertaking; or
- the invention was considerably facilitated by use of the undertaking's knowhow or resources.

301. If the employee passes the invention to the employer, they are entitled to an additional reasonable remuneration. However, if the employee is employed to make inventions and is also mostly occupied in doing so, an additional remuneration is only due insofar as a correspondingly higher wage has not been agreed upon in the employment contract any way. The Act also regulates guidelines as to these additional remunerations.

Chapter 3. Working Time and Leave, Sunday Rest, Annual Vacation, Holidays

§1. Working Time

I. General

302. The permissible working hours per day and week are primarily regulated by the Working Time Act (*Arbeitszeitgesetz*), according to which the 'normal daily' working time may not exceed eight hours, and the 'normal weekly' working time may not exceed forty hours. This statute also contains rules about work breaks and times of rest. It specifies, furthermore, that premiums have to be paid for overtime work, in addition to hourly wages. Finally, it contains numerous special regulations for particular job types. Apart from the Working Time Act, there exist special statutory regulations governing the working hours of young people (*see* paragraphs 557 et seq.) and medical staff in hospitals. Furthermore, it has to mentioned that management and senior personnel are exempt from the Working Time Act; hence, special statutory limits set on the working hours as well as provisions on overtime premiums do not apply to this group of employees.

303. The number of normal working hours can also be regulated by collective agreements, and they frequently do so by lowering the maximum amount of weekly working time. Longer working hours than provided for in the Working Time Act can only be specified in special cases listed in the Act itself. At the moment, many collective agreements prescribe a working week of less than forty hours, mostly thirty-eight hours. Any extra work up to forty hours per week must then be paid as extra work but is calculated without overtime premium, at the regular hourly rate unless provided for differently in the collective agreement.

304. In general, the number of working hours cannot be changed by works agreements. Only the temporary shortening or lengthening of working hours can be agreed this way. The main significance of works agreements as regards working time concerns the organization of working time: the allocation of weekly working hours on the individual days of the week, the beginning and end of daily work, and the time and length of work breaks. If there is no works agreement, these details have to be agreed upon individually and can only be changed unilaterally by employers if they have been granted such a right, have observed a notice period of at least two weeks and if no substantial interests of employees are opposed (§19c Working Time Act).

305. Due to numerous statutory rules and existing provisions in collective agreements, the individual employment contract does not have much significance for working hours. At most, it plays a part in settling matters of part-time activities and the duty to work overtime (within the legal boundaries).

II. Content of Limitation

A. Standard Hours of Work

306. Austrian working time law distinguishes between two types of working time limits: standard working time and maximum working time. The standard working time is the number of daily or weekly working hours that are agreed upon in the employment contract and that do not constitute overtime (which is subject to a surcharge of at least 50% of the hourly wage). Overtime work may only be delivered up to the maximum working time; if it exceeds the statutory maximum amount, the employer will be subject to an administrative fine.

307. For the vast majority of employees, the Working Time Act limits the number of standard (in other words, normal) working hours per week and per day. Since 1975, the number of standard working hours in general may not exceed:

- forty hours per week; and
- eight hours per day.

308. Principally, working time exceeding these limits is deemed to be overtime, for which an overtime premium of at least 50% has to be paid (for details *see* paragraph 319).

309. However, the forty weekly working hours can be arranged between the individual working days so that the standard working time on individual days is nine hours. This is allowed, in order to have a longer weekend break. Many establishments take advantage of this possibility so that for many employees, the work-free weekend begins as early as midday Friday.

310. Longer daily working hours are also permissible, in order to extend leisure time between public holidays. The deficiency in working hours (such as between Christmas and New Year) can then be made up in a period of thirteen consecutive weeks and even longer, if the applicable collective agreement permits it. During the reference period, the standard daily hours of work may be increased up to ten.

311. Flexible working hours, where allocation of working time is partly left to the employee's own decision (*Gleitzeit*), may be established by works agreement or, if no works council exists, by written agreement with each employee. In such a case, standard working hours may be extended up to ten or, under special circumstances, up to twelve hours per day.

312. A different form of flexible working hours, which enables the employer to allocate the working time, is possible if the collective agreement permits it: working hours during which no overtime premium is paid can generally cover up to forty-eight or even fifty hours per week. However, the weekly working time during the reference period must, on average, correspond to the weekly working hours as set out in the Working Time Act (forty hours per week) or the respective collective agreement. This is achieved through compensating extra work with time off.

B. *Maximum Working Time*

313. Principally, the maximum number of the working hours must not exceed (§9 Working Time Act):

- twelve hours per day; and
- sixty hours per week.

314. Additionally, the average weekly working time may not exceed forty-eight hours within a reference period of seventeen weeks (if the collective agreement permits, the reference period may not exceed twenty-six weeks and if there are technical and work-related organizational reasons, it may be extended up to fifty-two weeks).

315. Working hours may also be extended in legally laid down cases, such as special groups of employees or companies; for example, in public transportation companies, or if the employee's working time includes a regular and substantial availability rota (such as night clerks in a hotel or doctors in a hospital during their night shift). Furthermore, the maximum limits for working hours may be exceeded by business travel times (i.e., when workers leave their place of employment temporarily by order of their employer to perform work in other places), insofar as workers need not work while travelling.

316. In the case of a breach of these working time rules, the employer will be subject to an administrative fine.

C. *Overtime Work*

1. Definition

317. According to §6 Working Time Act, one speaks of overtime if:

- the permissible statutory standard daily; or
- the permissible statutory standard weekly working hours are being exceeded.

318. This double demarcation has the effect that overtime is also being worked if an employee works longer on one day of a week but does not achieve the normal weekly number of working hours (forty) because of lost time (illness). If employees work more than five days a week it is also possible for them to work more than forty hours during the week but not exceed the daily limit.

2. Overtime Premium

319. If an employee performs overtime work, in addition to regular hourly compensation he or she is entitled to a statutory overtime premium of 50% of the regular salary per hour of overtime. However, most collective agreements specify considerably higher overtime premiums (usually 100%) above a certain number of hours, as well as for overtime work performed at night, on Sundays or on public holidays.

320. Overtime may also be compensated with time off, if this is provided for in the applicable collective agreement/works agreement, or if so agreed between the employer and employee. The time in lieu has to take into account the overtime premium: if payment for overtime is 150% of the salary (including the premium), time off for overtime must also be granted in the same ratio; for example, a 1 to 1.5 (one-and-a-half hour) ratio. If the date for using the time credits is not agreed upon in advance and there is no agreement within six months after the overtime work, the employee may claim cash compensation (§19f Working Time Act).

3. Limitation of Overtime

321. Overtime work is not unrestrictedly permissible. Overtime can only be worked in the event of an 'increased need' ('greater demand') for work or when the employee is carrying out preparatory or concluding activities (cleaning or preparatory activities necessary to start work in an establishment). The Working Time Act thereby intends to prevent overtime becoming a permanent feature.

322. The amount of permissible overtime work is also limited. In the event of increased workload, overtime of twenty hours per week is permissible, but this sanctioned amount of overtime must be distributed so that no more than twelve hours are worked in a day, and no more than sixty hours are worked in any week. However, according to these overtime limitation terms, that were introduced only in 2018, employees may refuse to work overtime without stating a reason, if the overtime exceeds the daily working time of ten hours or the weekly working time of fifty hours. They must, therefore, not be disadvantaged by their employer due to the refusal. Furthermore, if employees work more than ten hours a day or more than fifty hours a week, they can choose whether they want time compensation or overtime premium.

D. Extra Work for Part-Time Workers

323. A full-time worker is a person who works the full amount of standard working hours permitted by law or the applicable collective agreement. Part-time workers are employees who work fewer than these standard working hours.

324. Before 2008, extra work by part-time workers, that is to say, working time beyond the agreed part-time hours, had to be paid at the normal hourly rate but without a premium. Only if the hours of work also exceeded the statutory standard working time (eight hours per day and forty hours per week) had an overtime premium to be paid. This legal situation had the effect that in some sectors of the economy (especially the retail trade), mostly part-time contracts (usually thirty hours per week) were offered, because by doing so, the employer was able to order extra time, up to forty hours a week, without paying overtime premiums.

325. Now, as regards part-time workers, the Working Time Act provides for an extra time premium of 25% of the hourly wage. However, this premium can be avoided, for example, if the extra work is compensated for by time off (on a 1:1 ratio) within a quarter year.

III. Rest Periods and Breaks

A. Breaks

326. The Working Time Act also specifies when and for how long work is to be interrupted by a break. It stipulates that at least a half-hour break must be allowed, if the day's hours of work exceed six (§11 Working Time Act). The half-hour break can be broken up, either into two breaks of fifteen minutes or three of ten minutes each. Furthermore, in the case of working at a computer, work has to be interrupted by breaks or different activities that have nothing to do with screens on a regular basis (§68 section 3 Health and Safety Act).

327. The times and length of work breaks must be agreed between employer and the employee or works council, in a works agreement.

328. Breaks are interruptions of work time. Thus, there is no payment during breaks unless otherwise agreed in a collective or individual employment agreement.

B. Rest Periods

329. After the end of the day's work, all employees are entitled to a continuous eleven-hour period of rest (§12 Working Time Act). This daily period of rest can be reduced to a minimum period of eight hours by collective agreement, or in the case of business travel times. However, such reduced rest periods should be made up, within the next ten calendar days, by an appropriate extension of another daily or weekly rest period. Furthermore, any reduction to less than ten hours is permitted only if other measures ensuring workers' recuperation are provided for by the collective agreement.

330. The Hours of Rest Act (*Arbeitsruhegesetz*) lays down a weekly interruption of work (rest period) of at least thirty-six hours. This weekly rest period normally has to include the Sunday and has to start on Saturday at 1 post meridiem (pm) (or earlier). Of course, there are many exceptions to this rule. In these exceptional cases, the weekly rest period may be transferred to another day of the week. If the employer calls on the employee to work during the employee's weekly rest, the employee is entitled to a substitute rest; this is paid working time off, equal to the hours worked during the weekly rest period.

IV. Exceptional Cases

331. The very detailed regulation of working hours covered by the Working Time Act does not, however, apply in 'exceptional cases' (§20 *leg cit*). These are cases of temporary work, not to be delayed, which:

- must be carried out immediately, in order to deal with a threat to the life or health of human beings; or
- is necessary to solve an urgent problem in the establishment or to avoid disproportionate losses.

Furthermore, the situation must not have been foreseeable or able to be dealt with in any other way.

332. In particular, the maximum permitted daily and weekly hours of work can be exceeded in such exceptional cases. Furthermore, the limits on overtime do not apply, and the prescribed breaks do not have to be given.

333. If the limits on working hours are exceeded in exceptional cases, the employer must inform the competent authority (Works Inspection Office) in writing and give the reasons.

V. Night Work

334. According to the Working Time Act (§12a), night is the period of time between 10 pm and 5 am. A night worker is an employee who works regularly or – if the collective agreement does not provide otherwise – at least forty-eight nights within a year, a minimum of three hours during the night. Night work, especially if it is done under difficult conditions, is subject to further limitations. Night workers are also entitled to regular health assessments. If they are suffering from health problems recognized as being connected with the fact that they perform night work, they have the right to be transferred, whenever possible, to suitable day work. The same applies in the case of imperatively necessary care for children up to the age of 12.

§2. Sundays and Public Holidays

I. Sundays

335. The Hours of Rest Act (*Arbeitsruhegesetz*) regulating Sunday rest fundamentally prohibits working on Sundays. However, it also allows for numerous exceptions. By ministerial decree, work on Sunday can be allowed for particular types of industry, if interrupting work is impracticable or if the work in question satisfies a particular public need (as in public transport).

336. Licence to work on Sundays is given to a whole range of establishments, particularly in the manufacturing or in the tourism sector. On the contrary, working on Sundays is prohibited in the retail trade (however, there are specific exceptions for several sites, such as shops in railway stations) and for work which is not 'productive' (e.g., office work).

337. In the event of Sunday work, there is no extra pay, but the employee is entitled to a substitute day of rest.

II. Public (Legal) Holidays

338. According to §7 Hours of Rest Act, work must similarly be stopped on public holidays. The public holidays are, according to the Act, New Year's Day, Epiphany, Easter Monday, 1 May (Labour) Day, Ascension, Whit Monday, Corpus Christi, Feast of the Assumption, 26 October (National Day), All Saints Day, Conception of the Virgin Mary, Christmas Day and 26 December. Most of these public holidays refer to Catholic feast days, but no account is taken of the employees' religious beliefs. Until 2018, Good Friday was also an additional holiday, but only for employees of protestant and certain other denominations. Due to its discriminating character, it has been replaced by a so-termed personal holiday (*see* paragraph 346). Many collective agreements also stipulate the cessation of work at midday on Christmas Eve and New Year's Eve. A few collective agreements provide additional holidays such as Yom Kippur for Jewish employees.

339. Exceptions to the prohibition against working on public holidays are determined by the Act and the individual regulations affecting it. For the most part, the same exceptions apply as for Sunday working.

340. Employers must continue to provide the regular pay for public holidays. However, that does not apply if the public holiday falls on a Sunday. In the case of work on public holidays – whether or not permitted – the employee receives double payment for the time worked. Most collective agreements also allow for special public holiday work and/or public holiday overtime premiums.

§3. ANNUAL VACATION

I. Sources

341. With a few exceptions, annual vacations are uniformly regulated for all types of employees by the Vacation Act (*Urlaubsgesetz*). Specific statutory regulations apply to employee categories, such as workers in the construction industry or workers in agriculture and forestry. They will not be dealt with here. Due to the extensive statutory regulation, the role of collective agreements in this regard is minimal. The same applies to individual employment contracts.

II. The Amount of Vacation

342. According to the Vacation Act, in every year of employment, the employee is entitled to a paid annual vacation of thirty 'business days', if the employee's period of service is less than twenty-five years. After more than twenty-five years of service, the annual holiday is thirty-six 'business days'. This means that the employee has five weeks or six weeks of vacation respectively per year, Saturday being counted as a 'business day'. In practice, though it is not laid down by law *expressis verbis*, vacation for employees working five-day weeks (Monday to Friday) is counted on the basis of 'working days', in other words, the days the employee actually has to work (Monday to Friday). Therefore, such an employee is entitled to twenty-five working days' holiday per year (thirty working days, after twenty-five years' service).

343. In the first year of employment, the full holiday entitlement becomes due only after six months' service. However, during the first six months, the holiday entitlement will increase in proportion to the time served with the employer. From the second year of employment onwards, the holiday entitlement arises at the beginning of the year.

344. The holiday year corresponds with the working year, that is to say, it starts on the day the employee commenced employment. It can be agreed that the annual leave should be calculated on the basis of the calendar year rather than the working year, if either a collective agreement or works agreement provides this option, or if such a calculation will not put the employee in a less favourable position.

III. The Use of Vacation Time

A. *Taking Vacations*

345. A basic condition for using vacation is a previous agreement between the employer and the employee, which has to be made before each vacation. This agreement between the employer and the employee determines when a vacation is to start. The requirements of the establishment, as well as the employee's opportunity to rest and to relax, are to be taken into consideration therein.

346. If no agreement is reached about the beginning of an employee's vacation, the employee is, in principle, not permitted to take a vacation at will. A comparatively complicated procedure (which, moreover, takes some time) is laid down for employees in an establishment with a works council, by which an employee can, under certain circumstances, take a vacation against the employer's will. Other cases of unilateral consumption of holidays, that is, without an agreement, are as follows: §16 Vacation Act provides the right to up to one week of time off twice per year and continued payment for this time, in the event that the employee has to look after a sick relative. After this basic entitlement has been used up, the employee may claim vacation time without an agreement with the employer in order to care for the sick relative. Another example of unilateral vacation consumption is the so-termed personal holiday, regulated in §7a Hours of Rest Act, which was introduced in 2019 as the consequence of a decision by the EJC, which considered the Austrian regulation on Good Friday as a holiday only for protestants to be discriminating. Accordingly, employees have the right to determine one day off per year out of their annual vacation amount without the employer's consent. This right comprises any day but can only be claimed once a year, and the date of the personal holiday should be announced at least three months in advance in writing.

347. Moreover, in establishments with a works council, guidelines for the taking of vacations can be laid down in a works agreement. However, it is not possible to fix the taking of vacations for individual employees by works agreement. Therefore, an establishment holiday ('company shutdown days'), during which all employees take their vacation at the same time, is subject to the employer's agreements with the individual employees; this means that a series of individual agreements covering all the employees is necessary. Also, this 'establishment holiday' must not exceed two weeks in duration and must allow employees to select individual dates for the (remaining and) larger parts of their annual holiday.

348. If the employer and the employee have reached an agreement on a proposed holiday, this agreement may only be revoked in particularly serious cases. In these cases, it is necessary to weigh the interests of the employee against those of the employer. Should the agreed leave be cancelled for justified reasons, the employer will have to compensate the employee for any financial loss that may have been suffered.

B. Splitting up Vacation Periods

349. The Vacation Act allows for the taking of vacations in two periods, whereby each part shall consist of at least six working days (in other words, one week). This is meant to prevent the employer from forcing an employee to use up vacation time simply on odd days. Shorter periods of holiday are only legal if they are in the interest of the employee; in other words, if the employee especially asked for them.

C. *The Ban on 'Paying-Off' Vacations*

350. The Vacation Act explicitly forbids payment in lieu of leave. Agreements between employers and employees providing for the non-use of vacation time in exchange for payment or other material reward are invalid.

D. *Illness During Vacations*

351. If an employee becomes ill during a vacation, the period of illness is not counted as vacation time, if the illness lasts more than three (calendar) days. It is also a prerequisite that the employee has not caused the illness or accident by gross negligence or intentionally. Moreover vacation is not interrupted if the illness (accident) is connected to gainful employment on the part of the employee during a vacation, and when this gainful employment was detrimental to the vacation as a period of rest and recreation. Decisions of the Supreme Court also apply these rules on 'interruption' of vacation to cases where the employee has to take care of sick close relatives (*see* paragraphs 431 et seq.). Hence, in such cases, the amount of vacation is not reduced, and the free days can be taken another time.

352. For the period of illness not to be counted as used vacation time, the employee must inform the employer of the illness in due time. The employee must also produce a doctor's certificate concerning the illness.

E. *Forfeiture of Annual Vacation*

353. Generally speaking, the entire vacation entitlement for one year should be taken within that year, but entitlements are not forfeited if they are not taken in full. The Vacation Act provides that entitlement to vacation is lost two years after the end of the vacation year in which it arose.

IV. Vacation Pay

354. If pay is calculated by week, month or longer periods, it may not be reduced for the period of vacation. The employee retains the right to pay during a vacation; that is to say, if the employee has regularly performed overtime work, any regular extra payments must also be continued. If pay is calculated in a different way (such as by the hour), the amount of pay due is that which employees would have received if they were not on vacation. Where payment is related to performance (e.g., piecework), payment is calculated according to the average earnings in the thirteen weeks previous to the vacation. The (continued) vacation pay just described should not be confused with the vacation benefit which constitutes an additional element of salary (thirteenth monthly payment, *see* paragraph 374).

V. The Termination of the Employment Relationship Before the Use of Vacation

355. If the employment relationship ends before an employee has taken all the due annual vacation, the employee is entitled to a pro rata vacation indemnity payment. The employee therefore receives one fifty-second part of vacation pay for each week which has elapsed since the beginning of the vacation year, minus the vacation pay already received. However, a pro rata vacation indemnity payment is not due at all if the employee prematurely resigns without good cause.

356. The employee usually does not have to pay back holiday pay for the leave already used exceeding the pro rata vacation entitlement (e.g., if the employment relationship ends after ten months and the employee has used up the full amount of vacation). This does not apply when the contract of employment is terminated, either by the employee resigning without good cause, or by summary dismissal for reasons attributable to the employee.

Chapter 4. Remuneration

§1. Remuneration and Reimbursement of Expenses

357. In labour law, remuneration (salary or payment) includes any benefit received by an employee in exchange for work. However, frequently employees also receive some payments which merely make up for special expenses incurred in order to do their work, such as payments for travelling and overnight expenses, made necessary by the work performed. These benefits are not remuneration but reimbursement of expenses. Moreover, it should be mentioned that there is no legal definition of remuneration (salary, payment) in Austrian labour law.

358. The difference between remuneration and reimbursement of expenses is important for the continuation of payment, for instance in the event of annual vacation, illness and so forth, in which cases remuneration but not reimbursement of expenses continue to be paid (*see also* paragraph 415). The differentiation between remuneration and reimbursement of expenses is also important in matters of tax assessment and social insurance contributions.

§2. Forms of Payment

I. Monetary Payments and Payments in Kind

359. Monetary payments are any earnings expressed in money terms. Monetary payment is not only payment in cash, but also by transfer into the employee's bank account, cheque or promissory notes.

360. Any other payments by the employer are payments in kind. These include, for instance, the provision of foodstuffs, fuel, accommodation or the private use of a company car or mobile phone, but also the granting of earning opportunities (such as the possibility of receiving tips).

361. The differences between monetary payments and payments in kind are important, because there are statutory restrictions on the agreement of a wage in kind. According to §78 of the Industrial Code (*Gewerbeordnung* 1859), employers are obliged to pay in cash. Payment in kind is only permitted exceptionally (e.g., accommodation or heating fuel). An agreement by which a blue-collar worker must acquire the necessities of life from particular sales outlets is expressly forbidden. The regulations mentioned are intended to prevent abuses which were widespread in the early days of capitalism. However, explicit similar statutory regulations do not exist for white-collar workers.

362. A requirement for cash payment results in general from the collective agreements. They virtually always specify monetary payment. According to collective agreements, a legally permissible agreement to payment in kind is therefore only permissible if it is more advantageous to the employee than purely monetary payments.

II. Time Pay and Payment by Results

A. Time Pay

363. If payment is calculated according to specific time units worked (hour, day, week and month), the term 'time pay' is used. If employees work for a time unit, they receive the agreed pay for that time unit. The 'success' or 'result' of the employee's work in the period has no effect on the amount of payment.

B. Payment by Results

1. General

364. Agreements are very often concluded, by which the amount of payment varies either as a whole or in part according to the results achieved. There are many different methods by which the effect of achievement on the amount of pay can be calculated.

2. Piecework

365. The simplest form of piecework pay is where a particular sum is paid for each unit produced. The number of units produced in the work period is then multiplied by the agreed sum ('money' piecework). However, the so-termed time form of piecework is more common. The major difference from 'money' piecework is that the average time necessary for each work process is calculated and agreed upon (time allowance). A certain sum is paid for each minute of this time period; usually it is one-sixtieth of the hourly wage paid to an employee on time pay.

366. Most collective agreements contain stipulations to ensure that an employee on piecework rates does not receive less remuneration than a comparable employee on time pay.

3. Commission

367. Payment by commission has much in common with piecework pay. It is usual for commercial white-collar workers (such as salespersons and representatives). These employees receive a certain percentage of the amount of business achieved. By agreement, payment can be either exclusively by commission, or be a combination of a fixed sum and supplementary commission.

368. The White-collar Workers Act contains several regulations regarding commission payments. In the absence of an agreement to the contrary, the right to the commission on a sale exists as soon as the employer receives a payment. Moreover, the employee has a right to inspect the employer's books. It is also specified that *ex post facto* price reductions by the employer do not reduce the commission.

4. Profit-sharing

369. Additional payments are often agreed for employees in management positions, based on the amount of enterprise profits. Alternately, agreements according to which all the employees have an interest in the commercial success of an undertaking are now becoming more and more frequent.

5. Agreements on Objectives

370. The concept of management by objectives has led to the widespread practice in many Austrian enterprises of concluding annual agreements on objectives to be fulfilled by the employees. A premium at the end of the year rewards the employee if the objectives are achieved. This payment is usually calculated on the basis of the achievement rate as well as on the economic situation of the company.

C. Employee Protection Where Payment Is by Results and 'All-In' Agreements

371. As already mentioned, most collective agreements contain provisions which secure substantially the same minimum wage for piecework employees as is received by employees on time pay. There are usually further provisions protecting employees against an *ex post facto* reduction of the piecework rate by an employer. In establishments with a works council, the introduction of certain result-related payments (in particular piecework pay) requires the agreement of the works council (*see* paragraph 812). Furthermore, current amendments lay down that an employer who does not give appropriate information on the initial basic amount (in writing) but pays 'all in' instead may be sued. In this case, the employee would have to be granted the amount that average employees receive for this job, including the 'usual' additional payment in this area (§2g Employment Contract Law Adaption Act).

III. Bonuses and Premiums

372. Employees often receive extra bonuses on special occasions in addition to their normal regular wage. For instance, Christmas bonuses and bonuses for the preparation of the balance sheet are very common. Loyalty or anniversary bonuses for long periods of service in the establishment are also frequent.

373. Employees do not have a statutory right to bonuses. An employer supplies these benefits because of collective or individual agreements, or often without any obligation to do so.

374. Principally, collective agreements in Austria state that salaries are paid fourteen times a year. The thirteenth salary is usually called 'vacation benefit' (*Urlaubszuschuss*) and the fourteenth 'Christmas pay' (*Weihnachtsremuneration*). This refers to the origin of this form of additional payment, a special occasion such as Christmas. Fourteen monthly salaries are usually standard, even for those employees not covered by collective agreements, as Austrian income tax law applies a very low flat rate of taxation to the thirteenth and fourteenth monthly salaries.

375. In contrast, premiums are those additional benefits with which employees are rewarded for particular success in their work, but where no direct relationship to performance exists as it does in the case of piecework pay. They may be determined either by the quality of the work or even by a certain manner or behaviour to do work (e.g., friendly way to treat customers).

IV. Severance Pay and Retirement Benefits (Company Pensions)

A. *Severance Pay – Old System – Commencement of Employment Before 1 January 2003*

376. Severance pay (*Abfertigung*) is a special (additional) payment paid at the end of an employment relationship. The purpose of severance pay is mainly to tide employees over after the end of an employment relationship. Besides, it is a premium for the loyalty of the employee as well, and it implies protection against (premature) termination.

377. According to the old system, applicable to employment relationships starting before 2003, severance pay is only due if the employment relationship has been terminated after at least three years of service (which does not play any role in practice any more, due to the temporal jurisdiction).

378. If the employment relationship is terminated by a premature resignation (*Austritt*) without substantial reasons on the part of the employee, by a summary dismissal where the employee is at fault, or by the employee's giving notice, there is no right to severance pay. However, in certain cases, there is an exceptional right to a severance payment although the employee him- or herself gives notice. Basically, these are cases where employees give notice because they have a right to the statutory old-age pension, or where employees terminate the employment relationship to take care of a child after its birth or parental leave afterwards.

379. The right to severance pay is reduced, or may cease altogether, if the company is wound up and the financial position has become so bad that the employer cannot reasonably be expected to meet it. However, this rule neither applies in the event of the employer's bankruptcy nor if the company is transferred, the acquirer (in other words, the new employer) offers to continue the employment relationship on the same conditions as before, but the employee refuses the offer.

380. The amount of severance pay depends on the length of the employment relationship. After three years, it is twice the last paid monthly wage. After five years, it increases to three times the last monthly wage, after ten years, four times as much, after fifteen years six times, after twenty years nine times and after twenty-five years, twelve times as much as the last monthly wage. Only periods of work for the same employer in an uninterrupted employment relationship count as periods of employment in this context. Here again, it has to be mentioned that the employment relationship must have already started before 2003 for the employee to be entitled to severance pay in this form. The amounts are much smaller under the new system.

381. If the employment relationship is ended by the employee's death, half the severance pay is due to legal heirs, for whose support the employee had been responsible. The right to severance pay is also quantitatively limited if the employee ends the employment relationship to take care of their newborn child.

B. *Severance Pay – New System – Commencement of Employment After 31 December 2002*

382. The new system of severance pay regulated by the Federal Corporate Staff and Self-Employment Provision Act (*Betriebliches Mitarbeiter-und Selbständigen-vorsorgegesetz*) applies to employment relationships starting after 31 December 2002 or to those employees (of the old system) who have opted into it. It does away with the past achievement-oriented severance pay system and establishes a contribution-oriented system, in which the financing of the severance payment takes place via monthly payments of contributions by the employers to special funds. The fund is selected either by the employer or – if a works council exists – in the form of a works agreement.

383. Employers have to make a contribution of 1.53% of the monthly salary during the employment relationship. These contributions are collected with the social security contributions and paid into funds which have specially been established for this purpose.

384. Unlike under the old system, in which the severance payment increased by abrupt jumps every couple of years, under the new system, the amount grows continuously month by month. In summary, the amount of the 'new' severance pay is made up by the severance pay contributions the employer has paid to the fund. The obligation to pay contributions begins with the second month of the employment relationship, the first month (usually a probationary period) being exempted from contributions.

385. The contributions are invested by the funds, which have to guarantee at least the payment of all contributions paid by the employer. The capital, as well as profits gained, are paid off upon request by the employee at the end of the employment relationship basically in those cases when the old severance payment was due: contributions must have been paid for a minimum of three years and the employment relationship must not have ended by the employee giving notice, or prematurely resigning without cause, or being summarily dismissed. However, unlike in the old system, the contributions are not forfeited in all other circumstances; they simply stay in the fund (backpack principle) and can be taken out if the above-mentioned requirements are met later.

386. For some employees, the new system might be a step towards more fairness and promoting mobility of employees. The winners are obviously those employees who would not have been paid a severance payment under the old system, that is to say, those with short-term contracts and those leaving the employer on their own account. In addition, unlike in the old system, not only employees but also free employees and self-employed persons are comprised and are allowed to benefit from the allowances. However, it is necessary to mention that the amount of the new severance pay that might be gained regularly is smaller than the one of the old system.

C. Retirement Benefits (Company Pensions)

387. In some undertakings, employees receive pension payments from the employer in addition to the statutory old-age pension, if they leave the establishment because they have reached a certain age or because of an occupational accident. There is no statutory obligation for any private employer to pay a retirement benefit. The duty to pay may be laid down in a collective agreement, a works agreement or in the individual labour contract. Occupational pension schemes are of great importance in the banking and insurance industries, and in parts of large-scale industry. In other fields, managers are often promised a retirement pension.

388. The Pension Funds Act (*Pensionskassengesetz*) allows special private corporations (pension funds) to be created. In the cases agreed upon in the pension agreement, the fund pays the pension to entitled employees or their entitled relatives. In this way, the risk of the employer becoming insolvent before having paid all the pension obligations can be evaded. However, the creation of or participation in such a pension fund needs the express consent of the works council (if one exists in the undertaking).

389. The Company Pension Act (*Betriebspensionsgesetz*) regulates the contract underlying the pension (scheme) and the rights and duties emanating from this contract. The contract may be as already mentioned, a collective agreement, or a works agreement, or an individual labour contract. The Act secures the employee's position, if the labour relationship is terminated before the employee is entitled to the pension. It also restricts employers' opportunities to reduce unilaterally their contractual obligations to company pension schemes.

§3. The Amount of Pay

I. Statutes

390. The amount payable to employees working for private employers is not statutorily determined. There is neither any general minimum wage for all employees nor is it clear whether or not the Austrian Constitution would permit the regulation of the amount of pay by statute at all. However, several statutes, such as the General Civil Code in its §1152, at least lay down that in the absence of collective rules or an individual agreement on this subject matter, the employee is entitled to 'adequate' payment.

391. Only in rare cases can the state specify the amount of pay by executive order, essentially where there is lack of employers' associations, and on application of competent bodies (such as associations on the employees' side entitled to make collective agreements, *see* paragraphs 746 et seq.).

II. Collective Agreements

A. Minimum Wages

392. Due to lack of minimum wages being laid down in statutes, the regulation of pay by collective agreement has pre-eminent practical significance. Based on the specific structure of collective labour law, by far the majority of employees and employers in the private sector are governed by collective agreements (paragraph 655). Due to its mandatory effect, wages specified by a collective agreement are minimum wages. This means that an individual agreement between employer and employee can only specify more, not less, pay.

B. Method of Stipulating Pay

393. The parties to a collective agreement are neither bound by statutory regulation in the determination of a minimum wage nor in the settlement of other details connected with payment. Due to the collective parties' great autonomy, types of wage vary a lot.

394. In stipulating a minimum wage, most collective agreements take the employees' different levels of training, sorts of job and periods of service into account. This results in numerous different wage scales. Further variety of collective wages arises from the fact that agreements lay down minimum basic salaries (which are the primary intention in collective bargaining in general), but a lot of different forms of additional wages as well. As to the latter, there are hardly any restrictions. These payments may vary according to the employee's function in the establishment (e.g., manager's bonuses), the employee's social situation (e.g., family allowances), or in terms of particular difficulties and risks connected with the job (such as danger premiums, night work supplements) or performance (such as efficiency bonuses).

III. Works Agreements

395. Works councils and employers are not generally competent to regulate pay by works agreement. According to the Labour Organization Act, they can only determine performance-related pay, profit-sharing plans and premiums for special company-related occasions (especially premiums for a certain amount of service time). Other payments (especially the 'time pay' or 'basic salary', *see* paragraph 363) can only be regulated by a works agreement, as explicitly allowed for by the collective agreement in force. Indeed, there are only a few collective agreements which empower works councils and employers to determine wages. However, it often happens that agreements on pay are in fact concluded between works council and employer in an establishment. These legally invalid 'works agreements' can only become effective as individual regulating agreements if they are applied in practice, and therefore can be legally qualified as a tacit amendment to the individual employment contract (as to such 'conclusive' agreements, *see also* paragraphs 82 and 191).

IV. Individual Agreements

396. As already mentioned, collective agreements apply to by far the majority of employees in the private sector. In such cases, only pay higher than that specified in the collective agreement can be agreed upon by an individual contract. The same applies if a valid works agreement is in force. Pay can only be specified in individual employment contracts alone in exceptional cases, where no collective regulation exists. Nevertheless, the practical importance of individual agreements is not insignificant. In many sectors of the Austrian economy, actual wages are above the minima laid down in collective agreements (de facto wages).

V. Increasing and Decreasing Pay

397. Pay regulated by a collective agreement can be either increased or decreased by a new collective agreement. The same applies to pay regulated by a works agreement, if allowed for.

398. Not only minimum wages but also the actually paid wages above that amount, which are based on individual agreements, are regularly increased by collective agreements. According to the prevailing opinion, this sort of collective agreement settlement is permissible. However, this does not mean that the actual increased wage becomes the new mandatory minimum wage as such, but only that the de facto wage has to be raised, and might be reduced by individual agreement afterwards.

399. Besides laying down wages which exceed the collective minimum wages, employment contracts sometimes also include clauses that provide for the offsetting of the de facto payment exceeding minimum wage against future wage increases resulting from collective agreements. After a certain time, the originally higher wage (i.e., the one exceeding the minimum wage) is therefore absorbed by wage raises. Without new bargaining of the contract terms, the employee may then only claim the collective minimum wage. These 'absorption clauses' (*Aufsaugklausel*) are valid, if they include a foreseeable number of wage increases (as a rule of thumb, about three).

400. The employer cannot *ex post facto* and by one-sided directive reduce the pay which has been agreed upon in an individual agreement down to the level of the minimum wage specified in a collective agreement. An agreement is always required. If the employee refuses, the employer can give 'conditional notice' (notice of termination pending a change of contract). That means that the notice becomes effective, in the event that the employee does not agree to the intended wage reduction (*see* paragraph 458).

§4. Time of Payment, Place of Payment, Statutory Limitation

I. Time of Payment

401. The White-collar Workers Act specifies that a white-collar worker's regular salary must be paid in two equal parts, on the fifteenth and on the last day of each month. However, it also permits agreements by which the entire wage is paid on the last day of each month. In practice, the payment of white-collar workers at the end of the month is the general rule.

402. There are no statutory regulations covering the times of payment for blue-collar workers, for whom compulsory provisions derive from either a collective agreement or a works agreement.

403. In any event, payment is due at the termination of the employment relationship.

II. Place of Payment

404. Insofar as nothing is specified by a collective, works or individual agreement, the place of payment is the establishment. Agreements (works agreements, individual employment contracts), according to which payment is made by bank transfer into the employee's account, are permissible and widespread.

III. Statutory Limitation

405. According to §1486 General Civil Code, employees' claims to remuneration lapse three years after their due date. This period may not be prolonged but can be reduced by a collective agreement or an employment contract, provided this does not make it impossible to pursue the claim. Principally, the minimum period must be at least three months.

406. In addition, (statutory) labour law prescribes different periods for some payment rights. For instance, all claims accruing from an unlawful termination of contract have to be raised within six months. The same applies to claims for damages due to the employee's or employer's withdrawal from the conclusion of an employment contract. In practice, collective agreements often provide for superannuation clauses and thereby set the minimum standard (usually six months) that cannot be reduced in an individual employment contract. If not provided for in a collective agreement the individual employment contract may also include a 'forfeiture clause' stating that claims not put forward in writing within a certain period of time (not less than three months) are forfeited.

§5. Earnings Safeguards

I. Protection of Earnings Against Execution

407. The Enforcement Code (*Exekutionsordnung*) specifies in a detailed manner to what extent an employee's salary may be subject to execution. As a general rule, payments based on employment relationships are only subject to execution insofar as they exceed a certain sum: the minimum of subsistence (*Existenzminimum*). As of 2022, EUR 1,030 of monthly payment (EUR 240 of weekly payment, EUR 34 of daily payment) cannot be subject to execution; in other words, the employee is entitled to this part of his or her salary even if it is subject to execution (the amounts are higher if the employee does not receive the thirteenth and fourteenth monthly salaries; *see* paragraph 374). If the employee has a legal obligation to support a spouse, children, or other relatives, the minimum of subsistence increases by EUR 206 per person (but not exceeding five persons) in the case of monthly payment (in the case of weekly payment: EUR 48, daily payment: EUR 6). If the employee earns more than the aforementioned amounts, a quota of 30% of the additional income is also free of execution, and in the case of relatives supported by the employee, this quota increases by another 10% per supported person. However, in every case, if the employee earns more than EUR 4,120 per month (EUR 960 per week, EUR 137 per day), the excess amount is fully subject to execution.

408. In exceptional cases, when the employee has special needs, and if it is a reasonable burden on the creditor, a court can allow the employee to retain further sums as exempt from execution. Also, there exist specific provisions in favour of employees if their salary is taken in execution to fulfil duties of family law (for instance, to support ex-spouses, children, or other relatives). Alternately, there are circumstances which allow for the reduction of the amount of payment that cannot be subject to execution.

II. Limitations on the Right to Dispose of Remuneration Rights

409. Insofar as remuneration is free from execution, an employee may not dispose of it by assignment or pledging. The purpose of this provision is that the employee should not be deprived of the basic means of living.

III. Employer's Insolvency

410. In the event of an employer's bankruptcy, it is not only the employees' jobs that are at risk, but also their as yet unpaid remuneration. Even if sufficient assets were available, the length of insolvency proceedings would at least delay the satisfaction of employees' claims. Therefore, in 1977, a form of insolvency insurance for the benefit of employees was created (Act on Safeguarding Employees' Claims in the Event of the Employer's Insolvency – *Insolvenz-Entgeltsicherungsgesetz*).

411. This Act entailed the creation of a central fund, which is mostly financed by state-prescribed employers' contributions. The fund takes over employees' claims, and then it makes claims to regain its expenses from the employer's bankruptcy assets, on its own behalf in place of the employees. The risk of lost remuneration in the event of insolvency is thus passed from the employees to the fund. Since 2010, besides employees and homeworkers, the Act has been protecting also 'free employees'.

IV. Measures Against Wage Dumping

412. In 2011, the lawmaker stipulated that non-compliance with rules on minimum wages should not only lead to consequences according to civil law, but, for the first time, also allowed for administrative penalties. Hence, all national or foreign employers who employ workers in Austria without granting them the wages due in law or by collective norms are liable to administrative fines. The main purpose of these provisions was to create fair and equal working and payment terms for all workers in Austria, and to ensure fair competition between national and foreign employers.

413. In 2016, a specific statute, the Law against Wage and Social Dumping, was introduced. This is a codification of provisions on the various forms of dumping, the authorities involved and administrative procedures. Besides the obligation to pay the minimum wages according to law or collective agreements and so on, the statute, *inter alia*, lays down that all employees usually working in Austria have the right to paid vacation. This also applies to posted workers or cross-border commuters, if the duration of vacation according to the 'posting' legal system would be shorter. Austrian working time provisions for comparable employment relationships, especially maximum working hours and minimum rest periods, have to be observed for posted workers as well. Moreover, employers have to provide for (electronic) documents on wages, social insurance registration and several other types of administrative permit.

Chapter 5. The Suspension or Interruption of the Performance of Work in the Individual Employment Relationship

414. When the obligation to work is not fulfilled by the employee, it is necessary to distinguish between different situations:

- If the employee is at fault, that is, if able to work but just does not want to, the employee is in breach of contract. The employer does not have to pay remuneration, is entitled to damages and usually has the right to summarily dismiss the employee.
- If the employee cannot, for some reason beyond his or her control and disposition, fulfil their contractual obligations, the employee is not in breach of contract. However, the employer does not have to pay remuneration, because the payment is connected to the provision of services by the employee. In other words, the execution or performance of the individual employment contract is suspended or interrupted. The contract between the parties remains in existence, but the rights and duties which exist towards each other are 'in abeyance' (i.e., they 'rest' either totally or partially).
- If the employee does not render services because of being 'not able' to work due to justified reasons (especially in cases of sickness and accidents or collisions of duties), the employee is not in breach of contract, either. Furthermore, labour law often deviates from civil law principles and obliges the employer to pay remuneration in such cases. This is provided because the employee is considered to be in need of social protection.
- If the non-performance of services is attributable to the employer; for example, if the employer is unable to give employees work because of lack of raw materials or electricity, the employment contract remains in existence. The employer has to continue payment but has the option of reducing the continued wages, to the extent of the employee's financial advantages because of the non-performance (such as money earned with another employer during the time the employee could not be employed).
- In rare cases, the reason for the non-performance of services might be attributable neither to the employer nor to the employee (e.g., in war or natural disaster). In those cases (the 'neutral sphere'), the rights and duties of the employment contract are 'in abeyance' on either side; the employer does not have to pay remuneration and the employee does not have to work. From a dogmatic point of view, epidemic and plague must also be attributed to the neutral sphere (*see* former editions of this monograph). As a consequence, in order to avoid massive social conflicts, the labour law regulations have been amended in the course of the pandemic and deviated from this principle (*see* paragraph 438).

§1. Sickness and Accidents of the Employee

I. General

A. Continuation of Wage Payments

415. If an employee is prevented from working by sickness or accident, in principle the employee retains the right to wage or salary payment for a certain period (sick pay; sick leave). Sickness and accident are not defined explicitly within the labour law system, but their understanding is based on general use of language and several indirect references to social security law. Examples for sickness are (head) cold, influenza, headache, cancer, heart attacks, diabetes or COVID-19, for accidents it is broken legs, cuts or concussions. However, there is no protection against losing a job because of illness. For instance, by law, an employer can give notice during the illness. Furthermore, an employee's illness can be justification for giving notice in procedures involving appealing against an otherwise socially unjust termination (*see* paragraph 498). In order to prevent employers from getting rid of sick employees too easily and thereby evading the continuation of wage payments, the employer has to continue to pay remuneration beyond the actual end of the employment relationship if the employee is still ill. This applies not only when the employer gives notice but also in the event of cancellation of the contract during illness by mutual consent (§9 White-collar Workers Act, §5 Continuation of Wages Act).

B. Statutory Basis

416. The continuation of wage payments is regulated in separate statutes for blue- and white-collar workers. The Continuation of Wages Act (*Entgeltfortzahlungsgesetz*) covers blue-collar workers, §8 of the White-collar Workers Act (*Angestelltengesetz*) regulates the continuation of payment in case of sickness and accidents for white-collar workers. There are also separate rules for artistic employees, journalists, apprentices and employees of public law bodies. Also, it should be mentioned that the employee's claims against the employer for continued payment are supplemented by social insurance allowances. When the continued payment by the employer ends, or is only paid in part, the employee is entitled to 'sickness' allowances granted by health insurance.

C. Privileged Treatment of Work Accidents and Occupational Diseases

417. Both groups of employees (i.e., white- and blue-collar workers) are particularly favoured as to the continued payment, if their incapacity to work is due to a work accident or occupational disease, that is, various forms of incapacities which have been caused in the course of work or due to work. Payment is continued for a longer period in such cases than in those of incapacity to work due to ordinary illness or private accident (for more details *see* paragraphs 424 et seq.). Labour law regulations on continued payment do not define these types of incapacity themselves but refer explicitly to social insurance law which defines 'work accidents' and 'occupational diseases'.

II. Conditions

418. Generally, wage payment is only continued where the incapacity to work is not due to gross negligence or deliberate intent on the part of the employee.

419. Furthermore, the employee must notify the employer without undue delay. If the employer requests it, the employee must produce a doctor's certificate of inability to work (sick note); this request may be repeated after a certain time. Although failure of the employee to produce a sick note does not constitute a ground for summary dismissal, the employee will lose any claim to sick pay for the duration of the delay.

III. The Period of Continued Wage Payment and the Amount of Sick Pay

420. In 2017, the legislature made a significant step towards equalization of the rights of blue- and white-collar workers, and, therefore, a (further) standardization of labour law in Austria. With effect on cases of incapacity of work due to illness or accident from 1 July 2018 on, the legal situation of all employees in the field of continued wage payment was adapted primarily to the situation of blue-collar workers. The amendment has thus eliminated some former privileges of white-collar workers such as the longer duration of continuation of payment. In compensation, the claims of the latter in case of work accidents and occupational diseases have been adapted to those of the blue-collar workers. In detail this means the following.

421. According to §8 section 1 White-collar Workers Act and §2 section 1 Continuation of Wages Act, within one work year, all categories of employees:

- with up to one year of service have a right to sick pay for six weeks;
- after one year and up to fifteen years, payment continues for eight weeks;
- after fifteen years up to twenty-five years, payment continues for ten weeks; and
- after twenty-five years the period increases to twelve weeks.

Within these limits, full wage payment continues. Furthermore, in each of these cases, there is an additional right to the payment of half the wage for a further four weeks. Therefore, an employee in the first year of service is entitled to a maximum of six weeks' full payment and four weeks' half payment per illness (within one work year). An employee in the second year of service is entitled to a maximum of eight weeks' full payment and four weeks' half payment per illness (within one work year).

422. If a second (or more) illness occurs in the same work year, wage payment will only be continued for the period which was not exhausted during the previous illness(es). For example:

- the employee (second year of service) is ill for twelve weeks, then later for two weeks: he or she receives eight weeks' full payment and four weeks' half payment during the first illness. For the subsequent, second illness (within one year), the employee is not entitled to continued wage payment by the employer;
- the employee (second year of service) is ill for three weeks, then later for seven weeks and a third time for four weeks (within one work year): he or she is entitled to three weeks of continued full payment for the first illness, and for the subsequent, second illness, the employee receives five weeks' full payment and two weeks' half payment. For the third illness, the employee gets two weeks' half payment, but for the remaining two weeks, there is no entitlement from the employer.

423. If an employee falls ill, and his or her entitlement has already been exhausted in the current work year, there is no further entitlement from the employer; however, if the new work year of the employee started during this illness, from this moment on, the employee would be entitled to continued wage payment again. For example:

- the employee started his or her work on 1 August 2018, which means that the work year will always run from 1 August to 31 July of the following year. If the employee falls ill for twelve weeks at the beginning of January 2023, and then later for six weeks in July: for the first illness, he or she is entitled to eight weeks of continued full payment and four weeks of continued half payment. For the subsequent, second illness, the employee receives nothing during July 2023 (four weeks). But for two weeks in August, the employee is entitled to full wage continuation again, because a new work year has begun.

424. In the event of specific types of incapacity to work, namely occupational diseases or accidents, all employees have a right to continued payment for eight weeks (ten weeks after fifteen years of service) in addition to the above-mentioned entitlements for 'ordinary' illness or accident. In other words, unlike 'ordinary' diseases or accidents, occupational diseases or accidents do not depend on the work year, but the entitlement to continued wage payment is 'case-related'. Each time such a specific disease or accident occurs, the employee receives his or her continued wage payment up to eight (ten) weeks. For example:

- the employee (second year of service) is ill for fourteen weeks (with an ordinary illness such as influenza), then later the employee suffers from an occupational disease for eight weeks: for the first illness, he or she is entitled to eight weeks' full payment and four weeks' half payment. For the second illness, the employee receives eight weeks' full payment, because in this case, it is an occupational disease;
- the employee (second year of service) suffers from an occupational disease for five weeks, then later from an 'ordinary' illness for fifteen weeks: for the first illness, he or she is entitled to five weeks' full payment. For the second illness, the

employee receives eight weeks' full payment and four weeks' half payment. For the remaining three weeks, there is no entitlement from the employer;
- the employee (second year of service) suffers from an occupational disease for five weeks, then later an occupational accident occurs, and the employee has to stay at home for eight weeks. Later again, another occupational accident occurs, and the employee cannot work for a further seven weeks: for the first period of incapacity of work, he or she is entitled to five weeks' full payment. For the second period, the employee receives eight weeks' full payment, and for the third period, he or she gets seven weeks' payment.

425. If an employee suffers from an occupational disease lasting longer than the legal period of continued wage payment, there is no further entitlement from the employer. This applies even if another work year for the employee has begun meanwhile. Unlike in the case of 'ordinary' sickness or accident, a new entitlement to continued wage payment requires the employee to resume work. For example:

- the employee started his or her work on 1 August 2018 (that means that his or her work year will run from 1 August to 31 July of the following year). If the employee suffers from an occupational disease for twelve weeks beginning in the middle of May 2023: for the first eight weeks, he or she is entitled to continued full payment. For the remaining weeks, from the middle of July until the middle of August, the employee receives nothing, although a new work year has begun.

426. In cases where the employee has more than one employment relationship, the regulations for occupational diseases and accidents only apply to the employment that actually causes the privileged incapacity to work. As regards the other employers, the employee is only entitled to continued wage payment by them in the case of ordinary illness or accident (§8 section 2a White-collar Workers Act and §2 section 1 Continuation of Wages Act).

427. Within the limits outlined above, an employee should not suffer any financial disadvantage because of illness. The principle of continuation of payment of the regular wage is, therefore, fundamental. Apart from the regular wage or salary, this also includes other benefits, of either a normal or exceptional sort, such as commission, incentive premiums or overtime pay. Alternately, payment of ordinary expense allowances such as travelling expenses does not continue.

§2. Other Important Grounds Related to the Employee's Person

I. General

428. An employee not only has the right to continued wage payment in the case of incapacity due to illness or accident, but also, in certain cases, where there are other important reasons for incapacity to work for personal reasons. In these cases, the employee's duties deriving from the employment relationship conflict with other higher duties of the employee such as duties towards the family, society, the state and so on. The legal basis for this entitlement to continued payment is contained in various statutory provisions: §1154b section 5 of the General Civil Code applies to blue-collar workers, and §8 section 3 of the White-collar Workers Act to white-collar workers.

429. The statutory regulations mentioned above do not regulate the right to continued wage payment in detail. They only specify that an employee retains the right to pay if – without any fault – he or she is prevented from working for 'important personal reasons'. These include, for instance, death of a close relative, birth of a child, accompaniment of a child to school where necessary, precautionary medical check-ups, actual prevention from attending, such as traffic accidents or delayed trains, essential appointments with an official body (e.g., tax examination, witness in a court trial) and so on. Also, if employees are affected personally by a catastrophe (for instance, they have to protect a family member in the house which is threatened by landslip, avalanches or flooding), the employee retains payment.

430. The period of continued wage payment is limited and must not exceed a 'relatively short' time (about a week, according to prevailing opinion) for each occasion.

II. Free Time to Look after Sick Relatives

431. Special statutory regulations applicable to all types of employees cover occasions when an employee's close relative who lives in the same household falls ill and must be looked after by the employee. In such cases, the employee has the right to continued payment, up to a limit of the weekly working time, in any one work year. In the case of sick children under 10, the employee also retains the right to continued payment while looking after the child during its stay in a hospital.

432. The employee is entitled to an additional week of continued payment, if the basic entitlement is used up and he or she has to look after their sick child of up to 12 years of age. The two entitlements must not be combined for one case of sickness, but may only be used for two different occasions. If the child falls sick again, the employee may use the rest of their vacation time without the employer's consent in order to take care of the child.

III. Military Service and Alternative Civilian Service

433. If an employee is called up for the statutory period of national service, the employment relationship is suspended for the period of service. This means that the duties to work and to provide pay are in abeyance. There is also special protection against dismissal (with or without notice) for such employees.

IV. Protection of the Working Mother

434. The Maternity Protection Act (*Mutterschutzgesetz*) proscribes certain jobs for expectant mothers and women after delivery. These include generally heavy physical work, or activities which are primarily performed standing up, as well as work in vehicles. In cases where no permissible work is available in the employer's establishment, and work is therefore impossible, the employee has the right to retain full pay. Also, there are special provisions for continued payment, despite interruption of work for a breastfeeding woman, such as additional breaks.

435. Furthermore, the Maternity Protection Act specifies an absolute work prohibition for certain periods (especially before and after giving birth, *see* paragraph 563). However, the right to wage payment does not exist in these cases: instead, the employee receives social insurance benefits compensating her fully for her loss in wages.

§3. The Suspension of Work for Reasons Within the Employer's Sphere of Responsibility

436. The cases described in the previous chapters are of incapacity to work for reasons attributable to the employee. According to §1155 section 1 of the General Civil Code, employees also have an entitlement to remuneration if they are ready and willing to work but prevented from doing so by circumstances on the employer's side. In this case, principally, there is no time limit on the continuation of wage payment.

437. Irrespective of the employer's actual fault, any incident concerned with the technical running of the establishment, the delivery of materials and supply of resources, the order-book and sales, and the legality of the establishment's activities is part of the employer's sphere of responsibility: for instance, the employer is responsible for the failure of machinery and energy supplies, the halting of production by fire and also lack of deliveries because of industrial action in other establishments.

438. Catastrophes of massive or supra-regional impacts (*force majeure*) are not part of the employer's sphere of responsibility: for example, widespread flooding, general paralysis of transport, war and so on. If work is halted for such reasons, there is no right to payment. Yet, this principle is limited in several ways, due to other provisions of continued payment as regards 'catastrophes': the Supreme Court has held that even snowfall over a larger region and preventing employees from driving to work entitles them to continued payment. Also, if employees are affected 'personally' by a catastrophe (for instance, they have to protect a family member in the house which is threatened by landslip), the employee retains payment (§1154b section 5 General Civil Code). Furthermore, by explicit stipulation, the employer had to continue payment also in the event of (temporary) shutdowns due to COVID-19-measures (§1155 sections 3 and 4 General Civil Code, effective from March to December 2020).

439. If work is halted by circumstances on the employer's side but wage payments must be continued, employees must allow the deduction from their wages of whatever they may have saved by the lack of work, whatever they have earned by doing other work, or whatever they have deliberately failed to earn.

440. §1155 of the General Civil Code, which lays down the employer's duty to continue wage payment if the suspension of work is lying within their sphere, is not binding. Divergent rules can be established by agreement. For many employees, such divergent rules apply because of collective agreements which, in particular, reduce the amount of continued payment and set time limits.

Chapter 6. The Termination of the Individual Employment Contract

§1. Fundamental Principles

I. Types of Termination

A. *Employment Relationships for an Indefinite Period*

441. In Austria, employment relationships for an indefinite period are general practice in employment. Such an employment contract exists, if the parties have not specified its length (paragraph 195). There are several ways of terminating it: it ends automatically with the employee's death. It can be ended by a legal act, the cancellation of the contract by mutual consent. One-sided forms of legal termination are notice given by either party (*Kündigung*), and premature termination for substantial reasons. If a premature termination for substantial reasons is initiated by an employer, it is classified as summary dismissal (*Entlassung*). If it is declared by an employee, it is designated as premature resignation (*Austritt*).

B. *Employment Relationships for a Definite Period*

442. An employment relationship for a definite period exists if the length of the employment relationship is defined in terms of the calendar, or if the ending of the employment relationship can be objectively established and determined in some other way (paragraph 196). Primarily, fixed duration employment relationships finish at the end of the period specified. Furthermore, they end with the employee's death, by a cancellation of the contract by mutual consent, or by termination for substantial reasons.

443. Giving notice is not permissible in a fixed duration employment relationship, unless especially allowed for by contract. However, this principle is only universally applied to termination by the employer. The employee can always give six months' notice after five years of service (*see* paragraphs 200, 203). As mentioned above, premature termination for important reasons is just as possible for limited as for unlimited employment relationships.

C. *Probationary Employment Relationships*

444. The peculiarity of a trial period relationship is that it can be terminated at any time by either party's giving notice (*see also* paragraphs 185, 202). Periods of notice are just as unnecessary as the existence of particular reasons. However, not every employment relationship counts as a trial period relationship at its commencement. A trial period relationship must be specifically agreed.

445. Due to 'easy' termination, the opportunities to conclude a trial period employment contract are limited. In general, they can only be concluded for a one-month period, and the trial period must be at the start of the employment relationship.

II. Special Situations

A. Change of Establishment Ownership

446. The sale of the undertaking does not end the employee's employment relationship with the selling employer automatically. Rather, the contract remains in existence, and no additional agreement between employee, previous employer (the transferor) and new owner (transferee) is necessary to transfer the employment relationship to the establishment's buyer (paragraph 207). The new employer enters *ex lege* into the contractual relationship. Furthermore, in addition to the general provisions on termination, the employer's right to dismissal in the case of transfer of business is restricted by law in order to protect the employees in this situation. On the contrary, in the event of impairment by an unfavourable collective or works agreement which is applicable after the sale of the undertaking, the employee has a specific right to terminate the employment contract.

B. Bankruptcy

447. An employer's bankruptcy does not automatically end the employment relationship, but it modifies and extends the termination possibilities. The liquidator of the employer's business (who is appointed by court) may terminate any employment relationship, whether or not it is of indefinite duration, within one month of the start of the various bankruptcy proceedings. The employment contract can be terminated with either the statutory minimum or the agreed period of notice, whichever is shorter, and with regard to statutory safeguards against unwarranted termination (such as the 'general protection against dismissal' or the 'early warning system on termination'). More or less the same applies to the employer in the case of bankruptcy where the employer, by court order, continues to be allowed to exercise 'usual' entrepreneurial actions ('insolvency with remaining administration by the employer'). In all these situations, the employee can terminate the employment relationship as well, similarly within one month after the start of bankruptcy proceedings, in particular by means of premature resignation, referring to the employer's bankruptcy as a substantial reason.

448. The employee's bankruptcy has principally no effect on the employment relationship as such. However, such an event can result in the loss of the employee's 'trustworthiness', which would constitute a ground for summary dismissal (as to the protection of employees' earnings from execution by third parties, *see* paragraphs 407 et seq.).

C. Age

449. If an employee reaches the statutory retirement age (at present, usually 65 for men and 60 for women; from 2024 on, the latter will rise gradually), there is no immediate effect on the legal continuity of the employment relationship. One of the usual forms of termination must again be used, and the event does not constitute a substantive reason for premature termination.

D. Impossibility of Performance

450. If the hindrance to performance of services is attributable to the employee (for instance, incapacity to work or loss of driving licence), the legal continuity of the employment relationship is not automatically affected, and in particular not even if the hindrance is long-term. However, in the latter case, the employer may terminate the employment contract by summary dismissal, because it is unacceptable to have to continue the employment relationship when it is foreseeable that the employee will not be able to perform the agreed upon work for a long time or even for good (*see* paragraphs 523 et seq.). Hindrances to work which are attributable to the employer do not automatically terminate the employment relationships as such either (*see also* paragraphs 436 et seq.).

III. Freedom to Give Notice and Protection Against Unwarranted Dismissal with Notice

451. Freedom to give notice is the legal right of both contracting parties to end the employment relationship unilaterally and at will. This freedom to terminate is a part of the general right of private autonomy. It implies, above all, that notice is not subject to any restraint. In the case of complete freedom to give notice, either party can terminate the employment relationship at any time and for any reason, by compliance with the legally laid down periods of notice or termination dates (unless, of course, *contra bonos mores*).

452. Although the freedom to give notice can be limited or excluded (according to the principle of private autonomy) by an agreement between employer and employee, this possibility is in practice not open to the majority of employees. The legislature has therefore created step-by-step mandatory legal standards to restrict the employer's freedom to give notice in a wide variety of ways:

- The weakest form of this protection consists of the relatively binding nature of the periods of notice and dates for giving notice in the General Civil Code and most individual special statutes.
- A much more effective restriction derives from the creation of general protection against unwarranted dismissal, which gives all employees in an establishment employing more than four workers the possibility of appealing against dismissal to the labour and social court on certain specific grounds.

- Special dismissal protection law specifies a ban on giving notice to groups of employees who are in special need of protection against unwarranted dismissal (e.g., pregnant women or employees with disabilities). The protection from termination is usually specified for the period of the special need. It only fails when an executive authority or the labour and social court has previously agreed and decided that specifically laid down grounds for a termination actually exist.

453. Yet, even 'general protection against unwarranted dismissal' has some distinct limits set by the establishment's economic situation. If the establishment's economic needs collide with the employee's interest in keeping his or her job, this might normally be a sufficient justification for dismissal. All in all, though, in Austrian labour law, actual freedom to give notice for the most part only applies in establishments which are not governed by works representation law.

IV. Termination Fee

454. Up to 31 December 2019, in the event of termination of a (free) employment contract, under certain circumstances, the employer had to pay the so-termed termination fee to the health insurance body. This was a federal tax, which mainly had to be used for the promotion of labour market policy, such as subsidies for enterprises employing older workers. The amount of the termination fee (in 2019: EUR 131) did not depend on the amount of payment, duration of the employment relationship or age of the employee, but on the type of termination. However, the fee was only due if the (free) employee's wages exceeded the statutory minimum income limit for social insurance contributions, and the employment relationship, therefore, was subject to unemployment insurance (i.e., in 2019, the employee had to earn more than EUR 446.81 per month).

455. Apart from the construction and building sector, the termination fee had to be paid, above all, in the event of:

- cancellation of the contract by mutual consent after the trial period;
- the employer's giving notice, even in the case of an assurance of re-employment;
- unwarranted dismissal by the employer;
- the employee's resignation for substantial reasons; or
- expiry of an employment relationship that has been agreed for a fixed term of more than six months.

§2. TERMINATION BY NOTICE

I. General Principles

A. The Concept

456. Notice of termination is a declaratory act by either party which is only valid if the other party duly receives it, and which has the effect of terminating the whole employment relationship for the future. It belongs to the category of rights by which legal relationships can be changed (for instance, brought into existence, altered or terminated) and enables a party to the contract to bring about a unilateral and complete termination of the employment relationship. Notice which is intended to remove only certain terms in a contract (such as the amount of pay) is only permissible if especially agreed on (partial termination). As giving notice is a legal act, the general conditions for the effectiveness of legal acts in civil law must be fulfilled: in particular, the person who gives notice must have the legal capacity to do so, and be serious.

B. Form and Legal Conditions

457. Principally, there is no legal requisite for a specified way of giving notice ('freedom of form'). It can therefore be declared (given) either expressly (orally, in writing or even via digital devices such as Short Message Service (SMS) or WhatsApp) or by 'conclusive' behaviour. Even the terms 'notice' or 'give notice' need not be used. It is enough that the declaration makes the intention objectively clear from the point of view of the recipient: that the employment relationship is to end at a particular time. It is not necessary to give reasons for giving notice.

458. In the interests of the recipient, notice may not be bound to conditions at will. After notice has been given, the recipient should know or be enabled to realize what their legal situation is. However, conditions which might be governed or influenced by the recipient's own actions are permissible. The most common example of this kind of 'conditional notice' is notice of termination pending a change of contract. Here, notice is given subject to the condition that the other party (usually the employee) does not agree to certain contractual adjustments within a certain specified period (e.g., wage reductions or changes of the work to be performed). If an agreement cannot be reached, the notice becomes effective. In contrast, an illegal conditional notice is invalid even if the employee agrees to the condition(s).

C. *Periods of Notice and Termination Deadlines*

1. Periods of Notice

459. Periods of employer's and employee's notice are specified by statute or collective agreements for almost all employment relationships. Therefore one can say that giving notice ends employment relationships after a certain period, and not at once.

460. The period of notice is the time which must elapse between the time of giving the notice and the end of the employment relationship. The period is specified either in days, weeks or months.

461. Until 2021, when the labour law reforms of 2017 in this area become effective, the length of periods of notice varied considerably for different employee groups. For the most part, the individual statutes for the different employee groups and, particularly for blue-collar workers, the various collective agreements were decisive. The above-mentioned reforms occurred because the differences between periods of notice applicable to various groups of employees were not always comprehensible – particularly as regards aspects of equality.

462. For most blue-collar workers, §77 of the Industrial Code (*Gewerbeordnung*) specified a fourteen-day period of notice for both contracting parties; in other words, the employer, as well as the blue-collar worker, could terminate the employment with a notice period of a fortnight. Additionally, the period could be reduced by (individual or collective) agreement, even if this reduction was less favourable to the employee. However, §77 of the Industrial Code only applied if there were no provisions in the employment contract or an applicable collective or works agreement. In practice, however, most collective agreements for blue-collar workers already contained provisions on notice periods that set binding minimum standards in favour of the employee.

463. As of October 2021, the periods of notice are the same for all groups of employees, though they are still laid down in different acts (such as §20 of the White-collar Workers Act or §1159 of the General Civil Code). The legal periods are relatively binding; they can only be changed in favour of the employee. Different periods exist depending on whether the employer or the employee gives notice. Furthermore, one universal principle does apply: for most employees, the period of notice to which the employer is bound increases with the employee's years of service ('seniority principle').

464. The employee can terminate the employment relationship with one month's notice, regardless of the years of service. Yet, the employee's notice period may be extended by mutual agreement, up to that to be observed by the employer.

465. The employer of a white-collar worker may terminate the employment of an employee having worked:

– up to two years of service with a notice period of six weeks;
– less than five years with a notice period of two months;
– less than fifteen years with a notice period of three months;
– less than twenty-five years with a notice period of four months; and
– more than twenty-five years with a notice period of five months.

2. Termination Date (When the Employment Relationship May End)

466. Besides the periods of notice, the White-collar Workers Act and several other statutes, for example, the Theatrical Work Act, the Agricultural Employment Act and as of 2021 also the General Civil Code provide for special termination dates.

467. The 'termination date' is defined as the moment when the employment relationship actually ends (*dies ad quem*); it is not the date that notice can be given (commencing date or *dies a quo*). Therefore, if a combination of a period of notice and a termination date are to be observed, this usually results in a longer time span between giving notice and the actual end of the employment relationship. For example, according to §20 of the White-collar Workers Act or §1159 of the General Civil Code, a notice period of six weeks and a termination date at the end of every calendar quarter apply. If an employer gives notice on 16 March, the employment ends only on 30 June, because the employer not only has to observe the notice period of six weeks, which would end on 27 April, but also the termination date, which is the end of June.

468. The above-mentioned White-collar Workers Act and the General Civil Code lay down that, principally, notice given by an employer terminates the contract only at the end of a calendar quarter. However, these Acts also permit agreements by which the last day of a month or the fifteenth of a month are the ending dates for the contract, in the case of a notice given by the employer, and in practice this possibility is often taken advantage of. In the above-mentioned example, the contract would end on 30 April.

469. In contrast, employees themselves can resign with a one-month period of notice to take effect on the last day of a month.

D. Unlawful Notice

1. Notice in Breach of Periods of Notice and Termination Dates

470. By their purpose, most periods of notice are minimum periods. Principally, especially if it is in favour of the employee, notice given with a longer period than that provided for statutorily, in a collective agreement or in an individual agreement, only terminates the employment relationship at the agreed upon time. Generally, the same applies if notice is given for later than the next legally permissible termination date (with rare exceptions – according to jurisprudence – for very unusual termination dates).

471. A different situation exists if notice is given with a shorter period or for an earlier date: according to court practice, such notice terminates the employment relationship at the earlier (i.e., the wrong or improper) date, but the termination is then treated as an unlawful premature dismissal. The legal result is that in the case of unlawful notice given by the employer, the employee is entitled to damages, that is, the pay for the time which would have passed until the proper termination of the employment relationship, in compliance with the correct period of notice and specified termination date (*Schadenersatzprinzip*).

2. Notice Where the Giving of Notice Is Precluded by Contract

472. Without any agreement to the contrary, notice cannot be given to terminate a definite employment contract (*see also* paragraph 443). A similar situation exists in cases where an employer has contractually promised an employee to refrain from giving notice. The employer agrees that notice cannot be given at all, or that giving of notice is bound to the existence of specific reasons. The two situations must be distinguished between, when deciding whether the notice nevertheless given is ineffective, or whether it ends the employment relationship but leaves the party terminating the employment contract liable for damages.

473. In the case of employment relationships for a definite period, the inadmissible notice to terminate is effective, that is to say, the contract is terminated by the notice, but the terminating party is liable for damages. If this is the employer, compensation has to be paid to the extent of the remuneration which would have been paid until the termination date the parties had originally agreed on in the employment contract.

474. Alternately, it is generally acknowledged that inadmissible notice is ineffective in the case of a contractual restriction on termination. If the right to give notice is completely precluded or bound to the existence of specific reasons, inadmissible notice of termination does not end the employment relationship. The same applies to lifetime employment relationships where the employer gives notice.

3. Other Unlawful or Unethical Notice

475. In the area of protection against unwarranted dismissal with notice, several statutory provisions specify particular procedures which have to be followed for notice to be valid or prohibit the giving of notice altogether for a certain length of time. If these provisions are violated, or if notice is given despite the prohibition, the notice is invalid and the employment relationship continues.

476. However, unlawful notice is sometimes only 'contestable'. If notice is given for discriminatory reasons covered by the Equal Treatment Act (*see* paragraphs 113 et seq.), or in order to penalize an employee for exercising rights under works representation law, it is initially effective although it violates the Equal Treatment Act or the Labour Organization Act, and can only be appealed against according to the provisions of these Acts.

477. Notice cannot only contravene legal prohibitions but may also violate ethical standards. This refers to the motives of whoever is giving notice (e.g., if it is based on the colour of the employee's hair). According to the prevailing view, unethical notice is null and void according to the general provisions of the Civil Code.

II. General Protection Against (Unwarranted) Dismissal with Notice

A. General

478. The provisions on protection against (unwarranted) dismissal are classified as a part of the employees' right of co-determination and are regulated in works representation law (§105 Labour Organization Act). Hence, despite its name, general protection against unwarranted dismissal does not apply to all employees, but only to those employed in an establishment governed by works representation law (*see* paragraph 452). Therefore, employees in an establishment with fewer than five regular workers are exempted from protection. Neither protection against unwarranted dismissal covers executive and senior personnel, because they are not considered to be employees in the sense of works representation law (*see* paragraph 61).

479. Moreover, the application of these rules of protection requires a declaration of notice which is valid according to contract (civil) law. An employee is only protected against notice (as well as unfounded dismissal), but not against other forms of termination. In particular, there is no protection when an employment relationship for a definite period comes to an end because the agreed on period ends (*see* paragraph 195). However, according to some current literature, general protection against unwarranted dismissal with notice might apply to termination of a trial employment relationship. Unfounded summary dismissal is covered by the law of protection against unwarranted summary dismissals.

480. Every intended notice of termination must be preceded by a procedure in which the competent works council must be involved. Thus, the main part of the protection against notice is the informing of the works council. Notice can only be given to an employee effectively if this procedure has been followed.

481. If the competent works council has been informed of the intended notice of termination and the actual termination as well, the termination is – at least for now – effective. Eventually, it can be challenged by filing a complaint with the labour and social court on specific grounds (unlawful motives or social injustice) laid down in §105 of the Labour Organization Act. If the complaint is successful, dismissal with notice will be cancelled by the decision of the labour and social court. That means notice is *ex post facto* declared ineffective and the employment relationship is – also for the future – considered to be continued and unbroken.

B. The Preliminary Procedure

1. Informing the Works Council

482. The employer must inform the competent works council before giving any employee notice. If an employer owns several establishments, the competent works council is that of the establishment in which the employee works.

483. No particular form is required for the notification though in practice the written form is recommended for reasons of provability in any later court procedure. It is enough that the employer's intention to give a particular employee notice is made clear. A specific date need not be given. If the establishment owner does not inform the works council, notice subsequently given is ineffective.

2. The Works Council States Its Position

484. After notification of the intended notice, the works council has the right to consult with the establishment owner about the notice, and also to comment on it within one week. The works council can decide on its reaction at an official meeting within this period or even by a circular resolution (e.g., by means of e-mail). In any case, it is at the works council's discretion how it comments on the notice (approval, disapproval, no reaction).

485. The support of a simple majority of the works council's members suffices for an objection to the intended notice. For the notice to be agreed to, the support of two-thirds of the votes cast is required. The works council may also decide not to respond at all and let the one-week period elapse. The reaction of the works council does not affect the validity of the termination itself, but will influence the appeal procedures that follow, that is to say, who may file the appeal, the deadlines for the application and so on.

486. If the works council's reaction is passed on to the owner only after one week, it is legally ineffective. This means that the situation is the same as if there had been no reaction of the works council at all.

487. If the employer gives notice to the employee after notifying the works council but before the end of the one-week period, or before the works council has stated its reaction, the dismissal is null and void.

3. Establishments Without a Works Council

488. If works representation law applies to an establishment (in other words, there are more than four employees working there) but it nevertheless does not have a works council, the procedure described above is not applicable. Up to this point, an employer is free to give notice; however, filing a complaint against the notice is still possible in such cases. The employee has to do it on his or her own, without the support of the works council (*see* paragraph 492).

C. Contesting Notice

1. Declaration of Notice

489. Notice can only be given effectively after the preliminary procedure involving the works council. After the employer's giving notice, the works council must again be notified. It is then relevant how the works council previously reacted to the intended dismissal:

- If the works council agreed to it, notice may only be contested on grounds of an unlawful motive (paragraphs 494 et seq.). Hence, the works council can bar the employee's appeal on grounds of 'social injustice' (paragraphs 497 et seq.). Also, the employee has to contest the notice on his or her own.
- If the works council expressly disapproved of the notice or did not react at all, the dismissal can be appealed against by either the works council or by the employee who has been given notice. Moreover, contest can be grounded both on 'unlawful motives' and 'social injustice'.

2. Appeal by the Works Council

490. If the works council expressly objected against the intended dismissal, the primary right to appeal is with the works council. Apart from the express protest on the part of the works council, it is also a prerequisite that the employee concerned asks the council to file a complaint.

491. The works council can file an appeal with the labour and social court within one week after being notified that notice has been given.

3. Appeal by the Employee Who Has Been Given Notice

492. The employee concerned has the right to appeal in three cases:

(1) If the works council has expressly lodged an objection against the employee's termination, it has the primary right of appeal. But for all that, if the works council does not comply with a request for appeal, the employee who has been given notice has the right to file a complaint on his or her own behalf. The employee can appeal within two weeks after the end of the period provided for the works council. Moreover, the employee can 'enter' into the procedures, in other words, the council's right of appeal passes to the employee concerned, if the council withdraws the complaint once it is already under consideration. Eventually, the employee can continue proceedings within fourteen days of being informed of the withdrawal.
(2) If the works council has not commented on the intended notice or if it has even approved of the termination, the employee who has been given notice immediately has the right to appeal him- or herself. The employee can file a complaint against notice with the labour and social court within two weeks of notice being given.
(3) If no competent group works council or even no works council at all has been established, the right of appeal passes to the employee concerned right from the start. The complaint must be filed within two weeks of notice being given.

D. Grounds of Appeal

493. An appeal against notice to the labour and social court can only succeed if the court finds the valid grounds for an appeal, as provided for in §105 section 3 of the Labour Organization Act, and therefore if the notice of termination is either based on 'unlawful motives' or if it is 'socially unjustified'.

1. Unlawful Motives

494. An appeal will be successful if the motive for giving the employee notice is the employee's:

- joining or being a member of a trade union;
- activities in a trade union;
- calling an assembly of employees;
- activities as a member of the election committee or an election commission, or as an electoral witness appointed by a candidate in a works council election;
- candidature for works council membership or previous activities as a works council member;
- activities as member of a conciliation board;
- activities as an employee representative responsible for works safety;
- impending call-up for national service;
- activities as a speaker according to European representation law;

– having claimed not obviously unjustified rights concerning the employment relationship (e.g., overtime pay).

495. If the works council agreed to the dismissal, the employee may nonetheless appeal against it and allege an unlawful motive.

496. Notice due to other unlawful motives, such as membership of a political party or religious group or because of political or religious activities or manifestations is not covered by the Labour Organization Act. Such notice may be covered by the Equal Treatment Act, or is otherwise *contra bonos mores* and therefore null and void, as unethical according to provisions of the General Civil Code.

2. Socially Unjustified Dismissal

497. If an employee has already been employed for six months, an appeal against notice of termination can be based on 'social injustice'. This means that the termination of the contract substantially impairs the interests of the employee concerned. The term 'substantial interests' leaves the court some discretion. In general, the employee's substantial interests are impaired if notice causes financial loss (as a general principle, more than 15% of the wages the employee earned in the job that has been terminated) or if a longer period of unemployment can be expected as a result of notice being given. In the case of older employees, any long service with the dismissing employer, as well as the difficulties which can be anticipated due to required adjustments to new work because of their advanced age, have to be taken into account.

However, according to amendments in 2017, there is only 'reduced' protection against socially unjustified dismissal for employees who did not begin their (current) employment relationship until after their fiftieth birthday. Difficulties due to their age with reintegration into the labour market after a termination cannot be referred to in a litigation on socially unjustified dismissal with as much impact as it could be previously.

498. Challenge to the termination will be successful if the employee's substantial interests are impaired by the notice in the above-mentioned way, and unless the employer is able to prove that:

– termination is based on grounds concerning personal characteristics of the employee that are adverse to the interests of the enterprise (such as frequent absences due to illness); or
– there are economic reasons preventing the continuation of employment (e.g., closure of a business).

499. This means that even if the loss of work impairs the employee's substantial interests hugely, it cannot be appealed against successfully if business interests conflict with continuation of the employment relationship. This is the case if an economic decision of the employer (such as closure of business, outsourcing or reduction of workforce due to acquisition of new machinery) results in the loss of the job the employee is doing. The economic decision itself is not reviewed by the court, but only its results as regards the cut back of the workforce. In this case, the court considers whether or not the employer has tried all possible avenues to avoid laying off the employee (e.g., by offering another suitable job in the establishment or vocational training).

500. Moreover, it cannot be appealed against notice successfully if there are 'personal reasons' concerning the employee which are opposed to the employer's or the undertaking's interests. These include a lack of physical, psychological or social capacities (such as regular illness) and an employee's light breaches of duty (such as repeated unpunctuality, bad work or teasing of colleagues).

501. If the works council has expressly lodged an objection, dismissed employees have an additional 'last resort': they may request a 'social comparison', which means that the judge compares the situation of an explicitly named employee of the establishment with the appealing employee. If such comparison of the two employees leads to the result that the employee concerned is hit harder by being given notice than another (e.g., a younger employee without children) would have been, the notice is not socially justified, either. The appeal against termination would be successful, the notice declared 'ineffective', and the employee can/must continue their work.

III. Special Protection Against Unwarranted Dismissal with Notice

A. General

502. A special and more comprehensive protection than the general protection outlined above is granted to certain categories of employees who, in the view of the lawmaker, especially require it. For the most part, this means that there are (temporary) legal proscriptions to give notice (e.g., during pregnancy), and the employer can only effectively give notice if the labour and social court or another official body has previously given permission after an application by the employer. Also, this permission can only be granted on specific and statutorily defined grounds. Special protection against unwarranted dismissal is regulated by various statutes, and for several groups of employees.

B. Works Council Members

1. Protected Persons

503. Special protection is laid down in favour of both current works council members and former members for three months after the end of membership (§§120 and 121 Labour Organization Act). Similarly, employees who have organized or initiated a works council election or have been election committee members are protected, although their special protection is limited in time. Protection against unwarranted dismissal also applies to substitute members of the works council under certain circumstances. Finally, the same protection is laid down for members of an establishment's 'young employees' council'.

2. Grounds for Assent to Dismissal with Notice

504. As long as special protection applies, all notice is null and void if the labour and social court has not agreed to it before the notice is given. In detail the court's permission can only be granted if:

– the establishment is being closed down or permanently reduced, and the employee concerned cannot continue to be occupied in another position within the establishment or the company; or
– the employee will not be able to do the contractually agreed work for an unforeseeable period, and the employer cannot reasonably be expected to give the employee different work; or
– the employee persistently fails in his or her duties and the employer cannot reasonably be expected to continue the employment for reasons of work discipline. However, in this case the labour and social court should refuse assent, if the works council member's behaviour in breach of duty is due to membership of the works council, and is excusable when all the circumstances are taken into consideration (such as intense discussions, or even quarrels, with the employer on employees' rights).

C. Protection of the Working Mother and Father

1. Protected Persons

505. According to §10 of the Maternity Protection Act, a female employee cannot be given notice without the consent of the court during pregnancy and for a minimum of four months after delivery. This is on condition that the pregnancy was known to the employer at the time of giving notice, or the employer has been notified of the pregnancy or delivery within five days of notice being given.

506. If a working mother or father takes parental leave or reduces their working time after the birth of a child (parental part-time), the special protection against dismissal ends four weeks after the end of the leave or of the reduced working hours. It ends with the child's fourth birthday. Afterwards, the protection is much weaker: if parents make use of parental part-time for a longer period of time, they may contest the termination on the basis that this fact was the motive of the dismissal ('individual protection against dismissal'). Furthermore, the law provides special protection against dismissal for fathers who make use of the Daddy's Month (*see* paragraph 569). The special protection against dismissal begins with the prior notification of intent to claim the Daddy's Month, but at the earliest, four months before the calculated date of birth; it ends four weeks after the end of the Daddy's Month.

2. Permissibility of Dismissal with Notice

507. Exceptionally, the court's consent is not necessary if the employer has closed down the establishment completely. Apart from that, pregnant women, mothers after delivery and so forth can only be dismissed with the consent of the court in cases of closure of a business or department, and if the employment relationship cannot be maintained without unreasonable burdens on the establishment. Otherwise, assent should be given, if the employee declares before court in the procedure that they accept notice.

508. Additionally, after the child's first birthday the court has to allow a dismissal if the continuation of the employment relationship would not be reasonable for the employer on grounds of business interests or of facts about the concerned employee.

D. Employees with Disabilities

509. According to the Employees with Disabilities Act, employees whose earning capacity is impaired, and not only temporarily, by at least 50% due to physical or psychological disabilities are afforded special protection against being given notice. The special protection is only granted if the employee has official certification of his or her status as person with disabilities. As to giving notice to people with disabilities, the employer must first receive prior consent from the Commission for Persons with Disabilities, a tripartite public authority. Furthermore, the employee with disabilities must have been working for forty-eight months in the establishment at the time of dismissal.

510. The authority's consent has to be given if the employer's interests outweigh those of the employee. The Act exemplifies three grounds for dismissal:

(1) the position of the employee with disabilities has been cut and the employee may not be employed in another appropriate position without considerable (financial) burdens to the employer; or
(2) the employee is not able to do the contractually agreed work any longer, rehabilitation is not to be expected within a reasonable period of time, and the employee may not be employed in another appropriate position without considerable (financial) burdens to the employer; or
(3) the employee persistently fails in his or her duties and the employer cannot reasonably be expected to continue to employ that person for reasons of work discipline.

511. There is no 'special protection against dismissal' if the employee's earning capacity is impaired by less than 50%, or if they lack official certification of status as a disabled person. However, the employee may contest the dismissal on the basis that it was discriminatory ('individual protection against dismissal').

E. Military Service and Alternative Civilian Service

512. Special protection exists according to an Act protecting the jobs of employees called up for national service (*Arbeitsplatz-Sicherungsgesetz*). Protection begins with the service of call-up papers and generally lasts for one month after the end of national service. During this period, notice given by the employer is, in principle, null and void. The precondition is that employees inform the employer that they have been called up for national service.

513. The employer can only give notice validly with prior consent of the labour and social court. Consent may only be given if the employer is closing down or cutting down the establishment or parts of it and cannot continue to employ the employee concerned without substantial (financial) burdens. Another reason for consent is the employee's long-term incapacity to work. Otherwise, the labour and social court consents, if the employee agrees to the termination of the employment contract before court in the procedure.

IV. Collective Redundancies

514. The Collective Redundancies Directive (*Massenentlassungsrichtlinie*), 98/59/EC, aims to protect the workplace in the event of redundancy of a larger number of workers. In Austria, the Directive was largely implemented by the Labour Market Promotion Act (*Arbeitsmarktförderungsgesetz*) and the Labour Organization Act. Accordingly, §45a Labour Market Promotion Act states that if the employer intends to reduce staff substantially, the local office of the Public Employment Service has to be notified thirty calendar days before giving notice to the first affected employee ('early warning system on termination'). This written notification should contain, *inter alia,* the reasons for the projected redundancies, the number of workers to be made redundant and the period over which the projected redundancies are to be effected, as well as details of the categories and sex of workers to be made redundant. This applies if the number of redundancies is at least:

- five employees, in businesses normally employing more than 20 and less than 100 workers; or
- 5% of the workforce, in businesses normally employing more than 100 and less than 600 employees; or
- thirty employees, in businesses normally employing more than 600; or
- five employees older than 50 years of age, irrespective of the number of employees in the establishment.

515. The notification of the local employment office also must show that the works council has already been informed of the mass redundancies. Following this notification, negotiations with the local employment office and the works council, as well as with the competent chambers of commerce and labour regarding the dismissal of the employees must take place.

516. Any dismissal prior to the end of the thirty-day 'waiting period' is null and void. The local employment office can, however, approve of the dismissals prior to the end of the thirty-day waiting period if a social plan (*see* paragraph 810) is filed, together with notification of the intended dismissals.

§3. Premature Termination for Substantive Reasons

I. General Principles

A. *Definition*

517. Premature termination is the act by which the employer or the employee immediately and unilaterally puts an immediate end to an employment contract for important reasons (just cause). The first difference to giving notice is that substantive reasons must exist, and the second, that the employment relationship ends prematurely (i.e., at once or without the prescribed period of notice).

518. The possibility of premature termination is based on the idea that reasons may occur which make the continuation of an employment relationship unacceptable and not endurable, even for the period of notice. Therefore the right to premature termination for substantive reasons need not be especially agreed upon in a contract – it is an implicit part of all employment relationships (and continuing obligations in general civil law as well). Thus, this also applies to definite contracts for a specified duration that may not be terminated by giving notice (*see also* paragraphs 442 et seq.).

519. If the employment relationship is terminated by the employer for substantive reasons, this is referred to as 'summary dismissal' (*Entlassung*). Termination of the employment relationship for substantive reasons by the employee is called 'constructive dismissal' or 'premature resignation' (*Austritt*). Like notice on termination, principally, the declaration need not be given in a special form though the written form is recommended, for reasons of provability. The general preconditions in civil law on declarations apply (in particular legal capacity, seriousness and so on).

520. Consequently, it is important for the premature termination to be declared without undue delay, if one party has good reason. If an employer or employee waits for too long, they lose their right to terminate prematurely. Adequate time to seek legal advice, to clarify the facts or to get the necessary intra-company consent to summarily dismiss is not considered undue delay.

521. If a premature termination is declared, the substantive reason itself need not be given in the declaration. It is sufficient that in the procedure before court, it can be proven that valid grounds existed at the time of the declaration. Valid reasons which come into existence only after the declaration cannot justify it; on the contrary, it is possible to base the termination on facts that already existed before the declaration but only became known afterwards.

B. Just Cause

522. Premature termination requires that one party cannot objectively be expected to continue the employment relationship, even for the period of notice. Whether such just cause exists, as well as its elements, is laid down in many different statutes and legal ways, hence, not uniformly for all employees. In part, it is only very generally specified that the employment relationship can be prematurely terminated for 'substantive reasons', without giving any further definition thereof (§1162 General Civil Code), in part, the reasons are listed exhaustively (§§82, 83 Industrial Code 1859, applicable to blue-collar workers, and in part, quite antiquated, *see* below), and in part, statutes contain a general clause and a demonstrative list of more or less concrete circumstances (e.g., §§25 et seq. White-collar Workers Act).

523. The most important reasons for the summary dismissal of white-collar workers are, among others:

- disloyalty or untrustworthiness of the employee;
- incapacity or failure to perform the promised or appropriate (reasonable) services;
- breach of contract or misconduct, such as disobeying orders, or attempts to induce others to disobedience, or refusing to work without any legitimate excuse;
- any breach of the prohibition on competition.

524. Grounds for summary dismissal for blue-collar workers according to the Industrial Code comprise the employee's:

- deception of the employer when concluding the contract;
- incapacity to do the agreed work;
- chronic alcoholism despite repeated warnings;
- certain criminal felonies (such as theft, personal offence or threatening of the employer);
- betrayal of industrial secrets and prejudicial sideline work;
- leaving work without permission or persistent neglect of duties; or
- 'repulsive' disease.

525. The reasons allowing employees to resign prematurely are also laid down in various Acts and are, for instance:

- if the employee is unable to continue work; or
- the employee cannot continue work without harm to life, health or integrity;
- if the employer does not pay salary properly; or
- the employer does not comply with other essential obligations of the employment contract.

526. Individual statutes set concrete standards, and they differ in detail but are mostly consistent with one another as to the central notions of 'just reasons'. The fundamental idea of all provisions relating to premature termination is that the circumstances of one party must make the continuation of the employment relationship unacceptable or unreasonable for the other side, even for the period of notice. Therefore, not every breach of the employment contract constitutes a valid reason for premature termination at the same time.

527. Vice versa, the principle of unreasonableness also implies that grounds for termination need not involve a breach of contract. This becomes obvious in the case of 'untrustworthiness' as a reason for summary dismissal. Untrustworthiness may even arise from actions or omissions on the part of the employee which are not connected to the employment relationship at all but to their private or even family life. Moreover, the reason does not need to be based on culpable behaviour (such as physical incapacity to work due to cancer). Only some statutory definitions of circumstances justifying termination presuppose fault. As to further financial consequences, one must make distinctions (*see* below).

C. Legal Consequences

528. Summary dismissal, as well as premature resignation, terminates the employment relationship with immediate effect.

529. If the employer is at fault for the employee's premature resignation, the latter is entitled to compensation for the loss of employment: the compensation covers the amount of wages for the remaining period of time, that is, until the date when a regular termination of the employment relationship, in accordance with the period of notice or lapse of time in the case of a definite contract, is possible ('compensation for notice'; as to its reduction after three months, *see* paragraph 537). Further rights to compensation may exist.

530. An employee who is to blame for dismissal is also liable for damages, although in practice they are only claimed rarely.

531. If the dismissal or resignation is based on material reasons, and where not only one party is at fault, but the other party is also to blame for the termination, a judge can decide at their own discretion whether and how much compensation is due.

532. All claims deriving from premature termination must, in the case of further damages, be asserted in court within six months from the date of premature termination.

533. Dismissal where the employee is at fault also leads to the loss of (immediate) claim to severance payment rights (*see* paragraphs 378, 385) and to the obligation to pay back holiday pay for leave already used in excess of their pro rata holiday entitlement (*see* paragraph 356).

II. Premature Termination Without Just Cause

A. General

534. If the employment relationship is prematurely terminated but without just cause, the employment relationship ends with immediate effect, all the same. This rule, which is provided for in individual statutes, is based on the consideration that it would be pointless to bind the parties to each other when the intention to terminate the contract had already been declared. Summary dismissal without justification only fails to end the employment relationship, if the employee is afforded special statutory or contractual protection against being dismissed.

B. Unfounded Summary Dismissal

535. Summary dismissal without just cause terminates the employment relationship with immediate effect. However, the employee is entitled to compensation covering the wages for the remaining period of time, that is, until the date when a regular termination of the employment relationship, in accordance with the period of notice or lapse of time in the case of a definite contract, is possible ('compensation for notice'). Besides this compensation for loss of employment, the employee can claim compensation for any further damages.

536. If the proper period up to termination does not exceed three months, the compensation for wrongful termination is due immediately. Furthermore, the income earned elsewhere during this period is not deducted from the compensation for notice. Therefore, if the employee immediately obtains a new job, perhaps better paid, the dismissed employee still receives full compensation for the loss of employment from the previous employer.

537. If the period in question exceeds three months, the due dates for wage payment remain in force, so that the employee receives compensation for notice at the time when the salary would be paid. Furthermore, after three months, the amount of compensation for notice may be reduced. It is allowable to subtract the expenses which are saved by the employee as a result of the discontinuation of the job (e.g., travelling expenses), wages earned through another employment elsewhere (such as in a new employment relationship), or deliberately not earned (as when the employee has turned down a reasonable job offer without good reason). The right to further damages, which only accrues in cases where the employer is at fault, can, for example, derive from the loss resulting from having to vacate duty accommodation.

C. *Unfounded Constructive Dismissal*

538. Unfounded premature resignation (constructive dismissal) by an employee ends the employment relationship immediately like summary dismissal without just cause. An employee who is at fault is liable for any consequent damages (such as the higher cost of a replacement worker for the regular period of notice). In any case, the employer does not have a claim for the employee's return to work, that is, fulfilment of the contract.

539. Other consequences are the loss of pro rata vacation payment (paragraph 356), as well as (immediate) severance payment (paragraphs 378, 385). Furthermore, it is not uncommon to incorporate contractual 'penalty clauses' into employment contracts, in case an employee resigns prematurely without just cause.

III. General Protection Against Summary Dismissal

A. *General Notion*

540. As summary dismissal without just cause also brings an end to the employment relationship, the employer might use it to circumvent legislation protecting the employee against unwarranted dismissal (with notice). To prevent this, general protection against unwarranted dismissal is supplemented by general protection against summary dismissal. Therefore, the legal basis is laid down in works representation law as well (§§106, 107 Labour Organization Act).

B. *Substantial Prerequisites: Summary Dismissal Without Good Cause, Unlawful Motives and Social Injustice*

541. The scope of protection against summary dismissal is identical to that of protection against unwarranted notice, that is to say, that it only applies if the employee works in an establishment of more than four workers (*see* paragraph 452). The operational method and legal structure are also the same. This means, to take the most important feature, that an appeal can be filed before the labour and social court against summary dismissal without good cause. Also, the employee has to claim that dismissal is based on 'unlawful motives' or that the dismissal is 'socially unjustified'. The court then declares the (previously effective) dismissal null and void, if just cause does not exist or the employer did not react to it in due time and, furthermore, grounds exist which would also justify the reversal of notice.

542. General protection against summary dismissal is directed against premature termination without just cause. It is no remedy against just summary dismissal. Furthermore, an appeal against unfounded summary dismissal only succeeds if the unfounded dismissal is based on an unlawful motive (*see* paragraph 494) or is socially unjustified because it impairs the employee's substantive interests (*see* paragraph 497). However in the latter case, the appeal, as an appeal against notice, will neither succeed if a summary dismissal is based on grounds of personal characteristics of the employee which conflict with the establishment's interests nor will an appeal succeed if the establishment's (bad) financial or economic situation outweighs the employee's interest in continued employment (*see* paragraph 499). If the summary dismissal lacks just cause but, nevertheless, is not socially unjust, the employee is entitled to damages (*see* paragraph 535). In this case, however, the employee has no right to be re-established in the job.

C. Participation of the Works Council

543. The employer must immediately inform the competent works council of every summary dismissal. However, unlike in the case of dismissal with notice, notification is not an absolute precondition for the effectiveness of the dismissal but only has to occur after the employee has been dismissed. The works council has the right, within three 'working days' of being notified, to discuss the premature dismissal with the employer and to react to it (consent, objection or no reaction). 'Working days' means the days on which the majority of the employees of the establishment are at work. The kind of reaction does not influence the dismissal itself, but it is significant as regards the existence and exercise of the right to appeal (i.e., who may file the appeal, the deadlines for the application and so on).

D. Contest of Termination

544. The appeal against premature termination without unjust reason can be filed as follows:

- If the works council has agreed to the summary dismissal, it may only be successfully contested if there was an unlawful motive. There is no right of appeal against the dismissal on the basis that is socially unjust.
- If the works council does not react within three working days, the employee concerned can immediately file an appeal him- or herself within two weeks.
- If the council has expressly objected to the dismissal, the right to appeal to the labour and social court belongs primarily to the works council. On request of the laid off employee, the works council must file the complaint before the court within one week. If the works council supports the dismissed employee's demand for an appeal only partly, or not at all, the right of appeal passes to the employee concerned. The complaint must then be filed within two weeks of the end of the period, to be observed by the works council.

- If the employee works in an establishment of more than four workers, but a works council has not actually been established, the right of appeal belongs to the employee right from the start. In this case, an appeal can be lodged within two weeks after the dismissal.

IV. Special Protection Against Summary Dismissal

A. General Observation

545. The 'special protection against unwarranted notice' which is afforded to particular groups of employees is routinely supplemented by special protection against summary dismissal, in order to prevent their avoidance. Therefore, the effectiveness of summary dismissal depends either on official consent and/or the existence of specific substantial reasons. The protection is regulated by various statutes, and for several groups of employees.

B. Works Council Members

546. The scope of special protection against summary dismissal mostly matches that of special protection against unwarranted notice (works council members, candidates in a works council election and so on; *see* paragraphs 503 et seq.). As a rule, these employees can only be dismissed if the labour and social court has already given its consent. An *ex post facto* consent to dismissal of a member of the works council only suffices in very serious cases (such as specific criminal felonies), but the consent must then be obtained immediately after the dismissal.

547. The grounds for authorizing summary dismissal (and also the court's consent) are listed exhaustively in §122 of the Labour Organization Act: deception when concluding the contract, particular criminal felonies, disloyalty and unauthorized acceptance of gifts, betrayal of secrets, prejudicial sideline activities and physical violence or defamation directed against the employer. Yet, even if such grounds exist, the court may not give its consent, if it is reasonable to expect the employer to continue to employ the employee concerned.

C. Working Mothers and Fathers

548. From the beginning of pregnancy until four months after delivery or (routinely) four weeks after the end of parental leave or parental part-time work, female employees can only be lawfully summarily dismissed after the court's consent and for reasons which are comprehensively listed in the Maternity Protection Act. An *ex post facto* consent to a pregnant woman's dismissal only suffices in the case of very serious reasons such as certain felonies.

549. Important grounds for premature dismissal are as follows: misconduct such as staying away from work without authorization, persistent neglect of duty, disloyalty and unauthorized acceptance of gifts, betrayal of secrets, prejudicial sideline activities, physical violence and substantial defamation, or certain criminal felonies. If such grounds for a summary dismissal exist, the court has also to consider whether the employee's behaviour might be mainly connected to the unusual state of mind resulting from pregnancy, miscarriage or childbirth.

550. Deliberate failure to mention pregnancy (for instance, at the job interview) cannot be a ground for summary dismissal.

551. Fathers on parental leave or on parental part-time work also enjoy the special protection against unfair dismissal granted to working mothers. The protection period starts with the notification about the parental leave or the parental part-time but at the earliest with the child's birth. The protection routinely does not expire until four weeks after the end of the leave or part-time work.

D. People with Disabilities

552. Actually, the conditions for valid summary dismissal of people with disabilities (*see* paragraph 509) are no stricter than for other employees. However, they differ insofar as any summary dismissal is null and void where substantial reasons do not exist. Thus, an unwarranted dismissal of a person with disability, that is to say, without just reason, has no terminating effect. On the contrary, there are no restrictions as to the justified summary dismissal of employees with disabilities, in other words, termination due to a good reason.

E. Military Service and Alternative Civilian Service

553. Protection against summary dismissal is granted from the issuing of the special call-up order and lasts until a month after the end of national service (*see also* paragraph 512). The precondition for protection is that the employee notifies the employer about being served with call-up papers.

554. The employee can only be summarily dismissed, if the labour and social court agrees to the summary dismissal, and specific grounds exist such as those that are listed exhaustively in §15 of the Job Protection Act: deception at the conclusion of the contract, leaving work without permission, persistent neglect of duties and the incitement of other employees to disobedience or unlawful behaviour, furthermore disloyalty, unauthorized acceptance of gifts, betrayal of secrets, prejudicial side-line activities, physical violence or substantial defamation directed against the employer or other employees of the establishment, or certain criminal acts. No consent is needed in the event of a complete shutdown of the establishment.

Chapter 7. Health and Safety Protection of Special Categories of Employee

§1. Young Employees

I. Ban on Child Labour

555. According to the Employment of Children and Juveniles Act (*Kinder- und Jugendlichen-Beschäftigungsgesetz*), the employment of children is generally forbidden. In this context, children normally are minors up to their fifteenth birthday. Employment for the purposes of instruction or education and the occupation of one's own children in occasional light household work do not count as child labour. Furthermore, the provincial authorities can permit the employment of children in musical or theatrical performances, films and so on.

556. Provided that their physical and psychological condition or education are not harmed by such work, children above the age of 13 may be given light and sporadic work, but essentially only in family businesses, in the household, on sports fields and in playgrounds – not in industrial establishments.

II. Protection of Young Persons

A. General

557. In this context, young persons are minors under the age of 18 or who have not yet completed an apprenticeship or other vocational training. The protection for this group of employees especially covers restrictions in the amount of working hours and bans on particular jobs.

B. Restrictions on the Number of Working Hours and Sunday Work

558. Generally, young persons' daily working hours may not exceed eight. Their weekly working hours may not exceed forty. However, arranging the weekly hours of work in order to achieve more free time for the weekly period of rest is permissible. Hours of instruction in a 'professional school', which the young employees or apprentices are obliged by law to attend, count as hours of work.

559. If the working day lasts more than four and a half hours, a break of at least one half-hour must be permitted. After the end of the daily period of work, a twelve-hour period of rest must be observed. In principle, young employees may not work between 8 pm and 6 am. Legal deviations are laid down for certain sectors, such as hotels, restaurants, theatrical performances and bakeries.

560. Moreover, each week, young employees must be given an unbroken period of free time of two days, which must include Sunday. Yet, as regards this, several legal deviations from general prohibition of Sunday work for young persons are laid down for sectors such as: hotels and restaurants, work in hospitals and clinics, musical and theatrical performances and work on sports fields.

C. Other Restrictions

561. Young persons under 16 must not be assigned to piecework or other work with 'performance oriented wages'. Furthermore, the physical conditions of young persons and public moral standards must particularly be taken into account. Thus, their employment in particular establishments or for particular work can be forbidden or restricted by an executive order or by order of the Works Inspection Office (e.g., work in sex shops, work exposing them to poisonous substances, heavy or dangerous work like mining, working on scaffolds or trains or ships).

562. The observance of the regulations on health and safety protection of young persons is supervised by the Works Inspection Office, a state authority. Breach of the regulations can lead to administrative sanctions such as fines. Where breaches occur repeatedly, the employer can also be forbidden to employ young persons for a certain period or forever.

§2. Protection of Working Parents

I. Absolute Employment Prohibition

563. According to the Maternity Protection Act, which also covers free employees, pregnant women may not be employed in the eight weeks preceding the expected date of delivery. The period is calculated on the basis of a doctor's certificate. To be able to comply with the prohibition, the employer must be informed of the pregnancy. After delivery, mothers may not be employed for further eight weeks, regardless of whether the child is born dead or alive. In the event of premature or multiple deliveries, the period increases to twelve weeks. During these protection periods, public health insurance grants the employee a maternity allowance of the full amount of her salary.

II. Further Employment Prohibitions

564. Pregnant women may not perform heavy physical work or work which might otherwise be harmful to mother or unborn child, for example due to materials or equipment used. The same applies to night work. Additionally, pregnant women must be especially protected from smoking colleagues. Bans on similar types of work exist for twelve weeks after delivery. Furthermore, there are specific restrictions for breastfeeding women. During the COVID-19 pandemic there existed also bans for pregnant women on work with a lot of physical contact with other people.

565. During these suspensions, mostly based on a certificate by the Works Inspection Office, the employer has to continue payment.

III. Maternity, Paternity or Parental Leave

566. After delivery, a working mother is entitled to an unpaid period of leave (maternity leave). Additionally, she has the right to return to work afterwards. The maximum period of maternity leave lasts until the child's second birthday. However, it is possible to postpone three months of this leave until the child's seventh birthday (for instance, to support the child's commencement of primary school). The mother may decide on her own on how long she will take the leave, but has to inform the employer of the start date and duration of the intended leave within a short period after the delivery. During and until four weeks after the end of the leave, the mother is specially protected against dismissal (paragraphs 505 et seq., 548 et seq.).

567. Since the 1990s, the right to 'maternity leave' has been continuously extended to the child's father as well. The parents may freely decide on which of them shall be entitled to claim the leave (with the right to return to work after the chosen period). In principle, mother and father cannot take the leave simultaneously (except for one month), but they may split the leave (with a minimum parental leave of two months) and take the leave in turns. The mother can share the leave up to twice with the father. For example, the mother can stay at home in the first year, and the father in the second year of the child's life. But each parent may also take two leaves of six months within two years.

568. During maternity or parental leave, payment by the employer is not continued. However, during the prohibition from working (until eight weeks after delivery), the health insurance grants maternity allowances, and afterwards, all parents, irrespective of work, are entitled to a specific state allowance, the federal 'child allowance' (*Kinderbetreuungsgeld*).

IV. The 'Daddy's Month'

569. In addition to the right to parental leave, fathers (or the other parent) are entitled to the so-termed Daddy's Month, regulated in § 1a Paternity Leave Act (*Väter-Karenzgesetz*). During this month, the employee's duty to work and the employer's duty to pay are suspended. If the employee intends to claim the Daddy's Month, he must notify the employer three months before the calculated date of delivery. Finally, the employee must inform the employer immediately of the birth and announce the date when the Daddy's Month begins no later than one week after the delivery. The Daddy's Month can be used during the period from the birth of the child until the expiry of the mother's absolute employment prohibition. From the time of notice until four weeks after the end of the Daddy's Month, the father is specially protected against dismissal (*see* paragraph 506). During the Daddy's Month, the employee has no remuneration claims against the employer, but the employee can claim the family time bonus (*Familienzeitbonus*) which is an allowance of about EUR 700 per month, provided by social security institutions.

V. Parental Part-Time Work

570. Parents are entitled to a reduction of working time after the birth of a child, until their seventh birthday. In principle, an agreement has to be reached on the number of hours to be worked and the allocation of working time.

571. The law provides for several different procedures to enforce this right, if an agreement on parental part-time cannot be reached. If the employee has been working for at least three years with the employer, and there are more than twenty employees in the establishment where they work, the employer has to explicitly oppose the employee's request, if that is what they want to do. The employer cannot then simply oppose the demand for part-time work *in toto* but has to propose another number of working hours or allocation that matches the business's interests better. The court then has to weigh the interests of the employee and those of the employer.

572. In other cases (for instance, smaller enterprises and/or less than three years of service) the employee may file a motion with the labour and social court to seek the employer's consent to their proposal of part-time work. It will be successful, if the employee's interests outweigh the interests of the employer.

VI. Working Time Restrictions

573. With a few exceptions (hospitals, theatres), pregnant and breastfeeding women must not be employed between 8 pm and 6 am. The same applies to work on Sundays and public holidays.

574. Moreover, pregnant or breastfeeding employees must not perform additional work beyond the statutory or collectively agreed working hours, and the weekly working hours must under no circumstances exceed forty.

Part II. Collective Labour Relations

Chapter 1. Trade Union Freedom

§1. The Term 'Affiliation'

575. Austrian law does not have a precisely defined term 'affiliation' or 'coalition' (*Koalition*). Primarily, these terms are taken in Austria to mean any association of employers and employees with the following characteristics:

- The association must be voluntary, which is only the case if the participants are independent of both state and other private individuals in the formation of the association, membership, withdrawal and the selection of further participants.
- Moreover, associations are only affiliations for the purposes of labour law if their aim is to influence the employment conditions of the participants and, if need be, to regulate them, as well as to look after and protect the interests of the participating employers and employees in connection with employment matters. Besides influencing employment conditions, affiliations can also aim at influencing economic conditions, regulating professional affairs, or even influencing cultural affairs.
- Furthermore, an affiliation must always be 'free of conflicts' and 'independent of opponents'. 'Freedom from conflict' means that only persons who typically have the same interests as to their situation in employment affairs may participate in the association. Put negatively, this means that nobody may be a member who belongs to the 'social opposition'. 'Independence from opponents' goes even further, also abolishing any influencing of the association itself or its decision-making procedures by the social opposition. The effect is that a coalition may not be directly or indirectly (financially) dependent on its social opponents in any way whatsoever.

576. Under the heading 'affiliation', there is a further distinction between *ad hoc* coalitions, which are more or less spontaneously created, and the so-termed free trade or professional associations, which are long-term associations of persons possessing an incorporated structure. They therefore have their own organs for decision-making and representation (which generally are subject to majority voting), and are independent of changes in their membership. Free professional associations of employees are generally known as 'trade unions'. Affiliations can also be categorized according to their modes of action. Some groups only use peaceful means to achieve their aims, in particular discussion and rousing public opinion, and the others, so-termed activist affiliations, also consider the use of industrial action where necessary.

§2. Legal Standards in International Law

577. Austria has ratified a series of multilateral agreements containing provisions relating to the law of association:

- The ILO Convention no. 11 on the Rights of Association and Combination of Agricultural Workers (BGBl 226/1924). The legal situation in Austria is fully in line with the convention.
- ILO Convention no. 87 on the Freedom of Association and Protection of the Right to Organise (BGBl 228/1950). Austrian law is in line with the convention. Besides, the convention is held to be directly applicable.
- ILO Convention no. 98 on the Application of the Principles of the Right to Organise and to Bargain Collectively (BGBl 20/1952). The Austrian legal situation is in line with Article 4 and parts of Article 1 of the convention. Article 1 no. 2(a) is not observed (*see* paragraph 598). Moreover, contrary to Article 2, Austrian law does not offer specific protection against interference by social opponents in an affiliation's internal affairs.
- The European Convention for the Protection of Human Rights and Fundamental Freedoms (BGBl 210/1958). In 1964, the Convention became a part of Austrian constitutional law (*see* paragraph 6, 579).
- The European Social Charter (BGBl 460/1969). Its contents are only directly applicable in Austria insofar as they are allowed for in a specific statute. Furthermore, the ESC allows for the states to declare themselves not bound by certain provisions. As to the right of association, Article 5 and Article 6 sections 1–3 are mandatory in Austria, and in this respect, Austrian law is in line with the charter. Yet, Austria declared itself not bound by Article 6 section 4, the right to collective action. This has not changed after the ratification of the ESC in its revised version (BGBl III 112/2011).
- ILO Convention no. 135 on Protection and Facilities to be Afforded to Workers' Representatives in the Undertaking (BGBl 88/1974). According to Article 5, appropriate measures shall be taken to ensure that the existence of elected representatives is not used to undermine the position of the trade unions concerned. Also, Article 3(b) refers to activities which are recognized as the exclusive prerogative of trade unions in the country concerned.
- The International Covenant on Economic, Social and Cultural Rights (BGBl 590/1978). Austrian law corresponds with Article 8, if this provision only covers the 'prohibition to strike'.
- The International Covenant on Civil and Political Rights (BGBl 591/1978). Austrian law corresponds with Article 22, laying down the right to freedom of association with others.

Other legal standards with effects on the law of association to be mentioned are:

- The EC Regulation 1612/68, Article 8 of Title 2, deals with the equality of rights as regards trade union membership and activities. This Regulation is directly applicable in Austria.
- The Charter of Fundamental Rights of the European Union (CFREU). Article 12 lays down the right to freedom of assembly and of association, and Article 28 enshrines the right of collective bargaining and action.

§3. Austrian Constitutional Law

578. Austrian constitutional law contains regulations concerning the freedoms of association and assembly in general and the freedom to form affiliations in particular, above all in Article 12 of the Fundamental Law on General Rights of Citizen 1867 (*Staatsgrundgesetz* 1867), in a constitutional statute from 1918 and in Article 11 of the European Convention on Human Rights. All these regulations are directly applicable constitutional standards, and are therefore binding on both legislature and executive. Special provisions concerning affiliation are contained in the European Convention on Human Rights but not the Fundamental Law on General Rights of Citizens. Also, the CFREU enshrines the right to freedom of association, and the right to negotiate and conclude collective agreements. According to the Austrian Constitutional Court, the rights of the CFREU are even constitutional rights. The other international covenants mentioned above in paragraph 577 are not part of the Austrian constitutional law, but when interpreting national statutes, these provisions are to be taken into consideration. These conventions are not, in general, self-executing, and their ratification only entails an obligation on the part of Austria to adapt its national legislation if necessary.

I. The General Freedom of Association

579. According to Article 12 of the Fundamental Law on General Rights of Citizens, Austrian citizens have the right 'of peaceful assembly and freedom of association. The exercise of these rights is regulated by a special statute'. A constitutional statute passed in 1918 also states that 'complete freedom of assembly and association is established'. Both regulations protect the creation and existence of associations, which are voluntary long-term organized affiliations of several persons in order to achieve a non-profit aim by continued associative activity. Therefore, the freedom of association does not apply to associations formed for commercial purposes.

580. Article 11 section 1 of the European Convention on Human Rights enshrines a provision similar to the one just mentioned, whereby, according to this provision, 'everyone has the right to freedom of peaceful assembly and to freedom of association with others, including the right to form and to join trade unions for the protection of his interests'. Unlike the Fundamental Law on General Rights of the Citizens from 1867, the provision of the European Convention on Human Rights also protects foreign citizens. Moreover, the Convention expressly specifies people's right to form 'trade unions' to protect their interests, and to belong to them.

581. In its Article 12 the CFREU lays down the right to freedom of assembly and of association. According to Article 28, workers and employers or their respective organizations have the right to negotiate and conclude collective agreements at the appropriate levels, and in cases of conflicts of interest, to take collective action to defend their interests, including strike actions.

582. The rights of association and collective bargaining can be held by individual people or by a group. From the individual's point of view, all workers or employers have the right to form and join associations of their choice, and to bargain collectively for the promotion and defence of occupational interests. Furthermore, the right to freedom of association is also a collective right, affording the association itself the right to be created and not to be disbanded by state interference, to choose its own members and to bargain collectively. The freedom of association allows for the independence of the organizations and for the protection of their right to defend all their rights.

583. Hence, the right to associate protects the employers' or employees' creation of affiliations and the associations' activities in order to promote occupational interests ('positive' aspects of the freedom of association). The 'negative' freedom of association refers to the right of individuals to refrain from associating with others in collective organizations, or the right to leave an organization and choose another one. Furthermore, the association's negative freedom of association would be infringed, if the state directly or indirectly leverages people not to join associations (e.g., rewarding employees if they only join federal organizations). The Austrian system of 'chambers' with mandatory membership can be considered lawful because, so far, it has not interfered with the individuals' right to association, in the sense that it would actually prevent them from joining free associations at the same time.

II. Freedom of Assembly

584. By this right, essentially, every gathering of several people to discuss, to demonstrate or to express their ideas collectively shall be protected. Some of the ad hoc coalitions which might not be considered to be covered by the freedom of association as well as some 'public' free trades association activities are regarded as at least covered by the freedom of assembly. Principally, a 'licence' or 'permission' system for assemblies would be incompatible with this constitutional right. However, a duty to notify the administrative authorities of the planned assembly in advance is permissible, in particular for meetings with unlimited participation. Prohibiting or breaking up meetings which have not been permitted or notified is also compatible with the constitutional principle. However, the legislature cannot categorically prevent spontaneous public meetings.

III. Specific Guarantees to Affiliations

585. The provisions in Article 12 of the Fundamental Law on General Rights of Citizens 1867 and the 1918 constitutional statute also apply, as already mentioned, to affiliations in labour law. However, they contain no special provisions for this type of affiliation, because they do not *expressis verbis* secure the specific forms of activity of such affiliations, such as autonomous collective creation of law (collective agreements), activities in establishments and undertakings, institutional participation in the legislature, the administration and the courts and industrial action. Austrian literature has been divided for a long time on whether or not all these rights might be implied in Article 12 and therefore protected as well. In particular, it has been contentious whether or not this provision includes the right to industrial action.

586. Many argue that Article 11 of the European Convention on Human Rights has decisively changed the legal situation; it explicitly secures people's 'right to form and to join trade unions for the protection of their interest'. According to jurisdiction, this includes the protection of the system of collective bargaining and collective agreements, the representation of interests against social opponents, and the toleration of industrial action in particular, as well as protecting the freedom of associations from outside private influence. However, it still is a matter of dispute to what extent it guarantees the freedom to strike. According to some current doctrine in Austria, the employer's power to dismiss a striking employee without notice is, in any case, no longer held to be compatible with Article 11 of the European Convention on Human Rights (*see* paragraphs 878, 916).

§4. The Non-constitutional Legal Situation

I. General

587. Two of the following chapters deal with the main areas of collective activities, that is to say, collective agreements (paragraphs 643 et seq.) and industrial action (paragraphs 876 et seq.). Beforehand, the chapters discuss: the connection between affiliation and criminal law; the 1870 Affiliations Act; the legal possibility of forming free trades associations and the regulation of their internal activities; the permissibility of ad hoc coalitions; freedom of affiliations from private 'outside' interference, and finally, activities of affiliations in the establishment and undertaking.

588. An extensive, non-constitutional statutory regulation of affiliation law exists for agriculture and forestry, where §423 of the Agricultural Employment Act 2021 lays down 'that employees are free to combine in order to promote their interests. Any impairment of this freedom of affiliation is forbidden'. According to the latter sentence of the provision, the freedom to collective activities goes beyond the contents of constitutional provisions; unlike fundamental rights in general, it also offers explicit protection against any private interference from outside.

II. Affiliation and Criminal Law

589. Punishment according to penal law (meaning imprisonment and so forth) concerning 'activist affiliations', in other words, those engaging in industrial action (especially strikes) or the joining or forming of such associations, was already mostly eliminated in 1870 by §1 of the Affiliations Act (*Koalitionsgesetz*). Now, only a few activities are subject to general criminal law, especially when performed in connection with intimidation.

III. The Affiliations Act (*Koalitionsgesetz* 1870)

590. The above-mentioned Affiliations Act from 1870 contains the only statutory provision which directly refers to activist coalitions; namely, its §2 states that the 'agreement' of employee action aiming at improvement of working conditions, by united work stoppage or similar actions of the equivalent employers' affiliations, 'are without legal effect'. The interpretation and validity of this provision have been much disputed. According to some literature, §2 means that agreeing to form an activist affiliation cannot be the content of a valid agreement under Austrian contract law, and therefore the obligation to take part in industrial action cannot be enforced by law. In any event, this does not mean that an 'activist affiliation' would not be a valid form of association; the intention to use means of industrial action where necessary in order to influence work conditions is also considered to be a permissible objective of association, and secured by jurisprudence of the European Court of Human Rights (ECHR).

IV. Organized Affiliations: Associations

591. Affiliations in Austria can exist in the form of 'incorporated associations' within the meaning of the Associations Act (*Vereinsgesetz*), that is to say, private law bodies with a non-profit purpose (such as local sports associations, regional associations of musicians, choirs, societies for traditional costumes and so forth). Such incorporated associations are legal entities in civil law, and as such they possess legal personality and also are entitled to accumulate assets. They are liable for damages caused by their representatives, directors or officials performing their functions.

592. No official licence is required for the formation of an association. However, the founders must report the creation to administrative authorities, which could then prohibit the association, in particular because of unlawfulness of its aims. The activities of the association are also subject to state supervision; for example, the names of the members of board must be reported. For other association activities or events, the Assemblies Act (*Versammlungsgesetz, see* paragraph 594) also applies. Any association can be disbanded by the administrative authorities for the reasons given in the Associations Act, for instance, if the association exceeds its articled spheres of activity (in other words, the purpose of the association) or passes resolutions which are contrary to criminal law.

593. The statute gives the administrative authorities considerable room for manoeuvring, but in every case, the grounds for prohibition or dissolution must be in accordance with Article 11 section 2 of the European Convention on Human Rights. An association or individual members thereof have the right to lodge a complaint with the Constitutional Court (*see* paragraphs 6, 16) against unlawful executive action. The legal position hence corresponds with Article 4 of the ILO Convention no. 87.

V. Assemblies

594. The Assemblies Act (*Versammlungsgesetz*) applies to the majority of ad hoc coalitions and public meetings of the free professional associations. All generally open meetings (i.e., meetings not restricted to individually invited guests) must be reported to the executive authorities, at least forty-eight hours beforehand. Meetings for a purpose contravening criminal law and meetings which threaten public security or public interests are to be prohibited and, if need be, broken up. Moreover, any meeting which is not registered, in particular any spontaneous meeting, can be broken up. Yet, the grounds for prohibition or interference must match Article 11 section 2 of the European Convention on Human Rights. The organizers and participants in the meeting have the right to lodge an objection with the Constitutional Court (*see* paragraphs 6, 16) against unlawful executive acts which infringe their constitutional right of assembly. Also, according to the courts, permitted assemblies have to be protected by the state from interference by third persons.

VI. Protection of the Freedom of Affiliation: Interference by Third Persons

A. General

595. The constitutional provisions protecting the freedom to affiliate mentioned above (paragraphs 578 et seq.) are not directly applicable to legal relationships between private persons. Therefore, the freedom to affiliate with regard to the relationships between private persons – in particular between employers and employees or between employees' affiliations and employers – is generally mainly protected by provisions of civil law, that is, the prohibition on 'unethical' legal acts (§879 of the Civil Code – contracts and declarations *contra bonos mores* are void), and the liability for damages in the event of 'unethical' infliction of damage (§1295 section 2 General Civil Code). However, there are some other regulations which will be outlined below.

596. If an employee or employer is influenced by other persons or entities (employers, employees, professional associations) in order to make them join an association or leave one, this is prohibited and therefore punishable when combined with either a serious threat to the employee's or employer's body, freedom, honour, or property or with force (§105 Criminal Code – Unlawful Compulsion). Similarly, §4 section 2 Anti-terror Act lays down that anyone forcing an employee by force or by intimidation to join or to leave an association shall be punished. Moreover, anyone persuading or attempting to persuade an employee to take part in a strike by intimidation or force shall be punished (§3 Affiliations Act).

B. Regulation of Closed or Union Shops

597. Closed or union shop clauses require that all the workers in a company belong to a (particular) trade union. The employer agrees to hire union members only, and employees must remain members of the union at all times in order to remain employed. In Austria, closed shops in collective or works agreements are illegal and null and void under §1 of the Anti-terror Act from 1930 (*Antiterrorgesetz*). Moreover, penalties are imposed on anyone who wants to enforce a closed shop by force or by threats (§4 section 1 Anti-terror Act). This includes a person's attempts or acts which aim to ensure, by intimidation or by force, that members of a trade union are generally not employed in an establishment. Despite all these regulations, it is a matter of dispute whether or not collective agreements may contain other clauses distinguishing between a union member's working conditions and those of a non-member.

C. Protection of Individual Employees' Right to Associate Against the Employer

598. Austrian labour law does not explicitly protect individual employees from an employer's refusal to conclude employment contracts with trade union members; this contravenes Article 1 section 2(a) of ILO Convention no. 98. Austrian law also accepts an employer's decision not to employ someone because of their non-membership of a trade union. However, a job applicant can untruthfully fail to reveal their membership of a trade union when asked without suffering any legal consequences.

599. After the start of the employment relationship, individual employees are better protected: in establishments in which a works council has to be established (because there are more than four workers, *see* paragraphs 452, 478), an appeal against any dismissal is possible, if it is based on the employee's joining or belonging to a trade union or on the employee's activities in a union. On the contrary, an employee is not expressly protected against dismissal due to their non-membership of a trade union, in which case the employee could only plead that the termination was *contra bonos mores* (paragraphs 117, 595). Moreover, there is no express protection against the employer's actions prejudicing an employee 'in other ways', such as transferring the employee because of their union activities. Insofar as there are no co-determination rights under works representation law, only regulations on employer's 'unethical' behaviour may apply here.

600. According to §2 section 2 of the Anti-terror Act, union dues can only be deducted from the wage directly by the employer and passed on to the affiliation, if the affiliation is entitled to conclude collective agreements (*see* paragraphs 677 et seq.) and if the employee has expressly given their consent to the deduction.

D. Protection of Affiliations as such, as Opposed to the Individual

601. Employers are prevented from giving non-union-members generally better employment conditions than union members. Yet, there is no specific legal protection against acts endangering the existence or the activities of the free trade association itself (such as blacklisting union members). It is only covered by the general ban on 'unethical' acts and prejudices (paragraphs 117, 595), which also covers in particular the boycotting of an affiliation by an employer or any other affiliation, and as a rule forbids it.

VII. Activities of Affiliations in Establishments and Undertakings

602. The rights of free professional associations with respect to individual establishments are stipulated in the regulations laying down the tasks and rights of the 'labour force' ('work representation law', for example definition of 'establishment' or 'works council'), namely in Part II of the Labour Organization Act. Fundamentally, these legally laid down rights apply only to those employees' and employers' associations which are entitled to conclude collective agreements (paragraphs 677 et seq.). As to these rights of associations in establishments, the following rules and principles must also be mentioned in particular:

- Works councils shall cooperate with the competent trade unions. For example, representatives of trade unions only have the right to enter the establishment if this is requested by the works council for the purposes of consultation.
- In the case of works councils with more than three members, officials and employees of the competent trade union can also be elected as members of the works council. However, at least three-quarters of the council members must still be employees of the establishment.
- Trade union representatives have the right to attend every general assembly of the workforce, but not a works council meeting. They even can call a general staff meeting, if there is no works council, in particular in order to elect one.

603. However, so far, in Austria the question of whether or not and how far unions do have statutory rights in the establishment or undertaking has had little significance in practice.

604. The reason is that union work in the establishment is also done by and 'through' the works council and its members. The works council is not seen as a competitor but as a 'complement' to the unions and a means to increase their influence.

605. In many cases, works council members are also union members, and many works council members are simultaneously active in trade unions. Therefore, the union's representatives in the establishment are mostly entitled to the representation of interests rights laid down in Austrian works representation law as well; that is to say, union representatives who are at the same time works council members also enjoy the special protection and rights afforded to the representatives of the labour force in an establishment. Furthermore, works councils may support the recruitment of union members or explain union policy to employees. The strength of the unions therefore depends significantly on the existence of works councils and the commitment of the works council to the union. For their part, the unions offer advice, further education and so forth to the works councils, and provide union backup in the event of disputes with the management.

Chapter 2. Organizations' Representation of the Interests of Employees and Employers

§1. Introduction

606. Austria has two organizations representing employees' interests at national level. These are the Austrian Trade Union Federation (*Österreichischer Gewerkschaftsbund* – ÖGB), based on voluntary membership, and the statutorily created chambers of labour (*Arbeiterkammern*), of which by far the majority of employees in the private sector are compulsory members (and pay compulsory fees of 0.5% of their income).

607. During the first Republic (1918–1934), there already existed 'neutral' chambers of labour, based on compulsory membership, besides the trade unions, which were mostly committed to political parties and split up according to professions. The chambers were recreated after the end of the Second World War. From a legal point of view, the chambers of labour are independent, representative institutions separated from the trade union organization. In fact, though, the top functionaries of the unions and the leaders of the chambers of labour have often been the same people.

608. As to the employers, there are statutorily created organizations for them as well, the chambers of economy or commerce (*Wirtschaftskammern*), to which the principle of compulsory membership and fees also applies. On acquiring a business licence, every employer automatically becomes a member of the respective chamber of economy. Furthermore, there exist several employers' organizations of a voluntary sort, but compared to the chambers of economy, their significance in employment matters is rather small. However, in the field of health and social management, and in the education sector, several associations on the employers' side have been formed, which also have been granted the right to conclude agreements.

609. In fact, rather than in law, the Austrian Trade Union Federation occupies a monopoly-like position. Apart from the numerically insignificant group of agricultural workers, it is the only trade union organization, that is to say, free association characterized by voluntary membership on the employee's side. Its unique position is not based on legal arrangements, but simply on *de facto* developments since the end of the Second World War. The Austrian Trade Union Federation is subdivided nowadays into seven specialized member unions, which between them cover all sectors of the economy.

610. Representation of employees' interests in Austria is not confined to national or supra-enterprise organizations only. There are also representative institutions at the establishment level. By statute, employees in an establishment have to elect their own staff bodies, for example, the works council, if there are more than four workers in the establishment (*see* paragraph 775). These statutory staff bodies are competent to represent the employees' interests in an establishment and also to participate in the establishment's running and administration (*see* paragraphs 798 et seq.).

§2. Trade Unions and Employers' Associations

I. General

611. Unlike the chambers of labour, which are established by law and have mandatory membership and fees, the free employees' associations (trade unions) are characterized by voluntary membership. Apart from organizations in the rural sector, there is only one significant trade union organization in Austria: the Austrian Trade Union Federation (*Österreichischer Gewerkschaftsbund* or ÖGB), which consists of seven specialized sub-unions (*see* paragraph 617).

612. On the employer side, apart from the Federation of Austrian Industry (*Vereinigung der Österreichischen Industrie*), which could but does not conclude collective agreements, there is no free professional association covering all sectors at once. Furthermore, only in some specific sectors like banking, the health and social management sector or the education sector do free professional associations exist at all, which also take part in collective bargaining. Employers' interests, including the regulation of employment conditions in collective agreements, are mostly represented by the economic chambers, the statutory employer representative bodies (*see* paragraphs 636 et seq.).

II. The Trade Unions

613. Apart from the representatives of agricultural workers, all unions are part of the Austrian Trade Union Federation. This concentration is not based on law, but is a result of historic and social developments since 1945. Before the Second World War (until 1934), 'political' unions with a predominantly ideological orientation existed. After the Second World War, in 1945, the unions agreed to have one 'united' trade union covering the most important employee groups, in order to improve Austria's political and economic situation. It was the understanding of that time that unions should not compete against one another but concentrate on improving the working conditions, and thereby also enable the reconstruction of Austria. Another result of that concept was good cooperation with the employers' side, the so-termed social partnership.

614. The Austrian Trade Union Federation is an incorporated association, that is to say, a non-profit private law body, in the sense of the Associations Act (paragraph 591). Its internal relationships and aims are laid down in the charter originally accepted in 1948, according to which the Austrian Trade Union Federation has the following tasks in particular: representing employees' economic and social interests; promoting union campaigns and improving employment conditions, where necessary by industrial action; concluding collective agreements; supporting individual employees, in particular in the event of legal disputes; ensuring the independence and neutrality of Austria and opposing fascism and all totalitarian regimes; influencing and participating in legislation; achieving equality between men and women; and cultivating international relations.

615. The most important organs of the Trade Union Federation are the Federal Congress, the Federal Executive, the Steering Committee and the Provincial Executives. None of these bodies is appointed by direct election by the union's members. Rather, their members are appointed throughout by means of step-by-step indirect elections in the specialized unions.

616. In 2021, Austria's average labour force was 4,306,000 (for more details *see* paragraph 25). According to its statistics, the Trade Union Federation had about 1,196,703 members in 2021, which signifies a union density of 27.8%. The figure varies strongly as regards employee categories and sectors of the economy; for example, it contains a great many manual workers in the production sector (manufacturing industry) and in the public services.

617. The Austrian Trade Union Federation is subdivided nowadays into seven specialized member unions, which between them cover all sectors of the economy. The system does not constitute 'industrial unionism', in the strict sense of there being only one union for each sector and hence only one for each establishment. This is specifically due to the fact that blue-collar and white-collar workers are organized in separate unions. The seven specialized sub-unions (*Fachgewerkschaften*) of the Austrian Trade Union Federation are:

(1) the Union of Production Workers (PRO-GE);
(2) the Union of Public Services (GÖD);
(3) the Union of Salaried Private Sector Employees and of Printers, Journalists and Paper Workers (GPA-DJP);
(4) the Union of Municipal Employees, Art, Media, Sport and Freelance Workers (*younion*)
(5) Union of Construction and Woodworkers (GBH);
(6) Transport and Service Union (*vida*);
(7) Union of Postal and Telecommunications Workers (GPF).

618. The sub-unions are legally not independent, but subsections, or more precisely 'institutions' (organs), of the Trade Union Federation. Although they themselves are legally entitled to conclude collective agreements, they always conclude them together with the Austrian Trade Union Federation.

619. The functions are divided between the Trade Union Federation and its seven specialized member unions, insofar as the federation is responsible for issues that affect all employees in Austria, whereas the member unions each represent the specific interests of employees within their respective economic branches. This means, in practice, that the 'umbrella organization' focuses on representing employees' interests vis-à-vis the government and the state, whereas the member unions' activities focus on collective bargaining. However, as mentioned above, the sub-unions always conclude collective agreements together with the Austrian Trade Union Federation.

620. The Austrian Trade Union Federation also supervises the internal structuring and activities of its specialized member unions. They act, on the whole, according to the general principles and directives laid down by the umbrella organization, which also supervises their financial management. In practice, the specialized unions certainly have more independence than is indicated by the legal situation described. This is particularly evident in collective bargaining affairs, and in the direct care of their members. Yet, comprehensive interlacing of personnel ensures that major controversies in important matters are virtually non-existent. The federation is not a loose umbrella organization split up into several strong autonomous individual unions, but a centrally run trade union. Together with its large scope (embracing one-third of Austrian employees), this has undoubtedly contributed to the homogeneity of the Austrian union movement and therefore to the considerable 'social power' of the Austrian Trade Union Federation. As mentioned above, in 2021, after all, the Trade Union Federation had about 1,196,703 members.

621. On an informal level, the Trade Union Federation is divided internally into ideological 'fractions', broadly mirroring the structure of Austria's party political system, each linked to the corresponding party through members who simultaneously occupy posts in both union and party. This ideological division strengthens the union's motivation, if needed, to find compromises, in other words, attempting to ensure that decisions have the support of all fractions, in order to safeguard the organization's unity.

622. For decades, top officials of the Trade Union Federation or its sub-unions and the members of the two largest political parties' top leadership used to be the same people ('multiple office holding'), relatively often. This meant that if needed, the achievement of trade union aims would be made possible by means of parliamentary political methods. Moreover, leaders of the Trade Union Federation or its sub-unions used to be members of the National Council. Also, since 1945, the position of Federal Minister of Social Administration or – as it is called now – the Federal Minister of Labour has often been held by high-ranking functionaries of the Trade Union Federation. This practice has been less common in recent years. Nowadays, the routes of influence are more informal but still very strong.

623. The territorial scope of both the Austrian Trade Union Federation and its sub-unions is Austria, but there are provincial executives of the federation in each province, and as a rule provincial groups of the sub-unions as well. There are also a number of further subdivisions, according to geographical criteria (local groups).

However, subdivisions for individual establishments or undertakings are not allowed in the union's charter, and, apart from de facto coincidence with a local group, virtually do not exist.

III. The Employers' Associations

624. Austria's most important employers' organizations, the economic chambers, are not 'free trade' associations (paragraph 576) but based on statutory membership. However, on the employer side, there are (several) free professional associations capable of concluding collective agreements in a few areas, but unlike on the employees' side these associations are not united under one organizational umbrella. The Federation of Austrian Industry (*Österreichische Industriellenvereinigung*) is a very important voluntary employers' association. Nevertheless, it does not conclude collective agreements itself but leaves this task to the economic chambers. Another example for an important employers' association is the Austrian Association of Banks (*Bankenverband*). As a rule, any overlapping in competence between the employers' statutory representation and the free employers' associations is sorted out by 'working agreements' between these organizations. Furthermore, there are employers' associations in sectors which are not covered by the chamber system, such as the Social Economy Austria (the *Sozialwirtschaft Österreich*, an association of employers in the field of social and health management) or the BABE (Association of Employers in the Field of Private Education Institutions).

§3. Statutory Representative Bodies

I. General

A. Definitions and Concepts

625. Statutory representative bodies are organizations established by statute: they are incorporated bodies with compulsory membership and fees, whose tasks (such as the representation of professional interests of their members) and structures are also prescribed by law. As a rule, they finance their activities by legally laid down contributions of their members. People who fulfil the statutorily defined preconditions of membership are *ex lege* members, irrespective of their will or intentions. The statutory representative bodies are legal entities, and therefore have full legal capacity, including the ability to own assets; they are legal bodies of public law and a part of Austrian self-governance (*see* below). In Austria, they are mainly referred to as chambers (*Kammern*). The chambers of labour (*Kammern für Arbeiterinnen und Angestellte*) and the economic chambers (*Wirtschaftskammern*) are the two most important groups of statutory representative bodies in Austrian industrial relations. They both consist of an 'umbrella' institution, competent for the whole of Austria, and a chamber in each of the nine provinces.

626. Other important statutory representative bodies are the agricultural chambers, the agricultural workers' chambers, and a number of chambers for the liberal professions (such as attorneys, notaries, accountants, dentists, veterinaries, doctors or civil engineers). As to some of the latter, it should be mentioned that there has been some controversy about their capacity to conclude collective agreements, because some of these chambers (such as the chambers of physicians or the attorneys) represent interests of self-employed people and of employees as well, without adequate organizational structures to guarantee separate decision-making within the chamber, and hence might not fulfil all the prerequisites in the following paragraph.

627. In order to play a relevant role in industrial relations, and to have the capacity to conclude collective agreements as well, the statutory representative bodies must fulfil two additional conditions, according to the Labour Organization Act: the chamber's activities must aim at the regulation (improvement) of working conditions, which is mostly no problem. However, statutory representative bodies which intend to influence employment conditions must furthermore always be 'free of conflicts' and independent of their social opponents (*see* paragraph 682). If a chamber cannot fulfil both requirements, it cannot conclude collective agreements as representative of all its members. As to some chambers, to clarify their legal status, the lawmaker has stipulated the capacity to conclude collective agreements *expressis verbis* in their specific constituting statutes from the start (such as in the Chamber of Veterinaries Act).

B. The Role of the Chambers Within the Austrian Administration

628. Chambers are legal bodies of public law which are, at the same time, part of the Austrian professional self-government. Self-governance in this area enables and allows groups of people to pursue their professional interests on their own, and to exercise at least the necessary functions of power without intervention from the state. Basically, statutory representative bodies have three typical spheres of operation, and each one corresponds to a particular form of the state's influence. These forms of interference are, in particular, not only the mere supervision of the statutory representative bodies' activities, but also the regulation of the conduct of a statutory representative body by directive. The following three spheres of operation can be distinguished, although only the first two spheres of operation are actually characteristic of a statutory representative body.

(1) Statutory representative bodies have to represent their members' interests, in particular in relation to the state and their social opponents. As to labour law questions, this sphere of operation mainly concerns the pursuit of professional or legal interests of its members. This representation of (professional) interests of the members is free of directives by the state, and state supervision is restricted, to ensure that the statutorily defined functions are not exceeded. Roughly, this sphere of operation includes comments on legislation, advising on (proposed) legislation or governmental measures, advising and supporting

members by offering legal advice, (vocational) training, and publications, furthermore, collective bargaining, that is, representing members' interests in relation to social opponents such as by concluding collective agreements, and cooperating with the social opposition in the context of social partnership (*see* paragraphs 638 et seq.).

(2) Second, certain state functions are fulfilled by the statutory representatives as a result of special statutory provisions. Here, the statutory representative bodies can act free of directives, too (if this is provided for by law), and, as a rule, state supervision only concerns the lawfulness of the fulfilment of these functions. Such state functions assigned to the statutory bodies are, for example, the legally laid down participation of statutory representative bodies in various public collegiate boards and authorities, participation in administrative proceedings, and the right to appoint representatives to the management of the social insurance bodies.

(3) Third, the statutory representative bodies carry out some actual state functions referred to as 'transferred' spheres of operation. In this area, the chambers are subject to the directives of the competent federal minister, and the supervision covers legality and efficiency of the activities. State functions taken over as 'transferred' spheres of operation are rare.

C. Practical Consequences

629. The numerous rights and competences of the chambers let them participate in the administration, and to a lesser extent, also in legislation. Together with the interdependences between chambers and trade unions and political parties, this has led to considerable influence of the chambers on Austria's political system, including the establishing of the social partnership (paragraphs 638 et seq.). Therefore, in recent decades, the system of statutory representative bodies has been discussed time and again in a controversial manner, for example, on the occasion of an amendment of the Austrian Constitution in 2008. Its Article 120a now states that 'the Republic recognizes the role of the Social Partners, respects their autonomy and promotes the Social Dialogue by establishing self-governing bodies' (i.e., chambers).

630. This recent development reflects the predominant view that this system is positive, on the whole. Namely, besides associations based on voluntary membership (the trade unions and employers' associations), only the chambers still represent the interests of the various social groups and classes – employers in trade and industry, employees, farmers – as professional group interests. Moreover, with their skilled officials, the chambers provide expertise that is indispensable to the functioning of the Austrian political system and often beneficially balances and corrects the influence of the state bureaucracy.

II. Chambers of Labour (*Kammern für Arbeiterinnen und Angestellte*)

A. Organization

631. The chambers of labour were first established in 1920, as a counterpart to the economic chambers, which were already in existence. In 1934, the new corporative state system enforced political conformity. In 1938, after the German invasion, they were disbanded, and after the Second World War, in 1945, they were re-established. It was then that they were also granted the capacity to conclude collective agreements.

632. The membership to the chambers of labour is mandatory, and comprises basically all employees in the private sector. The most important exceptions are senior personnel, directors, and employees who work in forestry and agriculture. The chambers of labour are financed by legally laid down dues collected from the members (0.5% of wages earned).

633. There is one chamber of labour in each province. Its most important organs are the plenary assembly, executive board, president and committees for particular purposes. The plenary assembly is elected by the members every five years in direct secret elections. The chambers of labour's umbrella organization is the Federal Chamber of Labour (*Bundesarbeitskammer*) in Vienna. Its administrative organs are elected by the functionaries of the provincial chambers of labour.

B. Functions

634. The chambers of labour are appointed to represent and promote the social, economic, professional, health and cultural interests of employees. In detail, the Chambers of Labour Act (*Arbeiterkammergesetz*) lays down, among others, the following tasks: to provide legislature and executive with reports, suggestions and opinions in all social and economic policy questions; to appraise draft statutes; to take part in the social and economic administration, insofar as is laid down by statute, and in particular to appoint representatives to collegiate boards (e.g., to the Federal Conciliation Board or the management organs of the social insurance bodies); to participate in the supervision of the enforcement of labour law; to advise and support works councils in performing their duties; and finally, to create any institutions necessary for the pursuit of their general representative duties. The chambers of labour have, by law, the capacity to conclude collective agreements but do not exercise this power, and leave collective bargaining to the trade unions.

635. The Chambers of Labour are not seen as competitors to the trade union movement but as an additional resource, by means of which advisory and other services and, in particular, expertise in matters of economic and social policy are made available to the employees' side. The 'chamber system' complements the representation of interests by the unions and increases their effectiveness. In practice, there is close cooperation between the chambers of labour and the Trade Union Federation, as to the function of representation. The chambers operate mainly as a source of expertise, both for the unions and for the government authorities, in matters relating to employees' interests. Furthermore, they provide a wide range of services to their members.

III. The Economic Chambers (*Wirtschaftskammern*)

636. The membership of the chambers of commerce comprises all the physical and legal persons entitled to run an undertaking in industry, trade, commerce, finance, credit, insurance, transport or tourism, as well as personal services such as temporary agency work and placement, care of the older people and life counselling. Membership commences *ex lege* with the acquisition of the entitlement concerned (in regular terms, the 'trade licence'). There is a chamber of commerce in every province, and the umbrella organization at the federal level is the Economic Chamber of Austria (*Wirtschaftskammer Österreich*). The provincial chambers and the federal chamber are each divided into sections according to their sectors or trades, which in turn are divided into craft groups (*Fachgruppen* – at provincial level) and craft organizations (*Fachverbände* – at federal level). The main competences of the federal chamber are supervision over the provincial chambers.

637. In industrial relations, the economic chambers, in particular, have the task of advising their members as employers and representing their interests vis-à-vis the state and their social opponents. They also have, by law, the capacity to conclude collective agreements: on the employers' side, some 95% of all collective agreements are, in practice, concluded by the economic chambers, which gives them a key position in collective bargaining.

§4. Social Partnership

638. The system of social partnership is the pre-eminent feature of industrial relations in Austria. Based on close voluntary cooperation between (representative institutions of) employers, employees and the state, this system constitutes the specifically Austrian manifestation of the system of reconciling interests, which in the social sciences is called corporatism. By international standards, Austria is one of the countries in which corporatist structures are most highly developed; yet, social partnership is not an institution regulated by law, but based on informal and legally non-binding agreement.

639. Within the social partnership, employers and employees are represented by a small circle of major organizations (the social partners). On the employees' side, these are the Austrian Trade Union Federation and the Federal Chamber of Labour, and on the employers' side, the Economic Chamber of Austria and the Standing Committee of Presidents of the Chambers of Agriculture.

640. Social partnership goes back to the violent class struggles and high unemployment rates in the years between the two world wars, culminating in the civil war of 1934 and the annexation of Austria by Germany in 1938. These bitter experiences unified employers' and employees' representatives, and motivated them, after 1945, to give shared interests and cooperation precedence over class interests and conflict. Social partnership has become a permanent and stable element of Austrian society, which is due to various factors.

641. First, there is a predominance of small and medium-sized enterprises in Austria's economic and labour market, which favours a system of collective regulation by the social partners at sector level. Also, after 1945 the employers' and employees' representatives agreed not to restore the ideologically divided system of organizations that had existed before the Second World War, but to create organizations which also represent common and comprehensive interests in favour of the whole economic and social system. Finally, the social partners are all connected to the major political parties, particularly to the Austrian Social Democratic Party and the conservative Austrian People's Party.

642. The cooperation between the state and the social partners is an important link between industrial relations and government policy. Legally, the social partners are involved in the following fields:

- governmental propositions for legal amendments are evaluated and commented on by the chambers of labour and the economic chambers;
- the chambers appoint the lay judges to the labour and social courts (paragraphs 91 et seq.), as well as the professional representatives to conciliation boards, which adjudicate in disputes over works agreements (paragraphs 97 et seq.), and to administrative authorities such as the Federal Conciliation Board (*see* paragraph 17);
- the Austrian social security system is based on public law bodies that are self-governed. This means that their boards consist of representatives of the persons concerned, who in turn are appointed to the boards by the respective statutory interest groups, in other words, the chambers;
- collective bargaining.

Chapter 3. Collective Bargaining and Collective Provisions

§1. The Main Features of Collective Regulations

I. Definition and Areas of Application

643. According to explicit Austrian statutory provisions, collective regulations (such as collective agreements) apply directly to the employment relationships they cover. This is mainly regulated by Part I of the Labour Organization Act (§§1–32 on the 'collective creation of law'). There also exist legal regulations especially governing the collective creation of law for agricultural and forestry workers, homeworkers, apprentices and janitors (since they mainly match the provisions of collective agreements in the Labour Organization Act and have less practical significance, they will only be described in brief).

644. 'Collective law' ('collective regulations') can be laid down for employment relationships of every type, based on a contract governed by civil law. This covers all employees in the sense of §1151 of the General Civil Code (*see* paragraphs 51 et seq.). Civil servants whose employment conditions are laid down by statute, as well as individuals who are not 'personally dependent' (in other words, free employees, *see* paragraph 54) are not included as well as employees of local authorities or of certain legal entities under public law, if the substantive content of their employment contract is determined by statute (contractual public servants, *see* paragraph 177). However, management employees or family members with an employment contract are principally covered by collective law, with some deviations in the area of works representation law.

II. Instruments of Regulation

645. The two main regulatory instruments of the collective creation of law are collective agreements (at the sector level) and works agreements (at the establishment level). At least at the sector level, if competent associations or collective agreements are lacking, there exists 'substitute' collective law, created by state intervention, as well: charters, minimum wage tariffs and minimum wage scales for apprentices (*see* paragraphs 650, 742 et seq.).

A. *Collective Agreements and Works Agreements*

646. Collective agreements and works agreements are forms of autonomous regulation, that is to say, they are created without the state's intervention. They do not come into existence by official resolution of a regulatory body composed of delegates appointed by employees and employers, but by the conclusion of a contract.

647. Works and collective agreements differ in terms of their personal and local scope. Works agreements are concluded at establishment level, the contractual parties being the individual employer (owner of the establishment) and the staff (labour force) represented by the works council. As a rule, the scope of collective agreements goes beyond the establishment. They are mostly concluded by a supra-establishment employees' organization with a supra-establishment employers' organization (in other words, for a whole economic sector).

648. Collective and works agreements also differ as regards the issues they can regulate. The regulatory powers of the collective agreement are laid down in §2 section 2 of the Labour Organization Act, and embrace almost all employment conditions in general, whereas the regulatory powers of the works agreement are enumerated in a restricted way in §§96, 96a and 97 of the Labour Organization Act, and in the Working Time Act. Apart from those legally delegated matters, they cannot be a valid subject for works agreements. Hence, having no such competence, the regulation of wages and wage policy is very much a part of the collective agreement's territory, whereas the activities of works councils are rather limited in this matter. However, in practice, works councils and employers ignore this lack of competence by concluding so-termed free works agreements.

649. Such agreements (on non-delegated issues) are not works agreements in the sense of the Labour Organization Act (*see* paragraph 820). They have no normative effects like works agreements, and can only be treated as contracts according to the general rules of civil law. If the employer fulfils the 'agreement' with the works council, this may lead to a ('conclusive') change in the staff's individual employment contracts (*see also* paragraphs 83, 191).

B. Substitute Forms

650. In case of lack of a competent association or an applicable collective agreement, the Labour Organization Act provides for substitute forms of collective labour law, in order to protect employees. The substitute instruments of collective law are not collectively bargained, as such, by the social partners but created by the state (*see also* paragraphs 645, 742 et seq.). The substitute forms are strictly subsidiary in relation to the collective agreement, mainly with regard to the constitutional right to affiliate and to bargain collectively (*see* paragraphs 585 et seq).

651. If employees work for an 'outsider', in other words, an employer who is not a member of an association, or there is not one in existence, the employees lack collective protection. In such cases, the Labour Organization Act allows for the 'extension' of the collective agreement to the non-covered employment relationships by adjudicating the collective agreement the status of a 'charter' (*Satzung*). Extending the scope of a collective agreement by declaring a collective agreement a charter (the charter declaration) is an administrative act of state. Therefore, the charter's contents derive directly from a collective agreement, but are made binding beyond its sphere of operation only by executive order (chartered collective agreement). With respect to the freedom of association and private autonomy, the state cannot 'charter' a collective agreement on its own initiative, but only on application by a competent employees' or employers' organization.

652. The minimum wage tariff is a governmental act decreed by the Federal Conciliation Board. As an intervention in private wage politics by authorities, the establishment and the possible personal scope of the minimum wage rate is strictly limited by law. According to the legal wording, the minimum wage tariff may only be established in the event of 'non-existence of an employers' association'. Furthermore, only a very small section of labour law terms – namely the payment – can be the subject of a minimum wage tariff. Unlike the charter, the state determines the whole contents of the minimum wage tariff but here also, the authority may act only on application of a competent employees' organization.

III. Practical Relevance of Collective Agreements

653. Though public law bodies (such as the federal provinces) are also entitled to conclude collective agreements, in Austria, the conclusion of collective agreements is essentially confined to the private sector. Moreover, these agreements are negotiated, almost without exception, at multi-employer and economic sector level.

654. Within the sectoral bargaining system, there are further distinctions, such as between employee categories (manual workers and white-collar workers) and also, in particular, in the area of goods production, between the sizes of enterprises (manufacturing industry or small-scale craft production). Most of the branch collective agreements cover the whole of Austria. The majority comprises small numbers of enterprises in narrowly defined sectors, and also separate agreements on specific issues. About 450 collective agreements are concluded per year, that is to say, more exactly, their minimum wages are bargained and raised.

655. On the employers' side, collective agreements are generally concluded by the chambers of commerce (with compulsory membership). As collective agreements apply to all employees of the covered employers (i.e., the outsider effect for employees, paragraph 712), there is a comprehensive coverage by collective agreements in most areas of industry and small-scale craft production (in summary about 95%, *see also* paragraphs 75, 392).

§2. Functions and Characteristics of the Collective Agreement

656. The collective agreement is a legally binding contract in the sense of civil law, based on the consensus of the contractual parties. Yet, in Austria, collective agreements are considered to be more than civil law contracts, due to their 'normative' effect, and therefore, they can only be concluded by associations of persons or by individual employers who have the legal capacity to conclude collective agreements (i.e., granted by law or by decree).

657. Collective agreements are not intended to regulate only the relationship of its parties, but above all, the elements of the individual employment relationships covered by it. As this concerns the legal relationships of persons who are not party to the collective agreements themselves (creation of 'objective law'), the conclusion of collective agreements needs the above-mentioned specific legal empowerment. According to express statutory appointment, the legal relationships between the individual employees and employers are directly regulated and influenced by a collective agreement; it has the same effects as a statute (paragraph 694 et seq). The contents of the collective agreement need not be made part of the individual employment contract expressly or conclusively. Therefore, collective agreements are also called 'normative contracts'. Moreover, the collective agreement not only directly regulates the relationships of individual employees and employers, but as a rule is also binding to the employees' advantage. This prohibits an individually agreed deviation from the collective agreement to the employees' disadvantage.

658. In summary, there is a distinction between two sorts of provisions in a collective agreement as regards their legal effects: the provisions concerning the parties of the employment contracts (normative provisions, the normative part), and the provisions concerning only the concluding parties to the collective agreement (provisions under the law of contract, the contractual part; *see also* paragraphs 666, 723 et seq.).

§3. The Conclusion of the Collective Agreement

I. General

659. Collective agreements are subject to general private contract law. Special regulations refer to the capacities of the contracting parties (paragraphs 677 et seq.), the contents (paragraphs 666 et seq.), and the form (paragraph 661).

660. As contracts under civil law, collective agreements are, therefore, (generally) concluded by consensus of the parties. There is one exception to this approach: by way of voluntary arbitration at the Federal Conciliation Board. Both parties to a dispute can request together that the competent conciliation authority make a decision (arbitration award), which would then be *ex lege* qualified as a collective agreement. However, this procedure has no practical significance. Moreover, so far, collective agreements based on compulsory arbitration are unknown in Austrian labour law practice.

II. Form

661. Written form is a prerequisite for the effectiveness of the conclusion of collective agreements. Due to their quasi-statutory effect, collective agreements also require a certain degree of 'publicity'. §14 of the Labour Organization Act specifies, therefore, that the collective agreement must be deposited with the Ministry of Labour, which then announces the conclusion of the collective agreement, though not its contents, in the official pages of the daily *Wiener Zeitung*. The announcement is a precondition of the validity of the collective agreement's normative provisions.

III. Nullity

662. If the conditions relating to the form of the conclusion or the publication of the agreement are not satisfied, the collective agreement is null and void and therefore invalid. The collective agreement is also invalid if it is *contra bonos mores* or not permissible, in the event of dissent and infringement of the limits set on the permissible contents of a collective agreement (*see* paragraphs 666 et seq.), and when one of the parties is not entitled to conclude collective agreements. If the grounds for nullity only apply to specific provisions, as a rule the rest of the collective agreement remains in force (partial nullity principle).

663. In all these cases, the nullity of the collective agreement can be asserted at any time and by anybody. If the collective agreement has been applied to employment relationships before, this is generally not reversed. This means, for example, that payments deriving from a void collective agreement cannot be recovered. Furthermore, there are no grounds for nullity, if the declaration of a party is not in accord with their true intentions. An appeal against the collective agreement on the grounds of fault in a party's intention only comes into consideration under certain circumstances, and can lead to the termination of the collective agreement (*see* paragraphs 729 et seq.).

IV. The Commencement of Legal Effectiveness

664. As regards its obligatory part, the contracting parties are bound to the collective agreement by law of contract, from the time of conclusion of the agreement.

665. The normative provisions only take effect from the day after the announcement of the agreement (paragraph 737). A later date can be specified in the collective agreement itself. In spite of this, collective agreements may also cover matters (i.e., rights or duties) which have accrued before the commencement of the agreement. Such 'retroactivity' on the part of a collective agreement is common but only permissible within narrow limits (especially if in favour of the employees). Vested rights which have already been achieved may not be affected, although simple expectations may be, in part.

§4. Content of the Collective Agreement

I. Normative Part and Obligatory Part

666. Like any other contract in civil law, collective agreements may regulate legal relationships between the parties which conclude them. The provisions of this 'contractual' or 'obligatory' part only concern the signatory parties (*see* paragraphs 723 et seq.) and relate solely to their mutual rights and obligations and implied duties, such as the 'peace obligation', that is to say, the obligation to refrain from industrial action (paragraph 727).

667. The majority of the provisions of a collective agreement refer to the individual contract of employment relationship and form the 'normative part' of the agreement. They have a directly mandatory effect on the employees and employers covered, as if laid down by statute ('normative effect'; *see* §11 Labour Organization Act). This power of collective agreements to set legal standards for employment contracts is quite comprehensive but still limited, insofar as it only covers matters specified by statute. Furthermore, if an issue is regulated both in a statute and in the normative part of the collective agreement, the regulatory powers of the collective agreement are limited due to the 'hierarchy of norms' (paragraph 85).

II. Permissible Matters of Regulation

668. According to §2 section 2 subsection 2 of the Labour Organization Act, collective agreements can regulate 'the mutual rights and duties of employers and employees accruing from the employment relationship' (content standards – *Inhaltsnormen*). Collective agreements may contain all matters relating to the (possible) typical contents of employment contracts and cover, for instance, terms about payment, suspension of work (for reasons such as employees' illness or other impediments), periods of notice, reasons for giving notice, and reasons for summary dismissal (termination standards), periods of vacation, severance pay, establishment retirement benefits, wealth aggregation from remuneration, conciliation clauses and regulations concerning good order in the establishment, such as establishment disciplinary measures.

669. Standards concerning the conclusion of employment contracts cannot be included in the normative part. Accordingly, the following provisions would be void: form specifications for employment contracts, hiring precepts, guidelines for selection in the hiring of employees and employment bars. Moreover, 'collective standards' such as arrangements for the benefit of the entire staff of an establishment or undertaking (e.g., provisions for a nursery or a sports-yard at the plant) do not count as 'content standards'.

670. Within certain limits §2 section 2 subsection 3 of the Labour Organization Act also empowers the parties to collective agreements to regulate the legal relationships of employees formerly covered by the collective agreement. This mainly concerns retirement benefits of ex-employees.

671. Generally, due to the absolutely binding effect of the works representation law, the collective agreement cannot lay down rules on such issues. In particular, it may not alter or augment the organization or powers of the staff of an establishment (paragraph 760). There exist only a few deviations, in particular §29 of the Labour Organization Act, which states that a collective agreement can extend the legally laid down subject matters of works agreements (paragraph 821) beyond what is statutorily provided for. On the question of whether or not a collective agreement can extend the works council's co-determination rights beyond statutory law, the predominant view deems such provisions to be void.

672. §2 section 2 subsection 7 of the Labour Organization Act permits a collective agreement to lay down rules about any institutions which are administered by both contracting parties. These are bodies created by the parties to the collective agreement together, such as vacation and severance funds for employees who regularly change their place of work, holiday homes, or institutions involved with employees' accrual of assets. In connection with such common institutions, a collective agreement can be directly binding and does not only regulate legal relationships between employers and employees, but also the legal relationship between an employer and the institution (contributions) and between the institution and employees (usually benefits).

III. Collective Agreement and Statutes

673. The subjects regulated by the normative provisions of a collective agreement are often already covered by statute. Whether or not the statute or the collective agreement applies, primarily depends on the effect of the regulations involved (non-mandatory, mandatory to the employee's advantage, or binding on both parties *see* paragraphs 47, 73).

674. In the case of absolutely mandatory effects of the statute concerned (i.e., binding on both parties), any divergence by collective agreement is prohibited. Such divergent collective agreement provisions would be null and void, whereas the rest of the provisions remain effective (partial nullity principle, *see* paragraph 193). In the case of statutory law which is mandatory to the employee's advantage, a comparison between the advantageousness of the statute and collective agreement is decisive (for comparing advantageousness in general, *see* paragraph 87). For the collective agreement to be legally valid, it suffices for it to be equally advantageous. A provision in the collective agreement is only null and void if it is less advantageous (for the employee) than that in the statute. The remaining provisions then basically remain effective (partial nullity principle). However, all provisions which are objectively or subjectively ('rights of claim and power') connected with the null and void (less advantageous) provision are also null and void.

675. Besides statutory provisions which possess the same binding effects in relation to all lower ranking instruments of regulation (collective agreements, works agreements, individual employment contracts and so on), there are also certain statutes with 'split legal effectiveness', for instance, statutory regulations which are non-mandatory only in relation to collective agreements. In this case, only the collective agreement can deviate from the statute's provisions, but regulate a subject matter even to the employees' disadvantage. In relation to all other instruments such as works agreements, individual agreements and employer's instructions, the provisions of the statute still are unilaterally (or bilaterally) binding.

676. The reason for introducing 'split effectiveness' of norms *v.* norms on a lower level was that collective agreement regulations can be adjusted to changing conditions more easily and quickly than statutes. Also, the parties to a collective agreement will be better informed on certain problems in an economic sector than is legislature. Furthermore, the bargaining power of the parties to a collective agreement is more balanced than that of the parties of an individual employment contract – provisions in a collective agreement can be more trusted than that in an employment contract to offer a fair solution for a certain problem given.

IV. The Capacity to Conclude Collective Agreements

A. General

677. In Austria, not every institution or person can conclude collective agreements. Only legal entities specifically entitled to conclude collective agreements can be parties to them. Due to the normative effect of the collective agreement, the capacity (also) implies the power to create objective law. The legal authorization to conclude collective agreements must therefore always be based on and derived from a statute.

678. The capacity to conclude collective agreements is referred to in various contexts, such as being a prerequisite for the rights of institutions or organizations to file applications (charters, minimum wage tariffs) or to take part in the co-determination at the enterprise level. In practice, this specific legal and contractual capacity gives employers' or employees' organizations the power needed to play a significant role in Austrian politics, and on the labour market as well.

679. §§4–7 of the Labour Organization Act, which regulate the capacity to conclude collective agreements in more detail, distinguish between three forms of institutions: free professional associations (especially trade unions), statutory representative bodies (i.e., chambers) and – most rarely – individual employers.

680. On the employee side, only organizations of individuals (i.e., natural persons) are entitled to conclude collective agreements. On the employer side, the organization may comprise individuals or legal entities (such as companies). Furthermore, besides their organizations, individual employers may also – by way of legal exception – have the capacity to conclude collective agreements. Moreover, if an association of individuals concludes a collective agreement, only the body as such (and not its individual members) is party to the agreement.

B. Associations with Voluntary Membership

681. The preconditions for the capacity of associations with voluntary membership (trade unions and employer associations) to conclude collective agreements are legally standardized in §4 section 2 of the Labour Organization Act. They substantially correspond to the general characteristics of an affiliation (paragraph 575). They prescribe a long-term association of individuals with incorporated character subject to civil law and based on voluntary membership. According to its charter, the aim of the association must be the regulation of employment conditions, and it must fulfil the conditions of 'freedom from the social opponent' (paragraph 575) and 'independence from social opponents'. Additionally, §4 section 2 of the Labour Organization Act requires that the association be intended to represent employees or employers on a large geographical and trade or professional scale, and, from the point of view of membership and the scope of its activities, that it in fact does already possess decisive 'economic significance' – a condition which may hamper the chances of any new association considerably, and gives much discretion to the Federal Conciliation Board as to its decision. On the contrary, preparedness to initiate or participate in industrial action is not a precondition for the capacity to conclude collective agreements.

C. Statutory Representative Bodies

682. According to §4 section 1 Labour Organization Act, chambers must fulfil two conditions to be entitled to conclude collective agreements: the statutory body representing employees or employers must be unrestrained by social opponents (*see also* paragraph 575) and independent of its social opponents, and it must include the regulation of employment conditions among its statutory tasks, whereby the latter does not regularly constitute a legal problem. As to chambers of which both employed and self-employed persons are members, they must, above all, have separate organs for decision-making, to fulfil the legal prerequisite of independence from social opponents.

683. The most important statutory representative bodies with the capacity to conclude collective agreements are the Economic Chambers in the provinces, the Austrian Economic Chamber and the subdivisions of these chambers (craft groups and craft organizations) on the employers' side, and on the employee's side, the

Chambers of Labour in the provinces and the Federal Chamber of Labour. In practice, mainly the Economic Chambers and their subdivisions take part in collective bargaining on the employer side; on the employees' side, collective agreements are concluded exclusively by the trade unions, as the Chambers of Labour do not exercise their statutory power to do so. Furthermore, in their economic branches, the chambers of the various liberal professions (e.g., those for attorneys, notaries, accountants, dentists, veterinaries, doctors or civil engineers) play a significant role in collective bargaining, due to the lack of free professional associations.

D. *Individual Employers (Company Collective Agreements)*

684. Austrian law does not promote the individual employer's capacity to conclude collective agreements only for one enterprise, and restrains it as far as possible. Apart from specific statutory provisions for companies of the (former) public sector, like the public broadcasting corporation, telecommunications, the postal services or federal museums, other individual employers are allowed to conclude collective agreements in just two cases: only public sector bodies (§7 Labour Organization Act), and certain societies of major social importance (§4 section 3 Labour Organization Act) may conclude collective agreements on the employer's side with their own employees ('company collective agreements'). For example, the Society of the Vienna Symphony Orchestra (as employer) has concluded a collective agreement with the trade union, covering only the employees (musicians, and so forth) of this orchestra. Furthermore, sectoral collective agreements concluded by an employer association which according to their personal scope would only apply to one individual establishment or undertaking are permissible.

E. *Acquisition and Loss (of the Capacity to Conclude a Collective Agreement)*

685. Statutory representative bodies and legal entities in public law (§4 section 1, §7 Labour Organization Act) acquire the capacity *ex lege*. This means that the capacity to conclude collective agreements exists automatically, if the statutory conditions are satisfied. On their application and after an administrative procedure, both an affiliation and a society of major social importance (§4 section 3 Labour Organization Act) may acquire the capacity by acknowledgement (decree) of the authorities, if they fulfil the legal prerequisites. The same applies, vice versa, to the loss of the capacity. In the case of free professional associations and societies, it can be lost only by express revocation. In the case of *ex lege* loss, there is no specific administrative procedure to decide whether or not the conditions are satisfied. Therefore, this question (as well as that on acquisition) can only be answered as a 'preliminary question' in any dispute before the courts, in which the issue is touched upon.

F. The Competence to Conclude a Collective Agreement

686. The capacity to conclude collective agreements does not always say anything, in itself, about which employment relationships or establishments are concerned or might be covered (i.e., which geographical areas, trades and professions, and personnel groups shall be concerned). The jurisdiction of statutory representative bodies derives from their statutory foundations. For example, based on the Physicians Act, the chamber of physicians' capacity may only cover the conclusion of collective agreements for 'physicians'. As regards the capacity of associations with voluntary membership, their jurisdiction derives from the contents of the Federal Conciliation Board's decree giving them the capacity to conclude collective agreements, and then from the associations' own charters. For example, the Tyrolean Federation of Agricultural Workers and Woodchoppers may only conclude collective agreements for workers in the rural sector in Tyrol. Legal entities in public law and specific associations are only entitled to conclude collective agreements covering their own establishment's employees.

G. Overlap of Capacities

687. The coexistence of associations with voluntary membership and of statutory representative bodies might result in the existence of several organizations that are capable of concluding collective agreements for a particular economic sector, job, group or establishment. Moreover, collective capacities may also overlap, when several associations with voluntary membership are involved covering similar sectors (e.g., banks and funds). However, there do not exist many rules to deal with such conflicts.

688. There are only two cases where statutory regulation specifies that one of the two contesting institutions loses its capacity:

(1) A legal entity in public law, or an incorporated society of major social importance, loses its capacity to conclude a collective agreement (i.e., a company collective agreement, paragraph 684) as an individual employer, if this employer (i.e., the public law body or society) belongs to or becomes member of an employer's organization which itself has collective contractual capacity ('priority of associations' capacity'). It is of no matter whether this employer organization has already concluded a collective agreement (§4 section 3, §7 Labour Organization Act).
(2) Whenever an association (of employers or employees with voluntary membership) concludes a collective agreement, the statutory representative body which is competent for this economic branch or professional group also loses its capacity as regards the members of the voluntary association who are covered by the agreement ('priority of free associations', *see also* paragraph 690).

689. In all other cases, contesting capacities exist in parallel. If several collective agreements are then actually concluded, and their spheres of application overlap (for instance, because an employer has various certificates of trade), the result is a conflict of collective agreements (*see* paragraphs 713 et seq.).

H. The Actual Situation

690. With a few less significant exceptions, only the Austrian Federation of Trade Unions (for more details, *see* paragraphs 611 et seq.) is currently entitled to conclude collective agreements on the employees' side. Since the federation in fact concludes collective agreements in practically every area, the chambers of labour therefore 'lost' the capacity to conclude collective agreements for trade union members (§6 Labour Organization Act). Furthermore, the chambers of labour, so far, have not made use of their capacity, in those economic areas where the trade unions have not yet concluded a collective agreement, or for those employees who are not union members. Due to the rather restrictive interpretation of 'actual economic significance', as to the acknowledgement of the capacity to conclude collective agreements with other associations (*see* paragraph 696), the Austrian Federation of Trade Unions has a *de facto* monopoly of collective contractual activity.

691. On the employer's side, there are various free professional associations, some of which have been granted collective contractual capacity. They by no means cover all employers or economic sectors, and for the most part do not even exercise their right to conclude collective agreements (paragraph 624). Collective agreements are quite predominantly concluded by the Economic Chambers, in particular the federal chamber and its professional subsections (paragraph 636 et seq.). Therefore, they also have a *de facto* monopoly in the field of collective bargaining, at least with respect to industry, trade and craft. Since the chamber system embraces all commercially active employers, and due to its *ex lege* compulsory membership, there are not any 'outsiders' in the area of trade and industry on the employers' side in Austria. In most areas of industry and small-scale craft production, there is virtual blanket coverage by collective agreements.

692. Besides the collective agreements concluded between the specialized unions and the Economic Chambers with their subsections, there are also so-termed general or top collective agreements (*Generalkollektivvertrag*, *Spitzenkollektivvertrag*), concluded between the Austrian Federation of Trade Unions itself and the Austrian Economic Chamber. As a rule, they apply to whole Austria and (almost) all economic sectors but cover only a small number of employment terms. For instance, a general collective agreement introduced the four-week vacation minimum and the forty-hour week, even before they were statutorily established. A more recent example for this type was a general collective agreement on amending measures in the case of permanent mask wearing during the COVID-19 pandemic.

V. Collective Agreements and the Individual Employment Relationship

693. As to the provisions in a collective agreement, it is important to distinguish whether or not a provision can affect an individual employment relationship.

A. *Normative Effect*

694. According to §11 of the Labour Organization Act, the entire normative part of a collective agreement is directly legally binding. This means that a collective agreement contains objective law, and is 'statutory' (statute-like), in a material sense. It influences and shapes individual employment relationships, independently of the knowledge or intentions of the parties to the individual employment contract.

B. *Mandatory Effect*

695. According to §3 of the Labour Organization Act, the normative provisions in a collective agreement are, as a rule, binding to the employee's advantage. Where the collective agreement itself does not expressly specify otherwise, these provisions therefore create minima for employment conditions. Deviating special regulations in works and individual agreements are only valid if they are more advantageous to the employee than the collective agreement, which otherwise applies (principle of comparative advantage; *see* paragraph 87).

696. Specifically, it is decisive whether or not an individual agreement already exists, when the collective agreement takes effect.

- Already existing individual agreements remain valid, insofar as they are more advantageous to the employee. Less advantageous individual agreements become ineffective until the lapse of the collective agreement (paragraphs 729 et seq.). Thereafter, they again come into effect, but cannot prevent any aftereffect of the particular collective stipulation (for details *see* paragraph 735). In other words, only a new (individual) agreement after the end of the collective agreement would change the working terms in question.
- Individual agreements concluded after the collective agreement takes effect are only valid, insofar as they are more advantageous to the employee. Otherwise, they are null and void, and remain so after the collective agreement ends, as well.

697. Whether an individual agreement is more advantageous to the employee than the corresponding provisions in the collective agreement can only be answered by 'comparison of advantageousness'. Its general principles (paragraph 87) also apply here. The individual agreement is only more advantageous if it (clearly) favours the employee. A 'neutral' provision does not suffice for its validity. The assessment must not only compare the divergent provisions in themselves, but also all the provisions which are objectively and subjectively connected to these provisions (e.g., not only the 'time pay' in the employment and in the collective agreement but also the rights to severance pay or additional remuneration would have to be taken into account). If an individual agreement provision is less advantageous, it is invalid, and the collective agreement provision applies. Due to the principle of partial nullity, the rest of the employment contract remains effective.

698. Hence, other provisions of the individual arrangement may be invalid, as well, if there is an objective or subjective connection to the primarily invalid provision, and if, additionally, the extended invalidity is compatible with the purpose of the collective agreement. However, the employment contract itself remains valid, even if the employer has made clear that they would not have contracted without the less advantageous provision.

699. The one-sided or relatively binding effect of collective agreements to the employee's advantage is the rule. However, §3 of the Labour Organization Act states that a collective agreement can be binding on both parties and can, therefore, exclude any special agreements on particular questions. Up to now, this possibility has been of no practical importance. Moreover, following the Supreme Court, a collective agreement may also provide its provisions with non-mandatory effects, although there is no legal provision explicitly allowing it. The argument supporting this opinion is that the parties of the collective agreement have no obligation at all to conclude an agreement, or to include any special provision – therefore, the non-mandatory effect would be more advantageous to the employee than no provision at all.

C. Wages above the Collective Minimum Wage

700. In practice, the minimum wages provided for in a collective agreement are often increased by individual agreements (*de facto* or actual additional wages; additional pay), which is generally permissible because of the unilaterally binding effectiveness of collective agreements to the employees' advantage. If a new collective agreement wage scale encounters *de facto* wages above the existing collective scales (i.e., extra payment based on the individual agreement), the result can be either 'absorption' or 'accumulation', on which agreement can be expressed in the individual or the collective agreement.

- Absorption means that the rise of collective wages is taken up, in part or completely, by the actual additional pay previously agreed on. As a result, the employee still gets the same payment as before (as long as de facto payment matches the payment in the collective agreement).
- In the case of accumulation, the employee receives the de facto payment exceeding the collective wages (additional pay) plus the increase specified by the new collective agreement.

701. If the collective agreement specifies accumulation, a distinction is made between 'simple' and 'qualified' actual wage clauses. 'Simple' actual wage clause means that the accumulated wage component has no mandatory effect, and the accumulation could be cancelled by individual agreement. In the case of 'qualified' actual wage clauses, the unilaterally binding effect of the collective agreement would also embrace the previously excess and now accumulated wage element, so that both together make up the new collectively agreed wage.

702. In practice, the wage scales of the collective agreements are negotiated annually, and usually the minimum wages as well as the *de facto* wages (additional pay) are raised. The way the additional pay is raised differs from sector to sector – collective agreements either include accumulation clauses, as described above, or they provide for a percentage by which the actual wages have to be raised (usually lower than the percentage applicable to the minimum wages).

703. It is not unusual for individual employment agreements to include an 'absorption clause' stipulating that future wage rises of de facto wages are to be absorbed in part, or completely, by the actual additional payment agreed on. This is valid, as no employer is obliged to pay above the collective minimum wage, and wages above the wage scales, combined with an absorption clause, are still more favourable for the employee than the payment of just the minimum wage. Court practice has established that such clauses may only include foreseeable actual wage rises, as a rule of thumb about two or three, depending on the amount of additional pay.

VI. The Sphere of Operation of the Normative Part of a Collective Agreement

A. General

704. With all its specific legal effects, a collective agreement is not valid for every conceivable employment relationship which may be implied by its contextual and geographical sphere of operation, but only for specific persons. This group is primarily defined in §§8 and 12 of the Labour Organization Act ('subjection to collective agreements'). Specifically, the scope of application of a collective agreement is defined by the statutory groundings and the prerequisites for application, and within the generally imposed framework, by grounds and prerequisites named in the collective agreement itself.

B. General Subjection to a Collective Agreement

705. Apart from the integration of outsiders on the employee side, according to §12 of the Labour Organization Act, it is §8 of the Labour Organization Act that lays down the main legal prerequisites of subjection to a collective agreement. It makes the following persons unconditionally subject to collective agreements:

- all those who are members of the employers' or employees' organization at the time of concluding the agreement, or become members afterwards;

- employers, to whom the establishment of an employer subject to the collective agreement gets transferred (unless the employer is already a subject to another collective agreement);
- if allowed, the employer concluding a company collective agreement (*see* paragraph 684).

706. Within the statutory limits outlined above, a collective agreement itself can then define its own sphere of operation (scope of application), whereby geographical (such as for a particular province), sectoral (e.g., for establishments in the chemical industry), trade or professional (for instance, based on the employees' jobs, such as all white-collar workers or carpenters), personnel (such as according to the level of education) and temporal spheres of operation (e.g., 'commencement of effects: 1 January 2023, indefinite duration') are identified. In order to be applicable to an establishment or employment relationship, it must lie within each scope of the collective agreement named above.

707. In defining its spheres of operation, a collective agreement must observe the (constitutional) principle of equality, which forbids discrimination without material grounds. The Equal Treatment Act makes unlawful and declares void all provisions which differentiate on grounds of sex, age, sexual orientation, ethnic origin, religion or belief without justification. Furthermore, these provisions especially forbid collective regulations resulting in directly or indirectly unequal pay.

708. If the temporal scopes of application of collective agreements between the same parties lead to an overlap (e.g., a collective agreement for mechanics in the metal industry concluded on 1 January 2023, followed by a collective agreement on 1 October 2023), the *lex posterior* principle applies, as with statutes. Therefore, the later collective agreement replaces the earlier one, insofar as the same sort of collective agreement (as well as concluding parties) are involved (branch agreements, special agreements), or the same questions dealt with. However, due to some specific regulations in the collective agreements themselves, the later specialized collective agreement does not, in general, affect the earlier general agreement.

709. If the spheres of operation of collective agreements concluded by different parties overlap, the conflict of laws rules for collective agreements (paragraphs 713 et seq.) apply, rather than these rules.

C. The Outsider Problem and Its Solution on the Employers' Side

710. Principally, the application of a collective agreement derives from and depends on the employee's and the employer's close relationship to the body concluding the agreement, which as a rule means membership of the body. On the contrary, 'outsiders' are persons who would not be subject to the collective agreement, due to the lack of such a relationship to a party of a collective agreement, because only the members of the concluding employers' organization or employers joining afterwards, are subject to the collective agreement. Hence, on the employer side, outsiders are not covered by the collective agreement. Overall, there are two solutions:

(1) In practice, most collective agreements are, in any case, concluded by the chambers. Due to their mandatory membership, they cover all employers of the concerned economic sector. As a result, apart from a few sectors, there are generally no employer outsiders in collective agreement practice.
(2) For the exceptional case where there are, indeed, outsiders, or for sectors without employers' organizations at all, Austrian labour law provides substitute collective instruments, such as charters or minimum wage tariffs, in order to include such employers and their employees within the collective protection as well.

D. The Outsider Problem and Its Solution on the Employees' Side

711. According to §8 of the Labour Organization Act, only the members of the concluding organizations are covered by the collective agreement concerned. However, as regards employees, the coverage is extended by statute in order to involve outsiders as well, that is to say, employees who are not members of a trade union. According to §12 of the Labour Organization Act (headed: outsider effect), collective agreements shall explicitly cover those employees who would actually not be subject to the agreement, because they lack membership of one of the concluding parties, but are employed by an employer who is a member of the concluding employers' association. In order to respect union plurality, and therefore freedom of affiliation, this 'outsider subjection' of employees under a collective agreement only applies when there is not already a collective agreement in force, based on an employee's actual association membership for the employment relationship in question.

712. The legal consequences of the outsiders' subjection to a collective agreement match those for actual members of the concluding trade union. Therefore, the normative part of the collective agreement is directly legally binding. The grounds for termination of application of the collective agreement are also the same. However, an additional reason for termination of application of the collective agreements would be the commencement of any subjection to a collective agreement, as a result of acquiring actual membership of a party of a collective agreement. This, again, ensures that a second free employee trade union (that exists in Austria only in theory, *see* paragraph 613) would have the opportunity to conclude a valid collective agreement for its members. Moreover, the predominant doctrine does not allow a collective agreement to differentiate between members and non-members of the contracting union, such as providing higher pay for members.

E. Conflicts of Collective Agreements

1. General: Principle of Uniformity of Collective Working Conditions

713. As to the individual employer and their employees, a conflict of collective agreements occurs if the spheres of operation of various collective agreements (concluded by different parties) all refer to the employer at once. This is mainly the case when the employer performs various economic activities related to different sectors (such as in the trade and hospitality industry, by running a liquor store and a little bar at the same premises). A permanent change or mixing of entitlements deriving from one or the other collective agreement would lead to an insecure situation, both for the employee and the employer; furthermore, it would lead to administrative and organizational difficulties. Consequently, the Labour Organization Act requires uniformity of collective working conditions at establishment level, and regarding the individual employee. It basically states that only one collective agreement can apply in one establishment, which then applies to all the employees in this establishment.

714. The principle of uniformity of collective working conditions applies, as explained above, to the individual employment relationships and, as a rule, to establishments. The following paragraphs describe how it is determined which collective agreement should apply, in the case of conflicting collective agreements.

2. Forms of Establishment

715. First, the structure of the establishment must be determined: if several activities are performed in an employer's establishment at the same time, for example, a liquor store and a little bar at the same premises, in this context it is referred to as 'mixed establishment' (*Mischbetrieb*). Furthermore, there exist establishments which consist of several separate departments, in each of which different activities are pursued. For example, an employer runs a liquor store and a little restaurant at the same place, but with strict separation as to employees, working hours and clients. Of course, there are also establishments, in each of which only one activity is pursued from the start (such as a liquor store in one part of a city and a little bar in another part).

3. Uniform Establishments or Departments

716. The two latter situations are treated equally in this context (§9 section 1 and 2 Labour Organization Act). If the employer pursues only one activity in an establishment, or an organizationally separate department thereof, only one collective agreement applies there ('principle of uniformity of working conditions in one establishment'). Mostly, this will be a sector collective agreement.

4. Mixed Establishments

717. §9 section 3 of the Labour Organization Act lays down that in a mixed establishment (in other words, several activities at the same premises without any organizational separation), only the collective agreement referring to the economic area which is commercially 'most important' for this establishment applies. In literature, it is often referred to as the activity which gives the establishment or separate department its 'economic character'. Routinely, this might be the collective agreement which covers those employer's activities that make the most profit within this establishment (often combined with the most sales, turnover and so forth).

718. If it is impossible to determine the 'most important' activity of the establishment (as when all activities make approximately the same average profit), this issue can be agreed upon in a works agreement which stipulates which collective agreement shall apply. If there is no such works agreement either, the Act lays down that the collective agreement applies which covers the most employees altogether within its scope of application (i.e., in the whole sector). In law, it is of no relevance in any of these cases which is the most favourable collective agreement to the employees.

5. Employees Working in More than One Establishment

719. If an establishment (or an organizationally independent department thereof) lies within the scope of several collective agreements, and none of the abovementioned exceptions applies, then one alone of the overlapping agreements can apply. Consequently, uniformity of collective working conditions as regards the individual employee is only at risk if the employee works simultaneously in more than one establishment (or department thereof) of the same employer, where different collective agreements apply (e.g., the employee works in two of the employer's establishments, the bar in one district and in the liquor store in another, that is, two separate organizational units). According to §10 of the Labour Organization Act, the collective agreement to apply is the one which covers the employee's main occupation; usually, this would be the job at which they spend most of their working time. If the employee works at both establishments alike, then the Act stipulates that the collective agreement applies which covers the most employees altogether, within its scope of application.

6. Further Considerations

720. Considering the whole labour law system, two or more collective agreements can be applied in one establishment in parallel, if:

– organizationally separate departments exist in the establishment which are covered by different collective agreements;

- one of the collective agreements is a 'top collective agreement' (*see* paragraph 692);
- two of the collective agreements have been concluded by the same parties, but one regulates specific issues which the other does not (such as sector agreement for the whole food and beverage industry, and specific sector agreement for certain beverage producers);
- collective agreements cover different groups of employees (white-collar and blue-collar workers); or
- union pluralism would make it necessary.

721. In summary, neither advantageousness to the concerned employee nor temporal precedence of a collective agreement matters, as regards which collective agreement is to apply in the event of conflicts of collective agreements.

VII. The Indirectly Operative Normative Part of the Collective Agreement

722. According to some literature, a further distinction has to be made between the 'operative' and 'non-operative' normative parts. The indirectly operative normative parts include all the permissible normative provisions in a collective agreement which do not directly interfere with the individual employment relationship, in particular, provisions relating to works representation law. Rather, these provisions directly affect the legal relationship between employer (establishment owner) and the establishment staff. Insofar as statutory works representation law can be modified by collective agreements at all, it has always to be to the employee's advantage, and binding on one party.

VIII. The Obligatory Part of a Collective Agreement

A. General

723. Besides the normative parts of collective agreements, there are also parts of a collective agreement which fall under the law of contract and regulate the legal relationships between the contractual parties ('contractual' or 'obligatory' parts, parts under the law of contract; §2 section 2 subsection 1 Labour Organization Act). As a rule, only the contractual parties, the bodies concerned, can be bound by such regulations, although they additionally have indirect impacts on the members of the associations. However, legal duties, as such, arising from the contractual parts of a collective agreement, always solely affect the contracting associations. Similarly, only an association can infringe the duties. Furthermore, this restriction means that the so-termed self-imposed duties of an association must be distinguished from contractual provisions, which are intended to have influence on the behaviour of the members of one of the concluding parties. In this case, the organization binds itself to influence its members in a certain direction (to do or not do something), but the members are not obliged to observe these provisions, or at least, not based on the collective agreement. Moreover, the implied terms in every collective agreement have to be distinguished from provisions which require express (collective) consensus. Of the former, the most important duties are those of implementation and 'keeping the peace' with respect to the other contractual party (in other words, the obligation to refrain from strikes, lockouts and other forms of industrial action, *see* below).

724. In summary, the contractual parts and the normative parts of collective agreements make up one homogeneous contract. The parts under the law of contract predominantly serve the purpose of carrying out and protecting the normative parts. The general principles of contract law also apply to the effects of the obligatory provisions, for example, those concerning the beginning and the end. Therefore, a mutual binding between the two parties only commences with a written consensus; furthermore, partial termination of the obligatory part – say, with reference to the duty to refrain from industrial action – is only permissible if it is expressly allowed for in the collective agreement.

B. The Duty of Implementation

725. As with every contract, each of the parties to a collective agreement takes on the obligation to fulfil it. In addition to the self-imposed duties which are in the nature of contracts, an inherent duty of implementation exists, which is characteristic of collective agreements and refers to the normative parts. The associations concluding the contract cannot guarantee that their members will obey the collective agreement's normative provisions, but they implicitly bind themselves to make any efforts possible to achieve observance by their members.

726. This promise of 'intervention' is unalterable and a necessary complement to each normative provision. In this sense, every collective agreement with normative provisions also has contractual components. The duty of implementation includes an association's commitment to make its members be loyal to the contract. For example, an association fulfils its duty by providing precise information about the conclusion and contents of a collective agreement, or by taking measures against recalcitrant members and even expelling them, if necessary. There is no standard in any detail regarding what measures an association should take, but a collective agreement could regulate the question more precisely. If either of the parties does not fulfil its duty of implementation, the other party can sue for fulfilment, insofar as there is sufficient interest in court enforcement; also, non-fulfilment may constitute a ground for premature termination (paragraph 732).

C. The Obligation to Refrain from Industrial Action

727. The 'duty of peace' is another implied term of a collective agreement. It refers to measures of industrial dispute, directed at changing the current collective agreement or the situation existing between the parties to the contract. It forbids the collective contractual parties to organize or support labour disputes. They are also obliged to hold back their members from industrial action, taking independent action, or continuing it. However, the more detailed nature of this obligation of restraint is not regulated by mandatory statute. Therefore, collective agreements themselves can settle the contents and extent of obligation. The obligation of restraint can also be suspended completely by a collective agreement. If, as is the usual practice, there is no regulation on these duties of restraint in a collective agreement, the following is regarded as implicitly agreed: the duties of restraint are limited to matters regulated by the collective agreement, but as regards the regulated matters, all industrial action is prohibited ('relative' obligation to restrain from industrial action). This binds the parties, as long as the collective agreement is valid.

D. Other Contents of the Collective Agreement

728. Apart from regulations on the duties of implementation and restraint from industrial action, a collective agreement can contain various other provisions, under the law of contract. These basically include agreements permissible in civil law in general, made by the parties to the collective agreement itself. Some important examples are conciliation or mediation clauses about the procedures to be followed in the case of collective disputes, mutual obligations such as nominating the members of arbitration and conciliation boards and so on. It is also considered permissible to include in the contractual part of a collective agreement all those regulations on employment conditions which could not be laid down otherwise (such as hiring standards; paragraph 669), or to which the parties to the collective agreement do not intend to give normative effectiveness.

IX. Terminating Collective Agreements

A. Forms of Termination

729. Principally, as with all contracts, the period of validity of a collective agreement ends with its termination (which means that it loses its legal effectiveness). The normative parts lose their directly binding effectiveness (though not all of it, *see* paragraph 735), and the parties are no longer subject to the duties of implementation and of restraint from industrial action.

730. A distinction should be made between several forms of termination of collective agreements. There are terms and reasons laid down in statutory law and the general provisions of contract law; also, there may be autonomous termination rules laid down by the agreement itself.

731. The terms and reasons of termination in statutory provisions and according to law of contract include:

– cancellation agreement or consensual termination;

- complete loss of the capacity to conclude collective agreements by one of the parties;
- summary termination by declaratory act on substantive grounds; and
- nullification of the agreement on grounds of fault in the intent.

732. One of the parties to a collective agreement can always terminate immediately on substantive grounds, if they cannot reasonably be expected to continue to be bound to the agreement. The substantive reason is usually based on the behaviour of the other party, but the other party need not be at fault. Like termination for substantive reasons, nullification on the grounds of fault in the intent also leads to the immediate ending of the collective agreement. This is because the declaration of intent given by one of the parties on the conclusion of the collective agreement was not in accord with their true intentions.

733. The rules of civil law in general apply to the prerequisites for nullification; the agreement can always be nullified by one party, if the other uses deception or coercion. However, if due to a simple error in the declaration's contents or the declaration of intent itself, the agreement can only be nullified if the error was caused by the other party (e.g., misleading information) or the other party should have been aware of the error. Permissible industrial action (*see* paragraphs 876 et seq.), however, or the threat of it (if intended to affect the collective agreement) are not grounds for nullification. The normative parts of the collective agreement can only be nullified with *pro futuro* effect.

734. According to non-mandatory statutory law (§17 Labour Organization Act), each of the parties to a collective agreement can give written notice after one year from its taking effect ('blocking period'), with a three-month period of notice. However, this statutory termination rule may be superseded by every autonomous rule for termination in the collective agreement itself. The autonomous rule can also specify a period of validity and the termination conditions. The collective agreement then ends automatically at the end of the period of validity, or if the condition is fulfilled. Moreover, a collective agreement can also lay down its own rules for termination and shorten or lengthen the duration of a collective agreement vis-à-vis statutory stipulations.

B. Aftereffect

735. A collective agreement does not lose all its effects at once on termination. First, it still applies to issues which arose before the termination, and second, by statute, the so-termed aftereffect applies to normative provisions. Namely, if the agreement ends for one of the reasons named above (with the exception of nullification because of fault in the intent), the direct effectiveness continues for all employment relationships which were already covered by the collective agreement before it ends (hence, not for employment contracts concluded after the termination of the collective agreement). However, it must be mentioned that the aftereffect is an 'alleviated' normative effect – because the relatively binding character of the collective agreement in favour of the employees ends. After the termination, its provisions only apply until a new collective agreement or individual agreement covering the same areas comes into force. The aftereffects end, regardless of whether these new regulations or individual agreements are more or less advantageous to employees.

736. Due to the absolutely binding effects of most of the provisions of the Labour Organization Act, the collective agreement itself can neither restrict nor extend its own statutory post-termination effectiveness.

X. Enforcing Collective Agreements

A. *Information and Publication*

737. The conclusion of a collective agreement and all its statutory effects alone will not be able to ensure that the agreement will (always) be observed in practice. Therefore, it is of great importance that the parties to the collective employment relationship, in particular the employees, also know about the collective agreement. As a rule, this is ensured by the organizations that are party to the contract. They have to send copies of the agreement to the Ministry of Labour, which has to publish the fact of the conclusion in the official part of the *Wiener Zeitung*, and afterwards the Ministry has to send copies to all competent labour and social courts. Furthermore, §15 of the Labour Organization Act obliges employers to publicly display the collective agreement in their establishments, and also to put information in a newsletter about where it is displayed.

B. *Interpretation*

738. The normative parts of collective agreements are interpreted like statutes, completely objectively and without probing into the true intentions of the contractual parties, that is to say, mainly based on the words of the agreement or their natural meaning. In the event of incomplete provisions, the gaps may even be filled by way of analogy; however, the collective agreement itself can provide for special organs entrusted with the task of settling differences of interpretation between the collective contractual parties. Moreover, the Federal Conciliation Board (paragraph 17) may provide an expert opinion on the interpretation of collective agreements, upon request by courts or administrative bodies.

C. *Arbitration and Conciliation Clauses*

739. A collective agreement can also allow for specific organs to decide on collective agreement disputes. Arbitration boards might be established, which 'replace' state courts (paragraphs 90 et seq.), and conciliation boards, which only delay but do not bar the appeal of the courts. Arbitration and conciliation clauses may refer to disputes between the contracting parties themselves, such as about interpretation or the fulfilment of the duties of implementation. They may also cover disputes between employers and employees deriving from the employment relationships which are subject to the collective agreement, in which case the agreement can prescribe a conciliation board but not arbitration boards.

D. Enforcement by the Courts

740. Any individual employee can go before the labour and social courts (paragraphs 91 et seq.) to achieve the enforcement of provisions in a collective agreement entitling them to a subjective right. This can only apply to (operative) normative provisions. In contrast, an employees' organization cannot, except in the case of company agreements, sue an individual employer directly for observance of the collective agreement because the employer as such is not obliged to the employees' association itself. However, a suit aiming at fulfilment of the contract by one of the two parties to the collective agreement is possible.

E. Recourse to Self-Help

741. In addition to enforcement by courts or boards created by a collective agreement, the parties to collective agreements, and in particular employees, have recourse to further means, in order to achieve enforcement of the collective agreement. The right of retention under civil law in general applies if the employer does not perform their duties duly, such as by not fulfilling their obligations to the employee under the normative provisions of the collective agreement. In such cases, the prevailing opinion holds that employees can refuse to work but retain the right to payment. Moreover, general non-observance of the collective agreement by a concluding organization or by its (the association's) members is a substantive ground for the other party to rightfully terminate the collective agreement. It is also possible to initiate industrial action against employers who do not fulfil their duties deriving from the collective agreement (for the risks involved for the individual employee, *see* paragraphs 913 et seq.).

§5. CHARTER (*SATZUNG*)

I. General

742. Collective agreements only apply within their scopes of application (paragraphs 704 et seq.). If an association with voluntary membership has concluded the collective agreement on the employers' side, the employees of outsiders, in other words, employers who are not members of the association, are not covered by this collective agreement. They lack collective protection.

743. In such cases, the Labour Organization Act allows for the extension of the collective agreement to the employment relationships which have not been covered up to that point, by adjudicating the collective agreement the status of a 'charter' (*Satzung*). Extending the scope of a collective agreement by declaring a collective agreement a charter (a charter declaration) is an administrative act of state. The competent administrative body is the Federal Conciliation Board (paragraph 17). The state has no influence on the contents of the charter as such, because the Board only extends the scope of application of an already existing collective agreement. Therefore, charters are sometimes referred to as 'partly autonomous' creation of (collective labour) law.

II. Prerequisites for Charter Status

744. First, a charter declaration requires a collective agreement which is still valid. Then, only the individual normative provisions of a collective agreement can be given charter status. Furthermore, if a collective agreement is to be chartered, its provisions have to be 'representative'. This means that the collective agreement must already apply to a 'greater number' of employees, or the major part of the employment relationships concerned. Also, the charter can only apply to employment relationships which are similar to those which are already covered by the collective agreement (e.g., the same or similar kind of work being done by the employees, the same or a similar type of establishment in which the employees work, similar trading or industrial classifications and so on). Also, a charter can never apply to employment relationships which are already covered by a collective agreement (because of the subsidiary character of the charter). Finally, a collective agreement can only be given charter status on the request, by of one of the parties to the collective agreement, to the Federal Conciliation Board.

III. The Legal Effects of a Charter

745. The Federal Conciliation Board not only names the parts of the collective agreement which are to be raised to charter status, but also lays down the (extended) geographical, temporal and the professional and personnel scope of application of the charter. The charter declaration must be made public in the Federal Law Gazette (*Bundesgesetzblatt*); whereupon, like a statute or a collective agreement, the charter has direct and binding effect on all the employers covered by the scopes of application of the charter. The duration of the charter depends mainly on the duration of the collective agreement it is based on, which it can never outlive. As mentioned above, in relation to the collective agreement, the charter is subsidiary. This also means that every new collective agreement will supersede the (existing) charter, for the employment relationships the agreement covers. Unlike collective agreements (paragraph 735), charters have no aftereffects, subsequent to their termination.

§6. Executive Regulation of Employment Conditions

746. Within collective creation of law in general, one can distinguish two sorts of executive or state regulation of employment conditions, namely 'minimum wage tariffs' (*Mindestlohntarif, see* §22–25 Labour Organization Act) and 'apprenticeship scales' (*Lehrlingsentschädigung, see* §§26–28 Labour Organization Act). In contrast to collective agreements and charters, it is the state which specifies the contents of these regulations. However, the executive specification of employment conditions should only intervene where there is no autonomous collective law (for instance, where no competent chambers or associations exist; 'subsidiary nature' of the minimum wage tariff), and there exists a lack of protection of employees.

747. Unlike the collective agreement, with its contractual character, the minimum wage tariff is a governmental act established by an official authority. Furthermore, only a very small section of labour law terms can be subject thereto. The minimum wage tariff, decreed by the Federal Conciliation Board, can only lay down minimum wages and minimum reimbursement of expenses, and no other employment conditions. The terms 'wages' or 'payment' include thereby any benefits provided by an employer in return for the employee's work. Minimum wage tariffs can only be laid down by decree, if the following conditions are fulfilled:

- application by an employees' body entitled to conclude collective agreements (statutory representative body, or union) to the Federal Conciliation Board;
- complete lack of any employer organization entitled to conclude collective agreements for the employees concerned, or for this economic sector; and
- lack of a charter specifying wages, for the employment relationships under consideration.

748. As an intervention in private wage politics by authorities, the establishment and the possible personal scope of a minimum wage tariff is strictly limited by law. According to the legal wording mentioned above, it may only be decreed in the event of 'non-existence of an employers' association'. There has been some controversy on just this issue, because, in order to protect employees, some jurisdiction and parts of literature have tended to interpret this criteria in a broad sense, and have accepted the application of minimum wage tariffs despite the existence of competent employers' associations; for instance, if a certain employer did not 'want to' join an association. Furthermore, the Federal Conciliation Board continued to 'change' already existing minimum wage tariffs despite the coming into existence of competent employers' organizations; in other words, it increased the wages laid down in the tariff. However, the Constitutional Court declared that even the mere increase of wages in an already existing minimum wage tariff opposes the legal criteria of stipulation mentioned above, if in the meantime, before the new decree, an employers' organization has been established.

749. In legal terms, the minimum wage tariff is an ordinance (executive order) by a state authority, the Federal Conciliation Board. It has directly mandatory effect, binding on one party and to the employees' advantage. Furthermore, there are after-effects, as is the case with collective agreements (*see* paragraph 735).

750. In summary, minimum wage tariffs can only be decreed for a few employees' groups in sectors without employers' organizations. The most important are the minimum wage tariffs for domestic helps, janitors, au pairs and private tutors. Hence, they apply to employees of private child care institutions (kindergartens or day nurseries), as well as to janitors and caretakers and all kinds of workers in households (such as domestic, gardening and child, or older people, care staff).

751. The 'apprentice scale' is very similar to the minimum wage tariff and is also an ordinance by the Federal Conciliation Board. It lays down the wages for apprentices, if there are no provisions for apprentices' wages in the collective agreement for this sector.

Chapter 4. Employee Participation at Establishment and Undertaking Level

§1. Basic Consideration and Definitions

I. Statutory Works Representation of Interest

752. For Austrian employees, besides unions and the chambers of labour, there is a third institution representing their interests, the works council (the best-known form of 'staff body'), which acts on the undertaking or company level. Statutory work representation law permits the employees to participate collectively in establishment and undertaking policy and decision-making.

753. Hence, to a certain extent, the Austrian works representation law lets employees participate in the management of 'their' establishment or undertaking. This institutionalized participation is the core of works representation or organization law (*Betriebsverfassungsrecht*, literally 'works constitution law'). In addition to civil, trade and economic law, it determines the employer's legal position with regard to employees' participation rights.

754. From the institutional point of view, this kind of employee participation has its basis in the 'establishment'; that is, the homogeneous producing unit (*see* paragraphs 762 et seq.). Some kind of natural unity of employees' interests is considered to exist within this common workplace. Works representation law has also established a structure of participation within the management at the level of the 'undertaking' (the commercial or economic organizational unit, which may consist of two or more establishments).

755. Statutory law organizes the employees of an establishment as a statutorily based association of individuals, the staff or labour force. Statutory law provides this association of individuals with its own representative staff bodies or organs, of which the most important is the works council (*Betriebsrat*). The law grants staff certain rights at establishment level (rights of participation or co-determination). These participation rights refer to decisions, or staff involvement, regarding order in the establishment, transferring and dismissing of individual employees, works inspection methods or workplace safety, but also decisions and involvement as to rationalization, closing down an establishment, outsourcing, investments and so forth. Besides this, institutionalized staff participation at undertaking level exists chiefly within the framework of the one-third participation by employees in the internal controlling body (supervisory board – *Aufsichtsrat*) of certain corporations (paragraphs 844 et seq.).

756. However, even where there are employee participation rights, managing the enterprise is always the owner's prerogative. Therefore, in the end, statutory works representation law does not restrict the employer's exclusive 'entrepreneurial discretion' and autonomy in economic matters.

757. Statutory works representation law neither can nor should change or eliminate the conflict between the employer's and the employees' interests in the establishment. Rather, it enables a 'balance of interests' to be reached for the benefit of the employees and the establishment.

758. Statutory law also intends that all staff in all establishments should actually establish the appropriate representative bodies, in order to exercise their statutory rights of participation. According to law, in each establishment where more than four employees work a works council 'has to be established'. However, neither the statutory obligation in itself, nor the employees, are subject to direct sanction in the event of non-compliance, which is the reason why only about 30% of establishments comply with this regulation. However, there is at least an indirect sanction, if employees do not establish a works council, for then the staff cannot exercise their statutory rights. The rights to participate of the labour force as a whole cannot be 'transferred' to individual employees. In general, participation rights presuppose the existence of a competent representative body.

II. Works Representation Law

759. Works representation law comprises all the statutory provisions legally organizing the staff of establishments and their representatives, and regulating the instruments of participation of the staff in the running of the establishment and undertaking. A major part of works representation law is organizational law, regulating the internal 'constitution' (in the sense of 'structure' or 'organization') of the staff, its representative bodies and their creation. It also provides the financial basis for the activities of works councils, and secures the position of staff representatives vis-à-vis the employer. The provisions on the competences form the core of works representation law. In the end, these rules give the staff establishment rights, which restrict either just the owner of the establishment (employer), or both parties to an individual contract, in freedom of disposition.

760. Regulations in statutory works representation law are absolutely mandatory. Staff of an establishment and their representatives only have the powers allowed for by statute; unless permitted explicitly by statute, they may not be extended, even in favour of the employees. To a great extent, legislation retains the exclusive right to determine issues of employee organization and powers, in order not to allow works representation to become a matter of dispute. Concerning this two-sided mandatory effect of organization law, there are only a few deviations regarding the regulation of powers, namely those in favour of collective agreements.

§2. The Scope of Works Representation Law

I. Works Representation According to the Labour Organization Act

761. For a place of work or an establishment to be covered by statutory works representation law under the Labour Organization Act, organizational, staff, professional and geographical conditions must all be fulfilled at the same time.

A. *Establishment, Undertaking, and Establishment Owner*

762. A primary condition for the application of statutory works representation law is the existence of an 'establishment', in the legal sense. An establishment is any place of work which forms an organizational (technical) unit, within which a person or legal entity (i.e., the establishment owner) intends to achieve a certain result (such as production of goods) through continuous work (§34 Labour Organization Act). The intention to make profit is not a prerequisite.

763. Therefore, a place of work is only an establishment from the point of view of works representation law if it is at least an organizational unit from the point of view of production, as well as being of long-term character, whereas legal independence is unnecessary. Often, several departments or other subunits working together make up such an establishment. Major elements of the 'unity' of an establishment are the owner, the means of production (equipment, facilities, funds and so on), an activity which is continuous, and the individuals employed at the place of work. Another mark of the required organizational unity is, as a rule, the 'united management' of production.

764. Hence, the first (and main) level of works representation law in the Labour Organization Act mainly concerns the 'establishment'. In order to become such an establishment despite the lack of the legal prerequisites mentioned above, the labour and social court can, on application, grant large subunits of an establishment, so-termed work places, the same legal status as the establishment itself, if they are at a significant distance from the main establishment and they are at least 'substantially' autonomous. Also, the labour and social court can decide on application (as a separate question) whether or not a 'work place' actually fulfils all the prerequisites of an establishment, in the legal sense.

765. If several establishments are run as an economic or commercial unit, they make up an 'undertaking' in the sense of works representation law, which is considered the next (second) level of works representation.

766. The establishment's 'owner', for the purposes of works representation law, is whoever has disposal of this establishment as legal owner or lessee, or for any other legally valid reason. As a rule, the establishment's owner is also the employer, for the purposes of works representation law, the partial exception being temporary workers.

B. Persons Covered

767. The statutory works representation law laid down in the Labour Organization Act applies to all persons working in the establishment in a condition of personal dependence. This essentially includes all employees, for the purposes of employment contract law (§1151 General Civil Code, *see* paragraphs 51 et seq.). However, employees who have a decisive influence on the management of the establishment (managers and senior personnel) are expressly excluded, whereas near relatives of the owner are among the persons to whom works representation law generally applies, the exception being, for example, the right to become member of the works council. As well as those employees with an employment contract, manual home workers (who have no employment contract and are free employees, *see* paragraph 54) are expressly covered by statutory works representation law.

C. Small Businesses

768. It is a precondition of the establishment of representative bodies that at least five employees (paragraph 775) over 16 be employed in the establishment. Hence, small enterprises with fewer than five employees are excluded entirely from works representation law. As a result, for example, individuals employed in small businesses are not afforded general protection against unwarranted dismissal, because the scope of this so-termed general protection against dismissal (paragraph 478) is identical to that of works representation law.

D. The Scope of the Works Representation Law in Terms of Professions and Trades

769. Works representation law is not applicable to places of work where habitual state functions are carried out, in particular courts and executive authorities (e.g., police, army, ministries). Furthermore, there are exemptions for public schools, private agricultural establishments, and finally, for private households (§33 Labour Organization Act). On the contrary, publicly owned economic enterprises, public hospitals and universities are included.

E. Special Provisions for Particular Types of Establishment

770. The Labour Organization Act distinguishes between different types of establishment, in respect of staff organization and the rights of participation. In matters of organization, there are deviations for theatrical and transport establishments; for example, concerning the definition of 'establishment', and additional subdivisions among the staff (such as 'flying' staff and 'ground' staff with airlines). Further exceptions exist, above all, for establishments in the field of politics, the press, education and churches (so-termed tendentious establishments or undertakings – *Tendenzbetriebe*; for details, *see* paragraph 853). As for all other establishments, organization law is binding on both sides and thereby very rigid, although the few statutory models of organization do not equally match all the conceivable sorts of establishment.

II. Staff Representation Outside the Scope of the Labour Organization Act

771. There are some further forms of statutory staff representation for workplaces excluded from the Labour Organization Act because of the nature of the professional activities carried out there. For instance, the Agricultural Employment Act (paragraph 160) contains works representation law very similar to the Labour Organization Act for private agricultural and forestry establishments. In the now partially privatized postal services, statutory works representation is provided for by a special Act, the Postal Labour Organization Act, which also agrees very largely with the provisions in the Labour Organization Act. According to the Universities' Organization Act, there exist separate work councils for the administrative and the scientific or teaching personnel. Specific statutes provide for personnel representation within federal and provincial authorities and various branches of the executive. However, participation rights in the public service sector are strictly limited to social and personnel matters. Finally, there is no statutory regulation of representation at the establishment level for other places of work not covered by the Labour Organization Act, and in particular, not for small businesses with fewer than five workers and households.

§3. Staff Organization

I. Definitions and Legal Position

772. The employees of a work place which fulfils all the conditions of §40 of the Labour Organization Act are united by law to form the staff or labour force (all the employees in the establishment). The Act provides for no specific representation concerning organizational levels below that of the establishment (such as establishment departments or shops), but does to levels above the establishment (i.e., undertaking and group of undertakings level). Moreover, works representation law partly focuses on special interests of particular parts of the staff, by grouping them into white-collar and blue-collar workers (*see also* paragraphs 153 et seq.), and, to a certain extent also in the case of young employees (paragraph 797), and employees with disabilities.

773. The existence of the staff as a statutorily organized association of individuals to which all employees in the establishment belong by statute, is independent of any changes of the corporeal members. The labour force has legal capacity, insofar as it is expressly granted rights and duties by law. In particular, the staff as a whole (and neither individual employees nor the representative bodies) are considered to be the bearer of employee participation rights. However, even staff bodies as a whole are not capable of owning property; they are not (comprehensive) legal bodies of private or public law and may only exercise rights *expressis verbis* laid down in the statute. They only take part in general legal or economic relations to third parties through the works council fund, which has legal personality (paragraphs 795 et seq.). Furthermore, the staff can only exercise their powers or rights if the representative bodies provided for in statutory law, in particular the works council, have been elected.

II. Staff Representatives and Representative Bodies

A. Representatives at Establishment Level

774. On the establishment level, two representative bodies, above all, are provided for by the Labour Organization Act:

(1) The 'staff assemblies' (establishment assemblies), which are composed of all employees of the establishment, or particular groups (e.g., all white-collar workers) thereof. These assemblies are in charge of preparing the elections of their competent works council, its control and revocation, as well as specifying works council contributions.
(2) The works council, which is the labour force's executive organ. It is directly elected by the competent staff and in charge of representing the interests of the staff; this is the body actually exercising the rights of participation.

775. Which staff bodies have to be established depends on the staff structure in the particular establishment:

- If both the group of white-collar and the group of blue-collar workers in an establishment consist of more than four employees, separate works councils are elected for each employee group (section or group works councils). For the various forms of so-termed white-collar workers *ex contractu* the law determines who belongs to which group of employees: if a blue-collar worker's individual employment contract irrevocably specifies that the worker be consistently treated as a white-collar worker (in other words, the whole White-collar Workers Act and the applicable collective agreement for white-collar workers have to be applied), the same applies in works representation law.
- If at least one of the employee groups generally does not consist of more than four employees, a 'joint' works council for both groups has to be established.
- The same applies if the (section) assemblies of white-collar and blue-collar workers both decide to elect a 'united works council' instead of divided ones.
- If section councils are to be elected, a section assembly and council election committee are provided for each section, as well as common institutions of both employee groups, the establishment's general assembly and works committee (*Betriebsausschuss*). The latter is composed of the members of both sectional works councils. In case of a 'joint' works council, there is only one establishment assembly and election committee.

776. Principally, all these institutions are 'collegiate' organs, consisting of several members. The number of works council members depends on the number of employees in the establishment or employee group. In an establishment with 5 to 9 employees, the works council consists of one member, from 10 to 19 employees it consists of 2 members, from 20 to 50 it is 3 members, from 51 to 100 it is 4 members. When there are over 100 members in the establishment, the works council consists of 4 members plus 1 additional member for each additional 100 employees (or fraction thereof), and over 1,000 employees the works council consists of 13 members plus 1 additional member for each additional 400 employees (or fraction thereof).

777. A united works council is elected by all the establishment's employees and a group works council by the employees belonging to the particular employee group. All employees over 18 are ex officio entitled to vote, regardless of nationality. Elections are equal, immediate, secret and direct. If fewer than three council members are to be elected, the majority voting system is used. Otherwise, election is proportional. As a rule, only employees of the establishment are entitled to be elected (though, in larger establishments, also employees and functionaries of a union or a statutory representative organization). The election principles and procedures are substantially based on those of political elections. Only persons who get the written support of a certain number of employees may be candidates. Principally, the works council's period of office ends after five years.

778. On application by entitled voters, fractions thereof, or also in certain cases the establishment owner, the labour and social court may decide on the legality of the election, for instance, on infringements of the election principles.

B. Institutions at Undertaking Level or Higher

779. In undertakings which consist of several component establishments, the members of all of the works councils make up the 'works councils assembly', whose members are entitled to elect a 'central works council' (*Zentralbetriebsrat*) from among themselves, by a secret ballot and using proportional representation. Like the works council, it is elected for five years. The vote of each voting entity is weighted according to the number of employees in the establishment it represents.

780. Furthermore, the Labour Organization Act provides for an employee's representation body at the level of an (affiliated) group of undertakings (*Konzern*), as well; that is to say, where two or more legally independent undertakings are in fact guided uniformly for economic purposes (especially where due to majority ownership). The (central) works councils of the individual undertakings are entitled to organize and elect a group of undertakings works council (*Konzernbetriebsrat*). As regards European representation, *see* paragraphs 860 et seq.

C. Management and Organization of the Representative Bodies

781. Works councils, works committees and central works councils, as well as group works of undertakings councils, must each elect a chairperson from among their members. Meetings of the staff assemblies are convoked by a works council. If none exists, assemblies can also be convoked by the establishment's individual employees or subsidiarily by the union or chamber of labour. Meetings of the works council, works committee, central works council and group works council, as well as staff assemblies, are not public. The establishment owner him- or herself can only attend after being expressly invited to do so. The decision-making process in all these institutions is based on majority voting, for which, usually, a circular resolution is even allowed, for example, via e-mail. However, in several cases, such as in a works committee meeting, one of the two group works councils can declare a veto, which can only be overruled by a two-thirds majority (protection of minority groups).

782. Works councils, works committees, central works councils and group of undertakings works councils are represented by their chairpersons. Apart from routine matters, a chairperson can only carry out actions based on the collegiate resolution. However, as to a recipient of a declaration in good faith (such as an employer), a chairperson's word is valid, even without any covering resolution in order to protect third parties. The staff assemblies do not, in themselves, deal with third parties.

D. Competence

1. General

783. Works councils, works committees, central works councils and group works councils are bodies whose main task is to exercise staff powers (rights and duties). The staff assemblies, the works council assemblies and auditors of staff funds, on the contrary, are primarily supervisory bodies.

784. A works council not only represents establishment personnel in relation to others (in particular the establishment owner) and thereby asserts the powers of participation they are granted; as a rule, it is also the 'source' of staff decisions.

785. The most important staff assembly powers are the electing of an election committee and thereby initiating and preparing works council elections, and further to this, determining whether or not works council contributions have to be paid by the employees and the amount thereof, dismissing the works council, and also receiving and passing resolutions on works council reports. In addition, the assembly elects the auditors of the works council's fund.

2. Competence to Exercise Participation Powers

786. The rights of participation may be exercised by any one of the following bodies: section works councils, united works councils, works committees, or central works councils. In its details, the statutory allocation of competences is extremely complicated and can only be described in outline here. The section works council has several very important competences. For example, it is always the competent section works council that has to be notified about the intended dismissal of an employee belonging to this group of workers. A joint works council is generally competent to exercise all powers, insofar as the central works council is not competent, in an undertaking made up of several establishments. In particular, the central works council is responsible for the appointment of supervisory board members (paragraphs 844 et seq.) and the exercise of all information and consultation rights, unless they only affect the staff of one single establishment.

787. If no works council or central works council is elected, the powers which would accrue to these bodies cannot be exercised. Generally, the participation rights cannot be transferred to the staff itself, individual employees or another non-competent staff body.

788. Hence, if section works councils should be elected in an establishment, but only one of them actually has been (e.g., only the white-collar works council), the elected council is competent with respect to all powers, insofar as they affect the employee group it represents. The participation powers cannot be exercised with respect to the other employee group. If both works councils (sectional) have been elected, the works committee is, as a rule, responsible for exercise of the powers which affect both employee groups (such as concluding a works agreement).

III. Preconditions for the Effective Action of Staff Bodies

A. *The Relation Between the Role of a Works Council Member and the Duties of an Employee*

789. As a result of express statutory provision, membership of a works council is an honorary office; the duties must principally be performed without disturbance of the ongoing work in the establishment, and in addition to the obligations resulting from the employment contract, that is, in the members' spare time and without extra payment.

790. However, there are several exemptions. An employer must grant every works council member fully paid time off during working hours to carry out their representative duties, if particular tasks can only be carried out during that time. Also, an employer has no right to give orders concerning the fulfilment of works council members' duties. A similar right to continued payment accrues to election committee members and auditors. A further right to continued payment exists for the advanced training of works council members, namely, two weeks during their term of office of the works council (i.e., five years).

791. Furthermore, beyond a certain number of employees, individual council members may be seconded from work completely (still receiving continued payment), without the actual need for this release from work having to be proved in each case. For 150 to 700 employees, one works council member must be exempted from work, and this figure increases, for instance, to two from 701 to 3,000 employees, to three from 3,001 employees, and to three plus one additional member for each additional 3,000 employees. Basically, the same applies to members of central works councils.

792. If a staff assembly (paragraph 774) takes place during working hours, an employer is obliged to grant employees free time, insofar as is reasonable and does not prejudice the employer's interests. However, there is no statutory right of continued wage payment for the employees with respect to this meeting time.

B. Protection Against Discrimination due to Activities Related to Works Representation

793. The Labour Organization Act expressly forbids discrimination of both works council members and all other personnel because of their exercise of statutory powers, within the context of works representation. In particular, works council members' activities may not lead to a reduction in their chances of career advancement. Measures taken by an establishment owner which conflict with these anti-discrimination rules are null and void, and, like default, make the employer liable for damages. Special protection also exists as to unwarranted dismissal and summary dismissal (paragraphs 503 et seq., 546).

C. Facilities for Carrying Out Works Council Activities

794. The Labour Organization Act expressly obliges the establishment owner to supply the works council, electoral committee, central works council and group of undertakings works council free of charge with any facilities which are 'necessary' for the proper fulfilment of their tasks (in particular this comprises proper premises, supporting staff and office equipment). The extent of supply depends on the objective requirements of the labour force or the works council and the establishment's capacity. For example, not all of the works councils need to be supported by secretaries. Any works council's expenditure on materials and personnel which does not have to be borne by the establishment owner may be financed by the works council fund (*see* below).

D. The Works Council Fund

795. The works council fund is an accumulation of assets with statutory legal personality which is primarily but not only financed by contributions of the employees. The establishment or section assembly can decide on whether or not all employees in the establishment or a staff group must pay a certain percentage (maximum 0.5%) of their wage over to the works council fund as a fund contribution. Voluntary bequests (such as from the establishment owner or the trade union), as well as profits from permissible commercial activities, can also form the basis of a works council fund.

796. The works council fund is administered by the works council. The funds bear the costs of running the council which need not be paid by the establishment owner, and contributions for welfare purposes or to welfare institutions (such as holiday homes or sports fields) for the benefit of employees or their relatives. The administration and management of the fund must be supervised by auditors and chambers of labour.

IV. Representation of Young Persons

797. Employees under 16 are not entitled to cast their votes either in the staff assembly or in the election of the works council. The Labour Organization Act provides for special representation of these young workers in certain cases. However, the representatives of the young mainly represent their interests in cooperation with the works council; direct representation of the young vis-à-vis the employer is only a subsidiary possibility. Accordingly, representatives of young employees have no rights of co-determination with the owner of the establishment.

§4. Duties and Powers of the Staff

I. General

798. It is the main task of staff bodies to represent the employees' interests in relation to the owner of an establishment. In order to fulfil this representative task, statutory law gives staff as a whole particular powers. The most important of these competences concern the owner, and aim at involving staff to a certain extent in the running of the establishment (powers of participation). In exercising these powers, the staff bodies must primarily consider and assert the interests of the establishment's employees and, second, also the prosperity of the establishment. Observance of these principles can only be supervised by the establishment's personnel themselves (especially by the employees' assemblies; *see* paragraph 774). Besides these powers, the staff also has the right to regulate several of its internal affairs autonomously (such as works council contributions, *see* paragraphs 795 et seq.). Nevertheless, despite various staff powers of participation, the direct management of the establishment is the owner's concern alone.

799. According to prevailing opinion, a specific ban on industrial action derives from the structure of statutory works representation law. The practical significance of this duty of restraint in works representation law is quite small, though. First, it (only) forbids the organization of industrial action by the elected staff bodies. However, this merely prevents staff functionaries from organizing industrial action in this capacity; the prohibition does not apply if they act as private individuals or union officials. Second, the prohibition only concerns industrial action aimed at changing (extending) staff co-participation rights, or referring to the conclusion, repeal, or changing of a works agreement.

800. In fulfilling the tasks and asserting their rights, staff bodies must nevertheless ensure that they pursue their actions appropriately, that is to say, without disturbing the ongoing work in the establishment. For example, works council meetings must basically be held out of working hours (in practice, this is not always the case in large establishments). On the contrary, the owner must neither hinder staff officials in performing their functions nor discriminate against them for doing so.

801. Members of a works council have a special ‘duty of confidentiality’, the breach of which is, in fact, punishable by law. This duty refers to establishment and business secrets, as well as the personal affairs of individual employees revealed to a works council member in the exercise of their function. However, other members of a staff body may be informed of secrets, if observance of the duty of confidentiality would hinder the effective representation of staff interests, and if the establishment or employee concerned would not be too severely prejudiced.

802. Staff officials have a ‘free’ mandate – this means that they cannot be bound by (individual) employees’ orders in fulfilling their representative duties. However, premature dismissal by the employees’ assembly of the works council as a whole is possible, as a sanction due to poor performance of their official functions. The staff assembly can dismiss the works council by a two-thirds majority. Premature dismissal of individual council members from office by the assembly is not provided for in the statute.

II. Types of Powers of Participation: A Survey

A. *Participation Powers: In Terms of Intensity*

803. The Labour Organization Act lays down several forms of participation:

- supervision;
- cooperation between staff representatives and establishment owner, which may be grouped as follows:
  - the right to ask for information – the employer needs to give information only after a request of the works council;

  - the right to receive information automatically without previous request – the employer must voluntarily provide the information unprompted;
  - the right to be heard – an establishment owner is allowed to act only after they have previously heard the works council's views;
  - right of consultation – the establishment owner is obliged to discuss measures with the works council before carrying them out;
- co-decision rights, which means that the staff bodies decide together with the employer, for example, because they are both members of a collegiate body entitled to make a decision on a particular question, or parties to an agreement. Co-decision rights, where the two sides stand on an equal footing, are called co-determination rights.

B. Participation Powers: In Terms of Issues

804. The subject of a participation right determines its practical significance as well as its intensity (e.g., mere supervision or co-determination). In terms of issues, participation rights may be distinguished as follows:

- economic matters regarding certain technical and financial aspects of the management of the establishment and undertaking;
- personnel questions concerning measures involving individual employees, such as 'hiring', 'firing' and transferring;
- social questions concerning the establishment's personnel and social policy, that is, general issues.

III. Co-determination in Social Affairs

A. General

805. From the viewpoint of Austrian labour law, co-determination means that the staff has the right to decide on an establishment or undertaking issue on an equal footing with the management. In these (rare) cases, the establishment owner or proprietor needs the works council's consent for their actions to be legal. Statutory law stipulates two forms of such a necessary consent: works agreement (agreement principle; *see also* paragraphs 820 et seq.) and *tacit* consent (objection principle).

806. Legally supervised co-determination means that the works council (or, respectively, the owner of the establishment) can rightfully refuse to agree to a measure for specific reasons, but its denial may be scrutinized by the labour and social court on application of the other party. Hence, the works council (or, respectively, the owner) can only block a planned or executed measure on reasonable grounds.

807. Labour law legislation has devised the forms of co-determination very thoughtfully and selectively. The most important areas of co-determination concern social affairs. At the moment, co-determination in commercial-economic affairs does not exist.

808. 'Social affairs' within the meaning of the Labour Organization Act are always general in character; they concern at least one whole group of employees. The main instrument of regulation for co-determination that is statutorily specified is the works agreement (*see also* paragraphs 820 et seq.). The following forms of co-determination may be identified:

- enforceable co-determination means that – where agreement is lacking – either side can apply for binding conciliation;
- compulsory co-determination gives the works council the right of co-decision, and its consent is not subject to (binding) conciliation; other means of regulating the issue (such as in an individual employment contract) are not allowed routinely;
- necessary co-determination gives the establishment owner the option of applying for replacement of the works council's consent, in the event that it is denied; other means of regulating the issue are not allowed;
- optional co-determination means that the conclusion of a works agreement is not legally enforceable; that is to say, there is no binding conciliation, or replacement of the missing consent of one party, but as a matter of course, the works council's refusal to agree does not hinder regulation of the issue in other ways.

B. Enforceable Co-determination

809. Generally, the initiative in concluding a works agreement can be taken by the owner of the establishment or its staff. If the works council opposes the conclusion of a works agreement proposed by the owner, which would deal with an issue of enforceable co-determination, the owner can appeal to the conciliation board (paragraphs 97 et seq., 857), which has to decide upon the appropriate measure in respect of the agreement. The board can deny the employer's application, but it can also approve of an arrangement against the will of the works council. This (imposed) arrangement has by law the effects of a works agreement. Similarly, the works council can appeal to the conciliation board, if the owner does not agree to its proposals. In summary, the conciliation board's decision replaces the consent of one of the two parties. Analogously, all this applies to changing or terminating such works agreements as well.

810. According to §97 subsection 1 no. 1–6a of the Labour Organization Act, above all, the following issues are subject to enforceable co-determination. They comprise:

- all of the agreements on general rules concerning employee behaviour in the establishment (including codes of conduct);

- guidelines for the employment of temporary workers in the establishment;
- the general regulation of the daily hours of work;
- 'social plans', in other words, works agreements about measures to reduce or prevent the consequences of changes in the establishment which may substantially prejudice major groups within the staff (such as the movement of the establishment or its reduction, changing the establishment's organization, introducing new methods).

C. Compulsory Co-determination

811. If the parties cannot achieve a works agreement on an issue of compulsory co-determination, any sort of alternative regulation (e.g., individual agreements) of the matter concerned is prohibited, and all forms of (compulsory) conciliation or arbitration are excluded, as well. Therefore, any action by an establishment owner concerning a matter of compulsory co-determination requires the works council's agreement in order to be lawful, in other words, the conclusion of a works agreement.

812. The following issues are subject to compulsory co-determination:

- the introduction of a works disciplinary code (i.e., with sanctions in the event of non-compliance, including codes of conduct);
- the universal introduction of personnel questionnaires;
- measures to supervise or control employees, where human dignity is affected, though it has to be mentioned that for this case there exists also the explicit stipulation that the measure can be laid down in an individual agreement, as well (*see* below);
- the introduction and regulation of schemes on 'payment by results', especially piece rates, their bases and calculation.

813. If the establishment owner takes one of these measures without the works council's agreement (i.e., without the conclusion of a works agreement), the measure itself (for instance, a works disciplinary code) is basically null and void, as well as any (disciplinary) measure based thereon (such as imposition of fines in the event of the employee's misbehaviour). For the same legal reason, there is no sanction against deliberately giving false answers to a non-agreed questionnaire, or refusing to fill it in. Also, the works council would have an enforceable right to the destruction of questionnaires which have already been filled in, and to stop their use. If an unlawful piece rate system is applied, an employee can refuse at any time to (continue to) work under the system. In the case of unlawful supervisory measures by the employer, the employees can refuse to work under this control, and the personnel have an enforceable right to their removal or suspension. However, according to express stipulation in §10 Employment Contract Law Adaptation Act, if no works council exists, exceptionally, the measure can be taken in the case of the individual employee's explicit consent.

D. Necessary Co-determination

814. On an issue of necessary co-determination, if the works council does not agree to the conclusion of a works agreement, the establishment owner can appeal to the conciliation board, which is competent to 'substitute' the consent of the works council which is lacking. Any other regulation of matters which were subject to necessary co-determination by works agreement would be unlawful without the works council's consent.

815. According to §96a of the Labour Organization Act, there are two cases of necessary co-determination:

(1) the introduction of electronic data processing (information technology), related to relevant personal data on the employees; and
(2) the introduction of systems to assess employees.

E. Optional Co-determination

816. Principally, the option of concluding works agreements gives the establishment owner and the works council the competence to create general rules for the whole establishment, in order to avoid multiple conclusions of individual contracts with all employees concerned. This facilitates the organization of the establishment: measures can be introduced for all employees equally and at the same time, and, if needed, similarly terminated; that is to say, without individually changing the clauses concerned in all the employment contracts.

817. According to §97 subsection 1 no. 7–26 of the Labour Organization Act, the issues which are subject to optional co-determination include, in particular:

- measures protecting employees' health and the 'benevolent' organization of work;
- temporary shortening or lengthening of working time (such as in times of economic crisis);
- principles for taking vacations;
- framework regulations of work in the home office;
- private occupational pension schemes in the establishment;
- employees' legal position in the event of illness or accidents;
- continuation of payment, in the event of attendance of staff assembly;
- periods of notice, and grounds for summary dismissal;
- promotion of working women, and of compatibility of family and career (work-life-balance);
- profit-sharing schemes, schemes for payment by results and several forms of premiums.

818. If the works council denies the conclusion of a works agreement on such issues, the establishment owner can regulate them on their own, using regulatory instruments other than a works agreement, such as general orders or employment contracts (at least, as long as no corresponding works or collective agreement exists).

819. The list of the covered issues shows, *inter alia,* that the size of basic salary is excluded from optional co-determination; in other words, minimum wages cannot be laid down, unless the applicable collective agreement would allow for regulation by works agreement (which is seldom the case). As regards wages, works agreements may principally only specify systems of payment by results, or 'premiums', and the size or calculation basis thereof.

IV. Works Agreements

A. Definition and Adoption

820. For the purposes of the Labour Organization Act, a works agreement is a written contract between the owner of an establishment and its staff, concluded in relation to a subject explicitly permitted by law, or by collective agreement, to be regulated by works agreement. At its conclusion, the staff is represented by the competent staff body (works council, establishment general works committee, central works council and so forth; *see* paragraphs 775, 779). Therefore, no works agreement can be concluded in an establishment without a works council.

821. Like a collective agreement, a works agreement is a legally binding contract in private law, which contains normative and contractual provisions (paragraph 673). 'Normative' provisions regulate individual employees' employment conditions; they shape the content of the individual contract, while 'contractual' provisions refer to the relationship between staff and their establishment's owner (in other words, the parties to the works agreement). Compared to the collective agreement, the works agreement has a smaller range of potential subject matters, because it can only cover issues which are specific and legally laid down (by statute or by collective agreement).

822. Works agreements are created by consensus, like any other contract in civil law. Moreover, in particular cases (i.e., enforceable and necessary co-determination; *see* paragraphs 809, 814), the Labour Organization Act also allows for the imposition of a works agreement by compulsory arbitration, after appealing to a conciliation board.

823. Written form is a prerequisite of validity for every works agreement. For normative provisions to be fully valid, it is also necessary for the works agreement to be displayed in the establishment. Basically, the legal validity of a works agreement is subject to the same principles as those outlined for collective agreements (paragraphs 659 et seq.).

B. Permissible Content

824. The Labour Organization Act restricts the regulatory powers of the parties establishing works agreements in two ways.

825. The first restriction concerns the permissible objects of regulation. Works agreements can only be concluded regarding matters which are provided for in the Labour Organization Act, or other acts like the Working Time Act, or matters which collective agreements allow to be settled by works agreement. These restrictions affect both the normative and the contractual parts of a works agreement. As a rule, therefore, a works agreement can principally include neither provisions laying down employee representation law nor, for instance, provisions regulating the establishment owner's relationships with ex-employees (exceptions here being pension schemes or social plans). Agreements between the owner of an establishment and a staff body, concerning matters others than those which may be regulated by works agreement, constitute a non-valid part of a works agreement. The potential relevance of such understandings depends exclusively on civil law. However, general standards *inter partes* would not usually be binding in character due to lack of legal personality on the part of the contracting party on the staff side.

826. The second restriction for the contents of works agreements relates to their position within the hierarchy of norms. Works agreements can contain regulations on issues which are already regulated by statute or collective agreement. Due to hierarchy of norms, the works agreement's provisions would principally be invalid if they were less advantageous than statutory provisions.

827. For the most part, once a collective agreement has regulated a matter, a works agreement can only regulate it in favour of the employee. However, in some cases, additionally, co-determination powers are modified. Several issues which are, by law, primarily subject to compulsory or necessary co-determination can be subject to optional co-determination, but only if they are already comprehensively regulated by the applicable collective agreement. The issues may then be the subject of an optional works agreement, if it regulates the matter more favourably for the employees. This 'conditional' co-determination applies to issues such as supervisory measures or data collection by means of information technology (*see* §97 section 1 no. 24 referring to §§96, 96a Labour Organization Act). In the case of only basic regulation in the collective agreement, the complementary regulation in a works agreement remains subject to compulsory or necessary co-determination.

C. Works Agreements and Individual Employment Relationships

828. The normative provisions in a works agreement are directly legally binding (§31 section 1 Labour Organization Act) on the employees and establishment owner concerned, and affect individual employment relationships in the same way as statutory law (*see* paragraphs 694 et seq.). This means that the parties to a works agreement are empowered to create 'objective law'. Moreover, the binding effects of the normative provisions are always to the employees' advantage. Where individual arrangements are neither less nor more advantageous, the works agreement applies (as to the 'comparison of advantageousness', *see* paragraphs 87, 697). Finally, unlike collective agreements, works agreements cannot give themselves absolutely binding effects on both contractual parties. The provisions of the works agreement cannot lay down absolutely unalterable working conditions which could not be changed even in the employees' favour (in other words, no overall 'fixed' working terms in works agreements).

829. A works agreement basically applies to all the employees in the establishment, or the employee group whose competent works council (for instance, the section works council of the blue-collar workers) concludes it. Within these limits, each works agreement can determine its own scope, thereby distinguishing individuals according to professional and personnel criteria (years of service, and so on). Principally, the *lex posterior* principle and the *lex specialis* principle apply, as with statutes, to the relationship between two works agreements of which the spheres of operation overlap.

D. Terminating Works Agreements

830. On the basis of its contractual features, every work agreement can be terminated by a termination contract (consensual or mutual cancellation), a unilateral termination for substantive reasons, or an appeal on the grounds of fault in the intention (*see* paragraphs 729 et seq. on collective agreements). Furthermore, there are differences regarding termination, depending on the type of co-determination (paragraphs 805 et seq.), as follows:

- As to optional or compulsory works agreements, an autonomous termination rule can be laid down and specified in the agreement itself (e.g., regarding time limitation, provisos, or notice of termination). If such an arrangement does not exist, both parties can terminate a works agreement on matters which are subject to compulsory co-determination, at any time and without notice. Optional agreements can only be terminated with three months' notice, to end on the last day of a calendar month (§32 section 1 Labour Organization Act). Notice of termination must be in writing. If the normative parts of a works agreement end due to notice of termination, there are, principally, aftereffects, as is the case with collective agreements (*see* paragraphs 735 et seq.). However, in the case of compulsory co-determination (e.g., works agreements on controlling measures affecting human dignity, *see* paragraphs 812 et seq.), aftereffects are explicitly exempted by law.
- In the cases of enforceable and necessary works agreements, statutory law does not allow for the giving of notice. If only one of the parties wants to change or terminate an enforceable works agreement, they must appeal to the conciliation board, which may substitute the opposing party's consent (*see* paragraphs 809,

814). Like other works agreements, enforceable and necessary works agreements can, in themselves, allow for time limitations or provisos as grounds for termination.

E. Enforcing Works Agreements

831. Normative provisions in a works agreement are to be interpreted like statutes. Disputes about both the interpretation and the implementation of normative provisions can be the object of litigation between individual employers and employees in the labour and social court. Hence, a staff body can have a legal dispute with an employer in the context of normative provisions. However, a works agreement cannot contain an arbitration clause. Finally, employee 'self-help' (paragraph 741) is permissible, in the event of a breach of a normative works agreement.

832. Contractual provisions imposing obligations on the parties to the agreement are to be treated like contracts. Disputes about the interpretation and implementation of such provisions, which are subject to Austrian civil law, can generally be dealt with in labour and social courts, by means of litigation between the staff and owner of an establishment. A specific procedure with respect to disputes about the conclusion, changing, or ending of a works agreement is only available in the case of enforceable and necessary works agreements.

V. Co-determination in Personnel Matters

A. General

833. Personnel matters relate to individual employees; examples include: measures on employment, grouping into a collective agreement's salary groups, regrouping, transfers and the termination of the employment relationship by dismissal with notice, or summary dismissal. Since some of the above-mentioned issues are laid down as rights to co-determination, the validity of an establishment owner's personnel measures may depend on the consent or involvement of the works council. Then, other ways of implementing such planned personnel measures are not available. However, in several situations, the works councils' actions are subject to legal supervision by the labour and social court.

B. Co-determination in Dismissals with Notice and Summary Dismissals

834. The most important right to co-determination in personnel matters concerns dismissals. A dismissal with notice is only valid if the works council is informed by the employer about the termination in advance. If the employer terminates the contract without informing the works council, or without waiting for its reaction, the dismissal is null and void (*see* paragraph 480).

C. Co-determination in Transfers, Disciplinary Action and Individual Productivity Payments

835. For the purposes of §101 of the Labour Organization Act, permanent transfer of an employee is a change of workplace for an indefinite period, or for a period exceeding thirteen weeks. Such a transfer is subject to co-determination if it has a negative effect on the employee's pay or other work conditions. If the required consent of the works council is denied, the transfer is null and void, and for this reason alone, the employee need not accept it. On application by the establishment owner, the labour and social court can substitute the lacking consent, if the transfer is justified on material grounds (such as being due to establishment necessity). Here, though, the labour and social court must scrutinize the choice of transferee from among all the possible candidates. Aside from works representation law, the transfer must also be permissible with regard to individual contract terms.

836. According to §102 of the Labour Organization Act, co-determination applies to all disciplinary measures, with the exception of dismissal with notice, summary dismissal or transfer. Disciplinary measures include warnings, promotion bans and fines. Generally, all disciplinary action is only permissible if it is allowed for in a collective or works agreement. Moreover, in individual cases, disciplinary action may only be taken if the works council has expressly agreed to it, or if it is imposed by an institution created in a works agreement (e.g., an establishment disciplinary board), and therefore with the council's agreement. Disciplinary action which does not fulfil all of these conditions is null and void.

VI. Participation 'below' the Level of Co-determination

837. The Labour Organization Act standardizes a number of further co-participation rights. These supersede all rights to information and are advisory, meaning that the establishment owner has to provide information, or the works council can demand additional consultation. Only the most important of these rights will be mentioned here. For example, as regards social issues, a works council has the right to know about the owner's future personnel plans, and to be informed about intended personnel measures (personnel planning, *see* §98 Labour Organization Act). The establishment owner must inform the works council about any acquisition of new employees, as well as the salary conditions of those hired (§99 Labour Organization Act) and planned promotions (§104 Labour Organization Act). Also, the employer has to consult with the works council about these issues, if required to do so. Other general participation rights to be mentioned are explained below.

838. §89 of the Labour Organization Act, according to which a works council has the right to monitor whether or not the general legal regulations (statutes, collective agreements, works agreements) concerning employees in the establishment are all being observed. For example, the staff body can inspect establishment records of working hours, or wage payments granted to employees, and of how the wages and so forth arc dctcrmincd.

839. §90 of the Labour Organization Act expressly guarantees the works council the right to intervene in all matters concerning the employees' interests at an establishment level and, where necessary, to involve supra-establishment representative bodies and executive authorities as well.

840. §91 of the Labour Organization Act sets out a general right to information. It compels the establishment owner to provide information, at the request of a works council, on all matters or questions concerning the establishment's employees. However, there are restrictions; for instance, a works council is only entitled to inspect an employee's 'personal files' with the employee's consent.

841. §92 of the Labour Organization Act obliges the establishment owner to consult with the works council every quarter year (and, if the works council so demands, as often as monthly) on current establishment affairs, the general principles of the management policy, and so on. Under certain circumstances, the establishment owner and works council are entitled to involve officials of their representative bodies in these consultative talks.

842. As regards economic and commercial matters, the owner must keep the works council informed about developments in the establishment's economic position, in particular about manufacturing, the order book, sales and investment projects. Moreover, in larger businesses, the works council must be given a copy of the balance sheet (§108 Labour Organization Act).

843. According to §109 of the Labour Organization Act, the owner of the establishment must inform the works council about planned changes in the establishment without undue delay (paragraph 804; also about changes such as any in the ownership or legal form of the establishment) and consult with it about them. If these changes affect a significant part of the staff, the development of a 'social plan' could be carried out (paragraph 810). Participation in economic and commercial matters also includes participation in supervisory boards or boards of directors (*see* below).

VII. Participation in the Supervisory Body

A. General

844. By means of this form of participation in economic and commercial affairs, employees are involved in supervisory boards of corporations, and thus may take part in forming the undertaking's policy and aims. In more detail, this participation varies according to the undertaking's legal form. For the most part, §110 of the Labour Organization Act only specifies this form of employee's participation for the de facto predominant forms of corporate enterprise in Austrian company law, the joint-stock company *Aktiengesellschaft* (*AG*) and the limited liability company *Gesellschaft mit beschränkter Haftung* (*GmbH*).

845. Usually, each of these companies has three major bodies: the meeting of all shareholders, an executive body and a supervisory body which continuously supervises the management (two-board system). In a joint-stock company, these are named the stockholders' meeting, the board of directors (*Vorstand, Vorstandsmitglieder*) and the supervisory board (*Aufsichtsrat*). A limited company has a general meeting, directors (*Geschäftsführer*) and – under certain circumstances – a supervisory board. Without exception, rules on employee co-participation are only specified with regard to the supervisory boards. It is also noteworthy that, with effect from 1 January 2018, protracted discussions on the gender diversity of corporate boards have resulted in the adoption of a mandatory quota of 30% for female members on corporate supervisory boards in Austria. The quota also applies to the appointment of Austrian members to the supervisory boards of the *Societas Europaea*.

B. Participation in Joint-stock Companies

846. Under Austrian law, joint-stock companies (*Aktiengesellschaften* or AG) are companies with legal personality, whose nominal capital, or stock, is divided between shares, and whose liability for debts is limited to the company assets. Every corporation has a supervisory board as its controlling organ. The number of supervisory board members appointed by the shareholders is settled by the general meeting. For every two of these members one employee representative is appointed in the body ('one-third' participation) by the works council or central works council (paragraph 786). The employees' representatives have to be workers in the undertaking. With effect from 1 January 2018, furthermore, in market-listed companies or enterprises with more than 1,000 employees, each gender has to have at least 30% representation on the board. This means that one-third of all the employee representatives on the supervisory board have to be female if the workforce as a whole consists of more than 20% women. Conversely, this percentage applies to male representatives on the board if the workforce comprises more than 20% men. With the decision of the works council, employee representatives automatically become members of the supervisory body. The appointments do not have to be confirmed at a general meeting. The employees appointed to an advisory board have a right to claim their expenses, but not any extra payment.

847. The main tasks of a supervisory body are to appoint and dismiss the executive board (*Vorstand*) and to supervise its activities. Members of the executive board are elected by the supervisory board. In the election, the approval of a majority of the members appointed by the shareholders is necessary, in addition to that of the majority of the supervisory body as a whole. The same 'double-majority' requirement applies to the election of the chairperson of the supervisory board.

848. For subcommittees of the supervisory board, the proportional (one-third) employee's representation is also compulsory. Only issues concerning the 'relations between corporation and members of the executive board', such as negotiations about the contracts of the members of the executive board with the company, may be delegated to a subcommittee without employees' representation. The board's 'basic obligations' (such as actual appointment of executive boards) may not be delegated to a subcommittee.

849. In order to supervise the management, the supervisory board can require reports from the executive board at any time. However, only the supervisory board as a whole can inspect the company books. The yearly balance sheet prepared by the executive board must be approved by the supervisory board.

C. Participation in Limited Liability Companies

850. Like the joint-stock company, a limited liability company is a corporative enterprise. A supervisory board must only be appointed as prescribed by statutory law, in particular if the company employs more than 300 employees. The company's charter or partnership agreement can also allow for a supervisory board. Essentially, what has been said about corporations applies correspondingly to employee representation on the supervisory board and the appointment of the employee representatives in a limited liability company. This includes the rules on the mandatory quota of 30% representation for each gender (*see* paragraph 846). However, in law, the supervisory board of a limited liability company has fewer powers than that of a joint-stock company. Above all, only the general meeting can appoint, dismiss and instruct directors. Therefore, the supervisory board's main function is to supervise the directors.

D. Participation in a Group of Undertakings (Multicorporate Enterprise)

851. If an undertaking is extensively dependent on another undertaking, the employees of the dependent unit should also be represented on the supervisory board of the controlling company, because that is where actual decisions are made. The employees of the controlled undertaking(s) have a right to be proportionally represented on the supervisory board of the parent company:

- if one undertaking controls another. This means it either has a 50% or more direct share of it, or runs it alone;
- if both the controlled and the controlling undertaking are a joint-stock company or limited liability company; and
- if the labour force of the controlled undertaking(s) is twice as big as that of the controlling undertaking.

VIII. Employees' Participation in 'Tendentious' Enterprises and Other Restrictions

852. The participation powers in the Labour Organization Act are not granted to all labour forces alike. The Act distinguishes between certain powers by reference to the number of employees (e.g., social plans, where establishments with at least twenty employees must be affected, paragraph 810) or the undertaking's legal form (e.g., sitting on the supervisory board of corporations, paragraphs 844 et seq.).

853. Furthermore, there are differences in the participation rights, depending on the purposes or intents of an enterprise. If an undertaking's entrepreneurial purposes and aims are primarily political (as with political parties), coalitional (as with unions), religious (as with denominational kindergartens), educational (as with private schools), charitable (as with the Red Cross) or scientific, it is referred to as a 'tendentious' establishment or undertaking, where, by law, the staff does not participate in economic decisions. According to the Act, the staff's powers are either completely excluded ('absolute' protection of tendentious enterprises) or only excluded, if exercising these powers would actually affect the non-profit purpose of the undertaking ('relative' protection of tendentious enterprises).

854. For example, the rules on economic participation according to §§110–112 of the Labour Organization Act do not apply in tendentious establishments and undertakings; in particular, this concerns employees' participation in the supervisory board. In establishments and undertakings which serve the religious purposes of an officially recognized religion or denomination, some rules on compulsory co-determination (e.g., works agreements on disciplinary codes) do not apply. Moreover, newspapers enjoy relative protection, with respect to rights under §§108–112 of the Labour Organization Act. Finally, there are specific regulations for the Austrian public radio and television corporation, the *ORF*.

IX. Exercising Powers and Types of Disputes

A. *Enforcing Participation Powers: Disputes of Rights*

855. The Labour Organization Act protects participation powers comprehensively, for the most part. For instance, an employer's act which does not have the necessary staff approval is often null and void (specified, *inter alia*, for dismissal with notice without prior notification of the staff body, *see* paragraph 480, 482; as regards transfer, *see* paragraph 835; disciplinary action, paragraph 836; and as regards issues where the conclusion of a works agreement (in other words, the consent of the staff body) is necessary, *see* paragraph 805). However, the nullity sanction does not suffice in all cases. For example, in the case of actual measures by the employer, a right to reversal of the measure also exists, which either the staff as a body or individual employees may apply for (for supervisory measures affecting human dignity, or questionnaires, *see* paragraph 813). The rights to information are principally enforceable by execution. Several participation powers are also protected by administrative sanctions.

856. Staff can apply for an official judgment on the legality of an employer's acts: the labour and social court has jurisdiction over disputes between staff and owner of the establishment. The labour and social courts, likewise, have jurisdiction over disputes between individual employees and the establishment owner, even if the dispute involves a staff right (such as whether or not works representation law makes an employee's transfer null and void).

B. Enforcing Participation Powers: Disputes of Interest

857. The Labour Organization Act also lays down procedures for some 'disputes of interests' between an establishment's owner and his or her staff, in other words, conflicts concerning the creation of new law. In particular, this applies to enforceable co-determination in social matters (and, in a wider sense, also to necessary co-determination; *see* paragraphs 809, 814). On application by one of the parties concerned, the conciliation board makes its decision (paragraphs 97 et seq.), which is regarded as a works agreement. The decision – which is also a type of arbitration award – will be considered reasonable, due to the composition of the conciliation board (which consists of representatives of both sides and an impartial representative as well) and the procedures laid down for it.

858. For other disputes of interest in works representation law, no special procedures are specified. Therefore, bearing in mind the ban on industrial action in works representation law (paragraph 799), a works council mainly depends on its bargaining skills, in order to implement its aims.

C. Enforcing Participation Powers: Other Disputes

859. Other disputes can arise within the framework of works representation, such as between individual employees when staff bodies are appointed, between works council members, between individual employees and the staff (or its institutions) over the exercise of rights, or between a works council or an establishment owner and supra-establishment representative bodies. As a rule, the labour and social court is competent, and general rules apply (paragraphs 91 et seq.).

§5. Employee Representation Bodies That Originate in European Law

I. Introduction

860. Inter alia, the following provisions concerning employee representation have been adopted within Austrian law:

- Directive 94/45/EC on the establishment of a European Works Council or a procedure in Community-scale undertakings and Community-scale groups of undertakings for the purposes of informing and consulting employees.
- Directive 2001/86/EC, supplementing the Statute for a European company with regard to the involvement of employees.

- Directive 2003/72/EC, supplementing the Statute for a European Cooperative Society with regard to the involvement of employees.
- Directive 2005/56/EC, on cross-border mergers of limited liability companies. and
- Directive 2009/38/EC, on the establishment of a European Works Council or a procedure in Community-scale undertakings and Community-scale groups of undertakings for the purposes of informing and consulting employees (Recast).

861. The relevant provisions of the Austrian implementation are grouped in chapters of their own within the Labour Organization Act ('European Works Organization', 'Employee Participation in the European Company', 'Employee Participation in the 'European Cooperative Society' and 'Employee Co-Determination in the case of Cross-Border Mergers of Limited Liability Companies'). The latter two mostly refer to provisions concerning European companies. Here, only the European works council will be discussed; the other forms of employee representation originating from European law still have no major practical significance in Austria.

II. The European Works Council

862. The Works Council Directive obliges enterprises with 1,000 employees in the Member States and 150 employees in each of at least two Member States to have a European works council, or a procedure in order to provide employees with information about consultation rights at European level. The original directive was implemented in Austrian law by integrating a new chapter ('European Works Organization') into the Labour Organization Act in 1996.

863. The purpose of the Works Council Directive, as well as of the corresponding Austrian provisions, is to improve the right to information and to consultation of employees in Community-scale undertakings and Community-scale groups of undertakings. They are to ensure, thereby, that the employees of undertakings or groups of undertakings operating in two or more Member States of the EU are properly informed and consulted, when decisions which affect them are taken in a Member State other than that in which they are employed. To promote this aim, the law provides for different bodies and procedures:

- a special negotiating body, responsible for an agreement with the central management, in order to establish a European works council or an information or consultation procedure;
- the European works council (its establishment either based on an agreement or directly on the law); and, as an alternative,
- an information and consultation procedure.

864. The European works council, as well as its social 'opponent', the central management, must work in a spirit of cooperation, with due regard to their reciprocal rights and obligations. The operating expenses of the European works council are to be borne by the central management.

A. Scope of Application

865. A European works council, or an information and consultation procedure, must be established:

- in Community-scale undertakings, in other words, any undertakings having at least 1,000 employees within the Member States, and at least 150 employees in each of at least two Member States;
- in Community-scale groups of undertakings, that is to say, any group of undertakings having at least 1,000 employees within the Member States and which have at least two group undertakings in different Member States, and at least one group undertaking with at least 150 employees in a Member State and another undertaking of the same group with at least 150 employees in another Member State.

866. The provisions of the Austrian Labour Organization Act concerning the European Works Organization are applicable to undertakings, or groups of undertakings, if the provisions mentioned above are fulfilled. Additionally, they must be covered by Austrian works organization law, and their central management must have its seat in Austria. If the central management has its seat outside of Austria, the law of the Member State where the central management is located applies.

B. Implementation

867. The 'European works council' is a body set up for the purpose of informing and consulting employees on transnational questions. Alternatively, the employees represented by the special negotiation body may agree on an information and consultation procedure without establishing a special representative body.

868. The procedure for establishing a European works council or an information and consultation procedure is initiated either by the central management or at the written request of 100 employees or their representatives. After this, a special negotiating body is set up. Its task is to determine, with the central management, the scope, composition, competence and term of office of the European works council, or arrangements for implementing one or more alternative procedures for the information and consultation of employees. The special negotiating body may decide to end the negotiations with the central management, or not to open negotiations at all.

869. The special negotiating body is composed of employees' representatives. Austrian employees' representatives can only be appointed from among the members of existing works councils. The members from other countries are appointed according to the applicable national law.

870. The agreement on the establishment of a European works council or the establishment of an information and consultation procedure must be in writing. The agreement on the establishment of a European works council must determine at least:

- the undertakings or the establishments which are covered by the agreement;
- the composition, the number of members, the allocation of seats and the term of office;
- the information and consultation procedure, as well as its functions;
- the venue, frequency and duration of meetings;
- the financial and material resources to be available for the council;
- the duration of the agreement and the procedure for its renegotiation.

871. The agreement on the establishment of one or more information and consultation procedures must stipulate:

- the obligation of the central management to inform and consult the existing employees' representatives on all transnational issues affecting the interests of the labour forces;
- under which circumstances the employees' representatives are to have the right to meet, in order to discuss the information conveyed to them.

C. *Subsidiary Requirements*

872. Subsidiary requirements apply if:

- the central management and the special negotiating body so decide;
- the central management refuses to negotiate with the special negotiating body within six months of the initial request;
- the central management and the special negotiating body fail to conclude an agreement within three years from the date when the procedure was initiated (exception: if the special negotiating body decides to end negotiations).

873. These subsidiary requirements stipulate that the European works council has the right to meet with the central management once a year, in order to be informed and consulted, on the basis of a report on the progress and prospects of the undertaking. In addition, the European works council or, if it exists, the select committee elected from among its members, has the right to be informed of exceptional circumstances having a significant effect on the interests of employees (relocations, closures, collective redundancies and so forth). Also, the select committee or the European works council has the right to meet with the central management, or any other suitable level of management, in order to be informed and consulted, on the basis of a report on measures significantly affecting employees' interests.

D. Links Between Austrian Works Councils and European Works Councils

874. Members of European works council representing employees working in Austria are appointed from among the members of the Austrian works councils. If no such representative body exists in an enterprise (because of its size, or if no works council has been established), its employees are not represented.

875. Members of the European works council must be afforded sufficient (paid) time off and facilities to carry out their functions, in particular to enable them to inform the employees' representatives of all the concerned establishments of the contents and results of the information and consultation procedures taking place on behalf of the European works council.

Chapter 5. Industrial Conflict

§1. General

I. Definitions and Notions

876. Austrian statutory law neither deals with the general term 'industrial action', nor defines its most important forms (strike, lockout and boycott). In general, industrial action is seen as the planned disturbance of the 'productive' or 'labour peace'. It comprises collective measures of one party to the employment contract (i.e., employees or employers), disturbing industrial production, which create enough pressure to achieve a specific goal (especially, improvement of working terms). The actual methods of carrying it out are defined as refusal to work (strike) or the denial of employment and payment (lockout). Another form – though only in a wider sense – is the boycott, a withdrawal from commercial or social relations with an enterprise, organization, or person as a punishment or protest. Furthermore, the collective use of individual rights may be considered a form of labour dispute; for example, if all employees go on vacation at the same time. Finally, labour disputes might be categorized in terms of the numbers of participating employers or employees: for example, in the case of a selective (pinpoint) strike, only certain establishments in a sector or certain key positions in an establishment are on strike, in order to cause intense impact despite the small number of striking employees.

II. Distinction Between Collective Action and Individual Behaviour

877. In this context, 'collective action' denotes the decision to take industrial action, and its planned collective execution. To take a strike as an example, this means the strike resolution, strike threat, strike call, the starting of the strike and the collective withdrawal of labour (the strike itself). The element of planning is usually subject to homogeneous allied leadership. According to the principle of 'freedom of industrial action' (*Prinzip der Arbeitskampffreiheit*), for the purposes of the legal appraisal of industrial action, collective action is differentiated from the behaviour of the individuals taking part in it (theory of separation – *Trennungstheorie*). As a result of this theory, the legitimacy of the collective action does not automatically imply the legitimacy of the individual participant's behaviour in a strike or lockout, and vice versa.

878. However, current developments in the international and EU legislation as well as the current jurisdiction of the ECJ and the ECHR must also be taken into account. A too strict interpretation of the theory of separation can no longer be maintained any more. Therefore, according to some Austrian literature, the recognition of the right to strike by jurisdiction even leads to the conclusion that participation in a lawful labour dispute does not constitute a breach of contractual duties.

III. The Actual Situation

879. Of the Western industrial countries, Austria is near the bottom of the statisticians' strike league (*see* Table 10). Furthermore, there have been virtually no lockouts since 1945.

Table 10 Strike Statistics

	Employees Participating	*Number of Days on Strike*	*Time Spent on Strike per Employee – Minutes*
1950	28,093	4,042,368	1,006.8
1951	31,555	677,461	165.5
1952	116,991	1,283,150	320.9
1953	12,695	304,817	77.0
1954	21,140	410,508	100.8
1955	2,601	464,167	108.5
1956	43,249	1,227,292	278.5
1957	19,555	364,841	81.0
1958	28,745	349,811	77.0
1959	47,007	404,290	87.7
1960	30,654	68,823	14.6
1961	38,338	113,878	23.8
1962	207,459	647,720	134.2
1963	16,501	34,017	7.0
1964	40,843	35,449	7.3
1965	146,009	423,473	86.2
1966	120,922	71,356	14.0
1967	7,469	16,411	3.0
1968	3,129	6,671	1.0
1969	17,449	18,517	3.8
1970	7,547	26,616	5.0
1971	2,431	3,702	0.5
1972	7,096	15,104	3.0
1973	78,251	160,138	33.5
1974	7,295	7,244	1.5
1975	3,783	5,512	1.0
1976	2,352	589	0.0
1977	43	11	0.0

	Employees Participating	*Number of Days on Strike*	*Time Spent on Strike per Employee – Minutes*
1978	699	10,222	2.0
1979	786	764	0.0
1980	24,181	16,961	3.0
1981	17,115	4,024	0.5
1982	91	344	0.1
1983	208	514	0.1
1984	268	544	0.1
1985	35,531	22,752	3.9
1986	3,222	3,253	0.6
1987	7,203	4,822	1.4
1988	24,252	8,542	1.5
1989	3,715	2,986	0.5
1990	5,274	8,870	1.5
1991	92,707	58,341	9.3
1992	18,039	23,437	3.7
1993	7,512	13,008	2.0
1994	0	0	0.0
1995	60	120	0.0
1996	0	0	0.0
1997	25,800	19,125	3.0
1998	0	0	0.0
1999	0	0	0.0
2000	19,439	2,947	0.5
2001	0	0	0.0
2002	6,305	9,306	1.4
2003	779,182	1,305,466	196.8
2004	30	178	0.0
2005	0	0	0.0
2006	0	0	0.0
2007	0	0	0.0
2008	0	0	0.0
2009	0	0	0.0
2010	0	0	0.0
2011	87,034	56,670	7.9

	Employees Participating	*Number of Days on Strike*	*Time Spent on Strike per Employee – Minutes*
2012	1,500	563	0.1
2013	5,529	3,277	0.5
2014	5,196	3,309	0.5
2015	0	0	0.0
2016	0	0	0.0
2017	0	0	0.0
2018	37,923	8,934	1.1
2019	5,262	1,973	0.2
2020	9,883	3,678	0.5

Source: http://wko.at/statistik/Extranet/Langzeit/lang-streiks.pdf.

§2. The Legal Sources of Industrial Action

880. Austrian law contains very few provisions covering the situation of industrial action, and even those provisions which do exist mostly only concern areas such as rights to work permits, temporary agency work, or unemployment insurance benefits. In particular, striking employees are not entitled to unemployment allowances, but, on the contrary, employee placement of unemployed persons, foreign, or temporary agency workers in strikebound establishments is prohibited by law. Since, in practice, industrial action is also very rare, and whatever industrial conflicts arise are mostly resolved out of court, there is also a lack of court decisions. Therefore, in summary, Austria has no complete, coordinated system of legal standards governing industrial action. For these reasons, the following outline of industrial action law can only be based, for the most part, on academic literature.

881. Austrian law recognizes no explicit, individual right of either employees or employers to take industrial action. This applies to economic strikes as well, because neither the fundamental freedom of association (paragraphs 579 et seq.) nor the statutory collective agreement system as a whole create a right to take industrial action.

882. Article 11 of the European Convention on Human Rights explicitly mentions the formation of trade unions, but the ECHR has so far not explicitly stated whether and under which circumstances, the previously ruled freedom of union activity (*Betätigungsfreiheit*) includes a right to organize and take part in industrial action; the court referred to this issue only indirectly. Therefore, Austrian doctrine is not conclusive, as to whether this constitutional rule provides for an individual and collective right to strike.

883. The ESC, which contains in Article 6 section 4 on the right to strike and to lockout, is not applicable, because Austria has added a provision in this respect, when signing it. This might be a strong argument that in national law, no constitutional right to organize or take part in industrial action is recognized. At least, the reservation can be considered as another evidence for the impartiality of the state.

884. Article 28 of the CFREU explicitly enshrines the right to collective bargaining at the appropriate levels 'and, in cases of conflicts of interest, to take collective action to defend their interests, including strike action'. Nevertheless, it is not considered a further securement of the right to strike, because the ECJ indeed acknowledged that the right to take collective action, including the right to strike, constitutes a fundamental right which forms an integral part of the general principles of the EU, even before the introduction of the CFR. The ECJ added that that right must, however, be reconciled with the fundamental freedoms within the internal market, such that exercise of that right may be subject to certain restrictions, in accordance with the principle of proportionality.

885. As a result, the legal appraisal is still open. As a first notion, however, and in order to avoid too many restrictions on the right to strike and with regard to the freedom of establishment and to provide services, the illegitimacy of industrial action should, in any case, only be assumed in the event of massive disproportionality (for further details *see* paragraphs 898 et seq.).

§3. The Principles of Legal Appraisal

886. As in the case of any other legal acts which are neither expressly permitted nor prohibited, the lawfulness of strikes and lockouts must be assessed according to the totality of law. Besides international law, for the most part, this concerns Austrian constitutional law, criminal law (paragraphs 890 et seq.), the law of contract, and tort law (paragraphs 894 et seq.).

887. Austrian law does not recognize explicitly a right of either employees or employers to take industrial action in the sense that a labour dispute would be a specifically protected, legal institute which would justify the breach of other public or private law provisions. On the contrary, there is no 'negative' notion either on the part of the Austrian lawmaker concerning industrial action, because neither criminal provisions nor provisions in private law explicitly forbid strikes, lockouts or other forms of industrial action. Therefore, Austrian literature on industrial action speaks of 'impartiality of the state' in this area.

888. In particular, the following points illustrate the state's neutrality concerning industrial action: compulsory arbitration only applies to very few disputes in works representation law (paragraphs 810, 815); striking employees or those who are affected by defensive lockout are not entitled to unemployment benefits; there is no provision for the state itself to take over production in strikebound establishments; the labour market service may not provide (unemployed) workers for strikebound establishments; similar rules apply to foreign or temporary agency workers.

889. In summary, the position of Austrian law on industrial action might best be described as a system of 'freedom of action', combined with 'the principle of state neutrality' on industrial action. Industrial action is neither legally, nor in any other way, favoured or discriminated against by the state. Within the scope of 'general freedom of action', anything is allowed within labour disputes that is not prohibited. As a result, insofar as industrial action is considered lawful (at least as collective action) in terms of Austrian law as a whole, the principle is accepted that the strength of the social opponents is crucial for the result of the industrial action. In other words, the 'right' of the strongest is recognized as a reasonable means of resolving labour disputes. This leads to an extensive permissibility of industrial action, which exists despite the fact that there is no (individual) right to take industrial action in Austria.

§4. Industrial Action and Criminal Law

890. Strikes and lockouts have not, in themselves, been especially penalized by any particular criminal standards since 1870 (paragraphs 103, 589 et seq.). However, most industrial action fulfils (at least formally) the statutory definition of the offence of unlawful compulsion in §105 of the Criminal Code, which lays down, among other things, that anybody is liable to punishment who attempts to coerce another into performing an action, or not doing so, by threats (causing material damage), if the threat as the means to the desired ends is *contra bonos mores*. Nevertheless, according to the view which currently predominates, this provision is not applicable to economic disputes, because their aim is not *contra bonos mores*. As to this, it has also to be mentioned that the legal appraisal in civil law and in criminal law is not the same. However, §105 of the Criminal Code may be applicable to strikes, if a claim is made that an employer or persons closely associated with an employer have been induced to do something.

891. Furthermore, strikes and lockouts can in themselves be punishable, if the stoppage of work directly affects life or health of others. The wilful or negligent general threat to health or life of a large number of people would be punishable, for example in the event of industrial action in hospitals and other important public utility areas (water, power). However, in this connection, the details are not clear; all that is certain is that not every strike in a public utility establishment is punishable. What applies to life and health principally also applies to public dangers and negligent damage to property, which is particularly significant where machines or goods are damaged by industrial action.

892. Other breaches of criminal law might occur, for instance in the event of injury or coercion of willing workers by pickets, or damage and unlawful entry, in cases of factory occupation.

893. Usually, not only direct participants but all 'activists' are liable to punishment, in law. In the case of a strike which is in breach of criminal law, the organizers of collective action are therefore liable to prosecution alongside the strikers. However, for the most part, the organizers of collective action may only be responsible in criminal law for individual punishable actions during an industrial dispute, if the punishable action is planned by them as a part of collective action.

§5. Industrial Action and Civil Law

894. For the most part, unlawfulness of collective action according to civil law rules occurs in the event of breach of specific statutory or contractual prohibitions, or action *contra bonos mores*. The consequences of organizing unlawful industrial action according to civil law may be claims for compensation, for forbearance (*Unterlassung*) or for disposal (*Beseitigung*).

I. Specific Statutory Prohibitions

895. Austria has no statutory law which expressly prohibits employees' industrial action in any form. Furthermore, it must be taken into account that industrial action mainly aims at and causes negative impacts (impairments) on 'mere property' which is principally not 'absolutely' protected by law. Hence, for the most part, unlawfulness according to §1295 section 1 of the General Civil Code does not occur.

896. The 'duty of restraint' in works representation law (based on §39 section 1 Labour Organization Act, *see* paragraph 799) does not generally prohibit any industrial action at establishment level, but it forbids the works council to organize industrial action itself, especially action aiming at the extension of competences or rights in works representation law. However, members of the works council as individuals may organize and take part in industrial action. Furthermore, this restriction may not be interpreted too narrowly and prevent members of staff bodies from fighting for improved working conditions in favour of the employees.

II. Contractual Prohibitions

897. In this context, mainly industrial action bans in collective agreements must be mentioned. As an implied rule, collective agreements forbid any industrial action based on issues which have already been regulated in the agreements – at least, as long as the agreement is valid ('duty of peace', *see also* paragraph 727). This also comprises the duty to 'influence' the members of the concluding parties not to take any actions. Collective agreements may expressly deviate from the implied duty of peace by laying down an absolute ban on all industrial action during their period of validity. Strikes or lockouts which contradict such relative or absolute bans would be unlawful.

III. Action *Contra Bonos Mores*

898. According to §1295 section 2 of the Civil Code, any deliberate damage which is *contra bonos mores* is prohibited. Behaviour is *contra bonos mores* if it is in breach of unwritten law, and in particular, general principles of law. For example, enormous disproportionality or inequity between the intended aims and the actual impacts of the industrial actions in question leads to unlawfulness.

899. For industrial action to be legal, it must concern the parties in employment relations. Additionally, the person against whom the strike or lockout is directed must have the actual capacity to fulfil the claims of the striking social opponent. Therefore, all political strikes, whose true target is a state organ, for example, the lawmaker, are unlawful. The same applies to 'sympathy' strikes, lockouts or boycotts, that is to say, all industrial action which is directed against other persons (or entities) rather than the strikebound employer (or the employers' association), or the locked-out employees. For this reason, sympathy actions which are primarily a gesture of solidarity with other employees or groups are widely considered unlawful as well, even if they support economic industrial action.

900. On the contrary, lawfulness does not depend on whether or not the organizer is a free professional association. Non-union strikes (often called wildcat strikes) can therefore be just as lawful as union organized ones.

901. Unlawfulness also relates to the 'inadequacy of purposes' of the industrial action due to a lack of any connection to employment conditions and work. Employment conditions must be taken in the widest sense, and it is irrelevant whether the aim of industrial action could be a matter for regulation by a collective agreement. Here, employment- or work-related means conditions such as pay, working and vacation hours, technical working conditions, rationalization, subjection to superiors, work with other employees, withdrawal of notice and the re-employment of an employee. Finally, this includes the general business policy of an undertaking (e.g., partial transfer of production abroad) as well, but not the political views of the employer or property relationships within the undertaking. Moreover, industrial action that intends to affect or even destroy the (financial) existence of the social opponent does not count as matters of 'employment conditions'. Furthermore, this unlawfulness applies to measures 'coercing' other employees, for example, if employees demand the dismissal of other employees without material grounds, or in the event of compulsory affiliation.

902. Moreover, economic industrial action is considered *contra bonos mores*, if its issues are subject to compulsory arbitration anyway. Such arbitration is laid down in works representation law concerning issues of enforceable co-determination (paragraph 809), about which, consequently, no lawful industrial action can be taken at establishment level. Otherwise, there exists no compulsory arbitration; only the voluntary conciliation and arbitration activities of the Federal Conciliation Board are available, which are only carried out if both parties to the dispute give their consent (*see also* paragraph 100).

903. For similar reasons, industrial action is considered *contra bonos mores*, if its aims can clearly and reasonably be achieved by resorting to litigation in the courts. Industrial action should serve the purpose of resolving conflicts of interest, not enforcing the law. However, this restriction is inapplicable if the employees concerned are collectively exercising a right to withhold, for example labour (for instance, for late wage payments, or because the industrial safety specifications have not been met); only employees who are directly affected have this right to withhold.

904. According to the predominant viewpoint in Austria, industrial action is not required to be the last resort (*ultima ratio*), only to be taken if all other efforts or arbitration measures and so on have failed. The law also does not require a pre-strike vote. It is considered to be the expression of a person's 'general freedom of action', to decide when to take measures in order to change from peaceful bargaining to industrial action. Of course, the above-mentioned limitations, especially proportionality of purposes and actual measures, have to be complied with. As a result, compulsory steps before taking industrial action do not exist *ex lege*. The observance of cooling-off periods or other forms of preceding negotiation procedures must be explicitly laid down as a contractual obligation, above all in a collective agreement.

905. Finally, collective action can be *contra bonos mores* because of the way it is carried out. In particular, as mentioned above, it is considered unreasonable, if there is an obvious lack of proportion between the actual form of action and its aims. This applies if the accompanying measures themselves are unlawful (e.g., planned damage to property or propagandist libel or slander against the social opponent), and if the position of the party against whom the industrial action is directed is intended to be decisively weakened by these measures. For example, collective action would be unlawful, if absolutely essential closing down safety work cannot be done; if strikebreakers who are willing to work are forcibly, and 'successfully', prevented by pickets from working; or if the public is informed of the reasons for action in a completely distorted and seditious way. That an action concerns public supply services is not sufficient for it to be unreasonable.

906. However, actions in a dispute (as accompanying or backup measures) can only be relevant to the legal assessment of the action as a whole if they are deliberately resorted to by the organizers of such collective action. If, on the contrary, the organizers of collective action do not sanction additional measures, but only passively tolerate or even denounce them, the activities are seen as infringements by individuals, which are not relevant to the collective action (or more precisely, to the legal assessment of the action). Moreover, if the unlawful accompanying measures to the action have no major effect on its results, they only lead to a liability to pay damages and do not affect the legality of the action as a whole.

IV. Consequences in Civil Law

907. The social opponent concerned has a right to forbearance against unlawful industrial action, and whoever is obliged to forbear need not be at fault. The right to forbearance can refer either to the collective action as a whole, or only to individual accompanying measures. It can be protected in advance by a preventive restraining injunction, even if only a future breach of the duty of forbearance is feared.

908. In the case of lockouts, the liability for damages is exhausted within the scope of individual labour law. If a strike is *contra bonos mores* as a collective act, or is in breach of a statutory prohibition, the organizers themselves are liable to damages, insofar as they have acted culpably. If the unlawfulness is on account of being *contra bonos mores*, intent is necessary. If the organizers (also) act on behalf of an association, such as a trade union, the association is liable for any behaviour on their part which creates a liability for damages, if they are its organs, have direct power of attorney from its official organs or are part of its leadership. An association is only liable for the behaviour of other persons for aiding and abetting within the limits of liability, that is, particularly if the helper (such as a strike picket appointed by the trade union) is 'incompetent or dangerous' (§1315 Civil Code).

909. If the collective action (only) breaches a contractual duty of restraint (paragraph 896), only persons affected by the duty of restraint are liable, such as the trade union or the employers' association which concluded the collective agreement. Associations are, in any event, liable for the behaviour of their official organs or helpers to the extent just outlined. Since the duty of restraint also protects members of the other contractual party, it is possible, as in the case of a union strike which breaches the duty of restraint, for individual strikebound employers to demand compensation from the union. Other organizers of a strike who are themselves not party to the collective agreement are not liable for damages in such cases.

910. General legal rules apply to measures in a dispute which go beyond actual strike measures. These include, for instance, damage and physical injuries caused by pickets attempting to stop strikebreakers ('blacklegs') working, or untrue public statements made by an employer about the purposes of a strike. Otherwise permissible behaviour does not become unlawful, because it is taken as part of an industrial action, just as otherwise unlawful behaviour is not permissible, because it is part of it. The organizers of collective action or the organizing association are only held liable for these measures in a dispute if they have expressly agreed to them (accompanying measures), but not in the case of simple toleration or clear denunciation.

911. In the case of lawful collective action, the organizers are not liable. Nor are they liable, say, for incitement to a breach of contract, or to affecting a right of claim, because individual strikers had breached their contractual terms by taking part in a strike (*see also* paragraphs 917 et seq.).

912. Liability of individual striking employees is only possible if they have culpably breached their contractual duties by striking (for a more precise outline, *see* below).

§6. EFFECTS ON THE (INDIVIDUAL) EMPLOYMENT RELATIONSHIP

I. Principles of Assessment in Individual Labour Law

913. If one follows the opinion that Austrian law does not recognize a right to take industrial action (paragraph 881), but only the general freedom to act, strikes and lockouts – taken to mean the withdrawal of labour or of work and earnings – are contrary to obligations resulting from the contract of employment, where the employment relationship remains in force. This assessment according to civil law is not affected by the legal assessment of the collective action. Lawful collective action can just as soon coincide with unlawful individual behaviour (e.g., lawful collective strike action without timely termination of employment relationships) as unlawful collective action with lawful behaviour (e.g., mass notice pending a change of contract with political industrial action). The employment contract is not breached in the case of collective notice as a measure of industrial action (mass notice pending a change of contract; paragraphs 400, 458) or collective exercise of the right to withhold.

914. A very important consequence of the strict approach mentioned above would be that strikes and lockouts neither suspend the obligations arising from an employment relationship (above all the duty to work and the duty to provide pay, but also secondary obligations) nor end the employment relationship itself. Usually, the employees withdraw their labour without (previously) ending their employment relationships. However, they can also resort to collective notice, pending a change of contract ('conditional' notice). In any case, a strike, as such, does not end employment relationships. A lockout similarly does not end employment relationships. However, employees can indeed link the strike to a generally permissible termination declaration, in particular premature resignation. The same applies to employers and lockouts. An employer can combine it with one of the generally permissible forms of termination.

915. Apart from a collective exercise of the right to withhold and the timely termination of employment relationships by giving tactical notice, every strike and lockout would therefore be a breach of contract in individual labour law.

916. Indeed, there have been several attempts in Austrian legal literature to adopt the predominant German view, that the legal assessment of collective action is also decisive at the level of the individual employment relationship. Until recently, most Austrian scholars have rejected this, just as attempts to make some modifications to individual contractual obligations in the event of industrial action have not been taken up. Now, however, other current developments in the international and EU legislation, as well as current decisions of the ECJ and the ECHR, have to be taken into account. According to some Austrian literature, the recognition by jurisdiction of the right to strike means that the participation in a lawful labour dispute does not, in any case, constitute a breach of the contractual duties.

II. Strikes

917. A striking employee is in breach of their obligation to work, and therefore always loses their right to pay. Even the recognition of a right to strike does not change this result. In the case of strikes organized by a union, the union usually pays strike support benefits, particularly to its members.

918. As a consequence of the above-mentioned current (European) decisions, literature now denies that the employer can end employment relationships at any time during the strike by means of summary dismissal (paragraph 519), and that premature termination is always justified. Rather, the lawfulness of a strike as a collective act, and especially its proportionality, have to be taken into account as well. This means that in the event of an unlawful strike, where the employee has intentionally not performed their work, the employer can dismiss them for reasons of persistent refusal to work. Vice versa, in the event of the employer's unlawful lockout and denial of payment, the employees also have the right to premature termination.

919. If an employer or employee has terminated the employment relationship, this termination is not affected by the end of the strike. If the employee is to be re-employed, a new employment contract must be concluded. This also applies after the end of a successful strike, if the re-employment of employees is laid down in a collective agreement. In general, there is no right to be re-employed, unless the employer acts arbitrarily in their choice of strikers for summary dismissal (or re-employment), in which case the termination of their employment relationships would be null and void.

920. Finally, according to general rules of the Civil Code, an employer can demand compensation for damages from strikers in breach of their employment contracts. In the case of unlawful collective action, strikers are collectively liable for all damage caused by it, if they have acted with intent. If they are only guilty of negligence, which is, in particular, possible if it would not be reasonable to have expected them to realize the unlawfulness of their behaviour, they are only liable for a proportion of the damages. In the case of lawful collective action, liability is only possible for damages which can be attributed directly to individual employees. Since this sort of attribution is normally impossible, in practice, in this event, the employees would remain free of liability.

III. Lockouts

921. In the case of lockouts, preventing employees from working only in exceptional cases leads to a breach of the duty to provide work (paragraph 288). In each case, if employees are willing to work despite the lockout, the employer is in default of acceptance and must continue to provide pay, despite work not being done (*see* paragraphs 436 et seq.). If the employer does not, they are in breach of their duty to provide pay, and the employees have the right to resign prematurely, with all the accompanying rights to compensation (paragraphs 198, 529). All this is independent of whether or not the collective action is lawful.

922. Valid grounds for summary dismissal are always lacking in offensive lockouts, if an employer combines the lockout with premature termination for this reason, and all the consequences of unjustified summary dismissal follow. In particular, employees have a right to compensation for dismissal (paragraph 529), and the system of general protection against summary dismissal applies. As a rule, summary dismissal will be socially unjustified, and therefore can be contested in court (paragraphs 540 et seq.).

923. If employers react to a sectional strike with a 'defensive' lockout, they lock out employees in a strikebound establishment who have not yet joined the strike. An employer does not always thereby breach their duty to provide work. A duty to provide pay to the non-strikers only affects the employer if the employees would really be willing to work (paragraph 436). It is subject to a scholarly dispute (as with all other questions concerning industrial action, no jurisprudence exists), whether or not an employer must, as a rule, pay wages to the non-strikers willing to work, in the event of a sectional strike (*see also* paragraph 928).

924. The system of general protection against summary dismissal (paragraphs 542 et seq.) is also applicable in the case of summary dismissals in the wake of a lockout, but summary dismissal is socially justified if work cannot continue in the establishment because of the sectional strike.

925. If no special regulation by collective agreement or individual contract exists, the general rules (paragraphs 436 et seq.) apply to the claims for payment of employees whose establishment is brought to a standstill by industrial action in another establishment (e.g., suppliers, transport, services and power suppliers). It follows from this provision that employees in an establishment which is indirectly affected by industrial action only lose their right to payment if the industrial action concerns the community as a whole, such as a strike in the power industry. If industrial action only affects specialized suppliers, the employer has to bear the risk.

IV. Liability vis-à-vis Third Parties

926. An employer whose employees are on strike is liable vis-à-vis third contractual partners such as clients, according to general rules on impairment of performance in §§918 et seq. of the General Civil Code which apply. In the event of a strike which occurs because of the employer's fault, they are liable vis-à-vis concerned third parties, according to the general rules on compensation for damages.

927. Due to a lack of contractual relations or other obligations to safeguard interests, striking employees are not liable vis-à-vis third parties such as clients or suppliers of the employer.

V. Selective Strike

928. During a selective strike, not all employees are on strike. As mentioned above, it is indubitable that striking employees are not entitled to payment. However, it is open to discussion whether this also applies to those employees in a selective strike who are willing and prepared to work, but cannot due to the strike and the lack of colleagues, material and so on. According to decisions from the 1920s, their claim for wages is principally upheld in a genuine selective strike which is only concerned with some parts of the establishment. Current decisions of the Austrian Supreme Court state the following: based on their duty of care, during a strike, the employer has to inform the employees willing to work explicitly that they cannot take on the employees' work. If the employer does not give such a notification, they have to pay the wages at any rate. If the employer does inform the employees about the 'non-acceptance' of services, there are two opinions in literature regarding entitlement to payment. According to the first, the costs of a labour dispute must not be unloaded onto the social opponent by imposing an obligation to continue paying wages to the employees who are indeed not striking but are benefitting from the labour dispute. The second opinion is based on the principle that it is, for the most part, the employer's responsibility to provide for running an enterprise. If there is a lack of work, equipment or human resources and so on, the suspension of work lies within the sphere of the employer and they have to continue wage payment, at least to all employees seriously willing and prepared to work. The lack of labour force due to a social dispute is treated like other cases of non-work.

Selected Bibliography

Books

In German:

Brodil W., Risak M., *Arbeitsrecht in Grundzügen* 11th ed 2022 (LexisNexis, Vienna).
Drs M., Arbeits- und Sozialrecht 6th ed 2021 (Manz, Vienna).
Födermayr B., Resch R., *Arbeitsrecht* 7th ed 2020 (Manz, Vienna).
Kietaibl C., Windisch-Graetz M., *Arbeitsrecht* 11th ed 2021 (Braumüller, Vienna).
Löschnigg G., *Arbeitsrecht* 13th ed 2017 (ÖGB-Verlag, Vienna).
Mazal W., Risak M. (eds), *Das Arbeitsrecht – System und Praxiskommentar* loose leaf 2022 (LexisNexis, Vienna).
Marhold F., Brameshuber E., Friedrich M., *Österreichisches Arbeitsrecht* 4th ed 2021 (Verlag Oesterreich, Vienna).
Reissner, Lern- und Übungsbuch Arbeitsrecht 6th ed 2020 (Manz, Vienna).

In English:

Laimer H-G., *Employment Law: A Basic Primer* 4th ed 2019 (NWV, Vienna).

Legislation

Stech, E. and Ercher-Lederer G., *Kodex Arbeitsrecht* (Linde Verlag, Vienna).

Cases

Weiß, D., *Sammlung arbeitsrechtlicher Entscheidungen*, 90 volumes (Manz, Vienna).

Journals

Arbeits- und Sozialrechtskartei (Linde Verlag, Vienna).
Informationen aus dem Arbeits- und Sozialrecht (AK Wien, Vienna).
Journal für Arbeitsrecht und Sozialrecht (Manz, Vienna).
Das Recht der Arbeit (Verlag des ÖGB, Vienna).
Zeitschrift für Arbeitsrecht und Sozialrecht (Manz, Vienna).

Websites

Legislation and court decisions (mainly in German) are available free of charge at http://www.ris.bka.gv.at.

Selected Bibliography

List of Laws

Act on Safeguarding Employees' Claims in the Event of the Employer's Insolvency = *Insolvenz- Entgeltsicherungsgesetz* BGBl 1977/324 idF BGBl I 2021/218
Affiliations Act = *Koalitionsgesetz* RGBl 1870/43 idF BGBl 1974/422
Agricultural Employment Act 1984 = *Landarbeitsgesetz* BGBl 1984/287 idF BGBl I 2019/93
Agricultural Employment Act 2021 = *Landarbeitsgesetz* 2021 BGBl I 2021/78 idF BGBl I 2021/121
Anti-terror Act = *Antiterrorgesetz* BGBl 1930/113 idF BGBl 1974/422
Assemblies Act = *Versammlungsgesetz* BGBl 1953/98 idF BGBl I 2017/63
Associations Act = *Vereinsgesetz* BGBl I 2002/66 idF BGBl I 2021/211
Chambers of Labour Act = *Arbeiterkammergesetz* BGBl 1991/626 idF BGBl I 2021/240
Civil Procedure Act = *Zivilprozessordnung* RGBl 1895/113 idF BGBl I 2022/61
Company Pension Act = *Betriebspensionsgesetz* BGBl 1990/282 idF BGBl I 2018/100
Construction Workers' Bad Weather Compensation Act = *Bauarbeiter- Schlechtwetterentschädigungsgesetz* BGBl 1957/129 idF BGBl I 2021/71
Construction Workers' Holiday and Severance Pay Act = *Bauarbeiter-Urlaubs- und Abfertigungsgesetz* BGBl 1972/414 idF BGBl I 2022/73
Continuation of Wages Act = *Entgeltfortzahlungsgesetz* BGBl 1974/399 idF BGBl I 2018/100
Contractual Public Servants Act = *Vertragsbedienstetengesetz* 1948 BGBl 1948/86 idF BGBl I 2022/81
Criminal Code = *Strafgesetzbuch* BGBl 1974/60 idF BGBl I 2021/242
Domestic Employees Act = *Hausgehilfen- und Hausangestelltengesetz* BGBl 1962/235 idF BGBl I 2018/100
Employees' Liability Act = *Dienstnehmerhaftpflichtgesetz* BGBl 1965/80 idF BGBl I 2021/61
Employment Contract Law Adaptation Act = *Arbeitsvertragsrechts-Anpassungsgesetz* BGBl 1993/459 idF BGBl I 2021/213
Employment of Children and Juveniles Act = *Kinder- und Jugendlichen-Beschäftigungsgesetz* BGBl 1987/599 idF BGBl I 2022/58
Employees with Disabilities Act = *Behinderteneinstellungsgesetz* BGBl 1970/22 idF BGBl I 2021/78
Enforcement Code = *Exekutionsordnung* RGBl 1896/79 idF I 2021/86
Equal Treatment Act 1979 = *Gleichbehandlungsgesetz* 1979 BGBl 1979/108
Equal Treatment Act = *Gleichbehandlungsgesetz* BGBl I 2004/66 idF BGBl I 2020/16
Estate Employees Act = *Gutsangestelltengesetz* BGBl 1923/538 idF BGBl I 2019/74
Federal Act Corporate Staff and Self-Employment Provision Act = *Betriebliches Mitarbeiter-und Selbständigenvorsorgegesetz* BGBl I 2002/100 idF BGBl I 2021/199
Federal Constitution Act = *Bundes-Verfassungsgesetz* BGBl 1930/1 idF BGBl I 2022/85

Foreign Nationals Employment Act = *Ausländerbeschäftigungsgesetz* BGBl 1975/218 idF BGBl I 2022/73
General Social Insurance Act = *Allgemeines Sozialversicherungsgesetz* BGBl 1955/189 idF BGBl I 2022/93
General Civil Code = *Allgemeines bürgerliches Gesetzbuch* JGS 1811/946 idF BGBl I 2021/175
House Care Act = *Hausbetreuungsgesetz* BGBl I 2007/33 idF BGBl I 2008/57
Health and Safety Act = *ArbeitnehmerInnenschutzgesetz* BGBl 1994/450 idF BGBl I 2018/100
Hours of Rest Act = *Arbeitsruhegesetz* BGBl 1983/144 idF BGBl I 2022/58
Industrial Code 1859 = *Gewerbeordnung* 1859 RGBl 1859/227 idF BGBl I 2017/153
International Private Law Act = *Internationales Privatrechtsgesetz* BGBl 1978/304 idF BGBl I 2019/72
Janitors Act = *Hausbesorgergesetz* BGBl 1970/16 idF BGBl I 2014/59
Job Protection Act = *Arbeitsplatz-Sicherungsgesetz* 1991 BGBl 1991/683 idF BGBl I 2021/78
Journalists Act = *Journalistengesetz* StGBl 1920/88 idF BGBl I 2007/102
Labour and Social Courts Act = *Arbeits- und Sozialgerichtsgesetz* BGBl 1985/104 idF BGBl I 2022/61
Labour Market Promotion Act = *Arbeitsmarktförderungsgesetz* BGBl 1969/31 idF BGBl I 2020/71
Labour Organization Act = *Arbeitsverfassungsgesetz* BGBl 1974/22 idF BGBl I 2021/61
Maternity Protection Act = *Mutterschutzgesetz* BGBl 1979/221 idF BGBl I 2022/87
Patents Act = *Patentgesetz* 1970 BGBl 1970/259 idF BGBl I 2022/61
Paternity Leave Act = *Väter-Karenzgesetz* BGBl 1989/651 idF BGBl I 2020/153
Pension Funds Act = *Pensionskassengesetz* BGBl 1990/281 idF BGBl I 2022/36
Salary Fund Act = *Gehaltskassengesetz* 2002 BGBl I 2001/154 idF BGBl I 2022/65
State Fundamental Law on General Rights of the Citizens 1867 = *Staatsgrundgesetz* 1967 RGBL 1867/142 idF BGBl 1988/684
Tobacco and Non-smoker Protection Act = *Tabak und Nichtraucherinnen- bzw. Nichtraucherschutzgesetz* BGBl 1995/431 idF BGBl I 2019/66
Temporary Agency Work Act = *Arbeitskräfteüberlassungsgesetz* BGBl 1988/196 idF BGBl I 2021/174
Theatrical Work Act = *Theaterarbeitsgesetz* BGBl I 2010/100 idF BGBl I 2013/138
Trades Representation Law = *Handelsvertretergesetz* 1993/88 idF BGBl I 2016/29
Unfair Trading Practices Act = *Bundesgesetz gegen den unlauteren Wettbewerb* BGBl 1884/448 idF BGBl I 2019/104
Universities' Organization Act = *Universitätsgesetz* 2002 BGBl I 2002/120 idF BGBl I 2021/177
Vacation Act = *Urlaubsgesetz* BGBl 1976/390 idF BGBl I 2013/3
Vocational Training Act = *Berufsausbildungsgesetz* BGBl 1969/142 idF BGBl I 2022/86
White-collar Workers Act = *Angestelltengesetz* BGBl 1921/292 idF BGBl I 2019/74
Working Time Act = *Arbeitszeitgesetz* BGBl 1969/461 idF BGBl I 2022/58

Selected Bibliography

Index

The numbers here refer to paragraph numbers.

Index

Index

Index

Index

www.ingramcontent.com/pod-product-compliance
Ingram Content Group UK Ltd.
Pitfield, Milton Keynes, MK11 3LW, UK
UKHW020136290926
15471UKWH00003B/518

9 789403 523262